THE DEVELOPMENT OF DOGMA

SACRA DOCTRINA SERIES

Series Editors

Chad C. Pecknold, *The Catholic University of America*

Thomas Joseph White, OP, *Dominican House of Studies*

THE DEVELOPMENT OF DOGMA

A SYSTEMATIC ACCOUNT

Guy Mansini, OSB

The Catholic University of America Press
Washington, D.C.

Copyright © 2023
The Catholic University of America Press
All rights reserved
The paper used in this publication meets the minimum requirements of American National
Standards for Information Science—Permanence of Paper for Printed Library Materials,
ANSI Z39.48-1992.
∞

Cataloging-in-Publication Data is available from the Library of Congress

ISBN: 978-0-8132-3745-9
eISBN: 978-0-8132-3746-6

CONTENTS

Acknowledgments		vii
Abbreviations		ix
Introduction		1
1.	What Is the Development of Doctrine?	5
2.	The Invention of Dogma	14

    Arius and the condemnation of his teaching at Nicaea 17

        Arius's problem 18

        Two very different readings of Sacred Scripture 18

        Arius and the frame within which he reads Scripture 20

        The teaching of Nicaea 21

    The logic of Nicaea 26

    An ecumenical council 34

    Dogma 35

    Nicaea and Christian philosophy 37

    Conclusion 39

3.	Framing the Development of Dogma Theologically	41

    Revelation 42

        What is revelation and how is it accomplished? 43

        Is revelation cognitive? 47

        Is it communal? 51

        Is it "closed"? 52

    Scripture and Tradition 55

    Magisterium and dogma 61

    "Dogma" in Scripture 65

4. Philosophical Presuppositions of Dogma
and Development 70

Knowing 72

The cognitive as the conceptual 76

Conceptual epistemological exclusivity and the upshot
for revelation and doctrine 81

Exclusivity 81

The upshot 82

Realism 88

Analogical words and ideas and realities 93

The historicity of revelation and Church teaching 96

The historical issue 97

The theoretical issue 99

5. The Logical Verification of Development 105

The justification of developments as genuine 106

Inevitable logic 110

Forms of the logical justification of developments 119

Confirmation by the logic of antecedent and converging
probabilities 126

6. Vatican I and the Dogma about Dogma 138

Dei Filius and the dogma about dogma 139

The reason for the dogma about dogma 142

The truth of the third canon of chapter 4 of *Dei Filius* 145

The Second Vatican Council and dogmatic continuity 147

The universal accessibility of dogma 154

The implication of accessibility 154

An objection 156

Person and nature 158

Common sense and the magisterium on dogmatic
language 162

Epilogue 170

Bibliography 177

Index 187

ACKNOWLEDGMENTS

Without the warm welcome of the professors and graduate students of the department of theology at Ave Maria University, this book would not exist. I thank them for their generosity of spirit and constant encouragement. I am indebted in a special way to Taylor Payne and Jim Kelly for their ardor and insight.

ABBREVIATIONS

Dei Filius The First Vatican Council's Dogmatic Constitution on the Catholic Faith. This can be found at the Vatican website or in *Decrees of the Ecumenical Councils*. Vol. 2, *Trent to Vatican II*, 804–811. Edited by Norman P. Tanner, SJ. London: Sheed and Ward, 1990.

Dei Verbum The Second Vatican Council's Dogmatic Constitution on Divine Revelation. In *Decrees of the Ecumenical Councils*. Vol. 2, *Trent to Vatican II*, 971–981. Edited by Norman P. Tanner, SJ. London: Sheed and Ward, 1990.

Dignitatis humanae The Second Vatican Council's Declaration on Religious Freedom. In *Decrees of the Ecumenical Councils*. Vol. 2, *Trent to Vatican II*, 1001–1011. Edited by Norman P. Tanner, SJ. London: Sheed and Ward, 1990.

DH Heinrich Denzinger, *Enchiridion symbolorum definitionum et declarationum de rebus fidei et morum/ Compendium of Creeds, Definitions, and Declarations on Matters of Faith and Morals*, ed. Peter Hünermann, and by Robert Fastiggi and Anne Englund Nash for the English edition, 43rd ed. San Francisco: Ignatius Press, 2012.

Mansi Johannes Dominicus Mansi, *Sacrorum Conciliorum Nova et Amplissima Collectio*. Graz: Akademische Druck – und Verlagsanstalt, 1961.

ND	J. Neuner and J. Dupuis, *The Christian Faith in the Doctrinal Documents of the Catholic Church*, 7th ed. New York: Alba House, 2001.
Pastor aeternus	The First Vatican Council's Dogmatic Constitution on the Church of Christ. In *Decrees of the Ecumenical Councils*. Vol. 2, *Trent to Vatican II*, 811–816. Edited by Norman P. Tanner, SJ. London: Sheed and Ward, 1990.

THE DEVELOPMENT OF DOGMA

INTRODUCTION

This book offers a Catholic theology of the development of doctrine. It is not a history of the theologies or accounts of dogmatic development. There are several good historical inventories of these accounts. There are the companion volumes of Owen Chadwick, *From Bossuet to Newman*, and of Aidan Nichols, OP, *From Newman to Congar: The Idea of Doctrinal Development from the Victorians to the Second Vatican Council*.[1] There is the older but excellent and very fine grained monograph by Herbert Hammans, which stretches from the Tübingen school of the nineteenth century to the mid-twentieth century.[2] Jan Walgrave's *Unfolding Revelation* takes us from the Fathers to his own theological synthesis of the contributions of major Catholic and other thinkers on development.[3] Very recently, there has appeared the theologically problematic but historically very insightful canvas of the history of Catholic thought on development in Michael Seewald's monograph.[4]

---

1. Owen Chadwick, *From Bossuet to Newman*, 2nd ed. (Cambridge: Cambridge University Press, 1987); Aidan Nichols, OP, *From Newman to Congar: The Idea of Doctrinal Development from the Victorians to the Second Vatican Council* (Edinburgh: T&T Clark, 1990). Nichols also offers a synthesis of the mid-twentieth century Catholic consensus on development.

2. Herbert Hammanns, *Die Neueren Katholischen Erklärungen der Dogmenentwicklung* (Essen: Ludgerus – Verlag Hubert Wingen KG, 1965).

3. Jan Hendrik Walgrave, *Unfolding Revelation: The Nature of Doctrinal Development* (Philadelphia: Westminster, 1972).

4. Michael Seewald, *Dogma im Wandel: Wie Glaubenslehren sich entwickeln* (Freiburg: Herder, 2018). It is insightful in showing the reality of development in every age of the Church and why

Nichols notes in his final chapter that the mid-twentieth century consensus on how to understand doctrinal development faced the challenges of postconciliar pluralism and the demands of modern hermeneutical theory. Such challenges have only increased in the last thirty years. The present volume intends to address some of them. Mostly, they have to do not with any new theological discovery or insight but with philosophical presuppositions, some of them relatively unexamined when assumed as forming the context for theological understanding.

The basic theoretical parameters of this book can be listed as follows. Anyone who thinks them hopelessly retrograde can thus abandon ship immediately. To the contrary, they are all very hopefully retrograde if historicism is false, post-Kantian positivism self-contradictory, and radical theological pluralism a denial that any revelation was ever made.

First, philosophically:

1. Knowledge is identity in act of knower and known (Aristotle), whose expression and flowering is the concept or interior word of the heart (Augustine).

2. The proper and exclusive human instrument of actually knowing the real in its intelligibility is the proposition, the composing and dividing of interior words, the linguistic expression of which is a statement, a sentence in the declarative mood. There is no other access to the real as intelligible except the proposition.

3. The logic suited to making sense of the world is the logic of Aristotle. In contrast to modern logic, it is only Aristotle who gives us to say what things are in themselves by distinguishing known essentials from non-essentials. Rather than merely systematizing our own various and changing impositions of self-made categories on the real, he gives us to say that things are of kinds, and describes how we in fact speak of kinds or natures, their properties, their differences, and their nonessential features. All the more is his logic suited to making sense of the world once we understand that the world is created.

4. Because the formal object of the intellect is being, the fundamental notions according to which human beings makes sense of themselves and

---

it emerges as a problem in the modern age; it is problematic in steering a little close to historicism. There is further note taken of Seewald in the epilogue.

of the world are in principle transempirical, transcultural, and so transhistorical. They must in principle be transempirical, moreover, if post-Kantian positivism is self-contradictory. And because being transcends culture as well as matter, radical historicism is false, and categories of thought can be transcultural, and so transhistorical. For the same reason—the formal object of the intellect as being—there is no untranslatable language, and all philosophies are commensurable.

For the exposition and defense of such principles, I call on such modern thinkers as Henry Babcock Veatch, Francisco Marín-Sola, OP, Robert Sokolowski, and Réginald Garrigou-Lagrange, OP. Such principles must be true, moreover, if the principles germane to a Catholic understanding of doctrine and doctrinal development are themselves true.

Second, the theological parameters or principles are as follows:

1. Revelation is cognitive and "realist." It is cognitive because, as recorded in Scripture, it evidently informs us and means to inform us about ourselves, the world, and God. It is realist because it is a continuation of the speech of God by which he created the world. God creates by his word—"God *said*, let there be light"; he calls things into being by naming them with names that can be rendered in Hebrew, Latin, and Greek. But God names things truly, according to how they really are, since they *are* only as expressions of some part of the Wisdom and Word by which he truly expresses himself. Our words can therefore aspire to and, on the lips of prophets and apostles, certainly succeed, in naming things truly, which is to indicate the essences of things. The speech of prophet and apostle prepares for, disposes to, repeats, paraphrases, and participates in the speech of the Incarnate Word. The cognitive and realist character of revelation and the grounding of theology in revelation together exclude the radical incommensurability of different theologies.

2. Revelation occurs in deeds and words and is therefore necessarily propositional. The historical deeds constituting the history of salvation are not brute facts but actions of an Agent and of intelligent agents who disclose or can disclose the meaning of their actions propositionally.

3. Revelation is "closed." It is not actualized, however, except when heard in faith; when it is so actualized, it is given over to history. This actualization across time and generations is not transformative but con-

INTRODUCTION   3

servative and sometimes enriching. That is, the Holy Spirit animates the Church, and Tradition is pneumatological and not historicist.

4. Church teaching is transculturally and transhistorically accessible to all men. This truth is grounded in the facts that (1) God wills all men to be saved and (2) the unity of the Church is the unity of faith, i.e. *fides quae creditur* as summed up, say, in the articles of the creed. The catholicity of the Church entails transcultural accessibility, and the apostolicity of the Church entails transhistorical accessibility. The ultimate agent of the maintenance of this accessibility is the Holy Spirit, and its proximate agent is the Church herself. This fourth truth depends on the fourth philosophical principle listed above.

For the exposition and defense of the theological principles, I call on John Henry Newman, Bernard Lonergan, SJ, Yves Congar, OP, and Joseph Ratzinger. Contrasting clarifications are sometimes provided by Maurice Blondel, Pierre Rousselot, SJ, Henri de Lubac, SJ, Karl Rahner, SJ, and Edward Schillebeeckx, OP.

If the dogma of the Council of Nicaea in 325 is confessed as true, and if the dogma about dogma enunciated at the First Vatican Council is true, then they are so confessed on the implicit understanding that the above four theological and the above four philosophical principles are all true. In other words, the theological and the philosophical principles are not facultative. They are denied by the theologian on pain of ceasing to be a Catholic theologian at all.

In what follows, there is an initial determination of what the development of dogma is (chapter 1). Next, there is an account of the Church's discovery of dogma at the Council of Nicaea in 325, which also manifests the causes of dogmatic development (chapter 2). There follows an outline of the broader framework of fundamental theological realties in which the development of dogma is intelligible (chapter 3). Basic philosophical presuppositions of development are then outlined (chapter 4). Special attention has then to be given to the role of logic, not so much in arriving at new dogmatic formulations, but in showing that they belong to the deposit of faith (chapter 5). Last, the dogma about dogma of the First Vatican Council and its implications of universal accessibility have then to be explored (chapter 6).

CHAPTER 1

WHAT IS THE DEVELOPMENT OF DOCTRINE?

The "development of doctrine" commonly refers to the unfolding of Christian faith into hitherto unformulated and undefined doctrinal propositions. It is the successive unfolding of the one, once-and-for-all revelation of God, completed by and in Christ and first possessed by apostolic faith, into newly articulated doctrines. Suppose here at the outset that the "thing" of revelation, the original formulation of faith, was itself propositional, something located above all in the propositions of the Bible. Perhaps it was not exclusively propositional (we will say more on this later), but suppose that it is contained importantly and preeminently and also very accessibly in such dicta as the confession that "Jesus is Lord," and that "he has risen from the dead," and that "he will come again to judge the living and the dead." Let us call such propositions "revelatory propositions." They are propositions that contain the fundamentals of faith insofar as they formulate fundamental realities of faith—the Lordship of Christ, his resurrection, his second coming; the realities and the formulations in language that report them are revealed by God. The realities themselves are works of God; the formulations reporting them are words of God.

It is important to see from the outset that these realities (and so the truths that report them) are not discoverable by human beings, either by us today or by the apostles in the first century. They are realities that are received from God revealing Christ and revealing himself in Christ. And we have to be *told* of these realities, even insofar as they are facts of history, because they do not bear their meaning in themselves in such a way that we can know them without words. So for instance, the Lord's resurrection is not simply a matter of an empty tomb and his appearances to the disciples. No, no—"resurrection" means raised *by God*, and we do not get the "by God" part by reports of appearances and of empty tombs, and the original disciples did not get the "by God" part simply by looking at the risen Jesus and noticing that the tomb was empty. So we have to be told of these realities, even as were the original Christian disciples. And, to be sure, we have to be told them by God. So, to stick with the Resurrection, God in his Son tells us beforehand of his resurrection from the dead when he predicts his passion and death; he speaks of it to the disciples on the road to Emmaus after it; on Easter morning, the angel tells the women at the tomb that Christ is risen. And for us, too, we have to be told, by God, whether the telling comes from our parents or our parish priest or our catechist or our bishop. When any of these tell us that "Christ has been raised from the dead by God," then we are hearing God say that to us (more will be said about this, too).

Now sometimes revelatory propositions summarize a narrative of events, and this is not unimportant, since certain truths about God cannot be manifested except on the basis of a history captured in narrative. When Isaiah reflects on the Old Testament story of Israel's exodus from Egypt, her establishment in the Promised Land, the kingdom of David and then the kingdoms of Israel and Judah, Jewish exile, and return from exile, he makes statements about God's providence (Is 43) and eternity (Is 44). That God is provident and eternal are truths about God. The course of events is in part constituted by words of divine promise and di-

6   CHAPTER 1

vine threat. And the course of events as a whole is captured in a narrative that stretches from the book of Exodus to 2 Kings. The narrative itself, however, is the prior and necessary demonstration of God's providence and eternity, without which Isaiah cannot formulate his teaching about them, and without which any talk of them would amount to dealing in abstractions and possibilities. In a similar way, the narrative of the mission of Jesus and its conclusion are the necessary presupposition of what St. Paul teaches us, quite "didactically" (propositionally) in his letters to the Galatians and Romans, and when he tells us such things as that we are reconciled to God in Christ with our trespasses not being counted against us (2 Cor 5:19). And there are smaller narrative communications of truth, too: the narrative of Jesus's walking on the Sea of Galilee and calming the wind and the subsequent worship of the disciples is a declaration of his divinity (Mt 14:22–33). What is to be noticed, however, is this: that the original possession of revelation, and so every initial access to the Realities disclosed by revelation through deed and event—namely, the Triune God, the Incarnation, the Eucharist, and so on—is in *language*. And although saving assent to revelation requires the interior assistance of the Holy Spirit (cf. Jn 6:44), it remains a saving assent to the exterior word of ecclesial and biblical truth, the exterior word spoken by apostle and evangelist (cf. Rom 10:14–17) and bishop (2 Tm 3:15–16; Ti 1:9). The point of departure for the development of doctrine, therefore, is not in the first place some wordless experience, either historical or transcendental,[1] of God and his Christ, but assent in faith to the creed and the reading of Scripture that the creed enables and controls.

Let us try to fix more analytically what "development" entails. Evidently, the phenomenon of development requires a recognition, first, that there is a "one," an integral cognitive whole, "revelation" as such, which we have referred to by adverting to certain articles of the creed—that Jesus is Lord, that he was raised from the dead, that he will come again. Revelation as received in the mind of the believer and of the Church as a whole is what Cardinal Newman called the "idea" of Christianity.[2] He

---

1. A wordless historical experience is constituted by sense-perceptible things and persons, if such a thing be possible; a wordless transcendental experience is a perception interior to consciousness of nameless states, objects, and conditions within our subjectivity and its constitutive structures.

2. John Henry Cardinal Newman, *An Essay on the Development of Christian Doctrine*, 6th ed.,

understands it as an integral intelligible whole,[3] not all of which is necessarily reflexively possessed by the believer.[4] That revelation and the idea of it is a "one" is evident from the unity of the Apostles' Creed. The Creed is not a hodgepodge, but a "one" in several ways: it possesses a Trinitarian unity in the three articles devoted to Father, Son, and Spirit; it possesses an economic or salvation-historical unity in that it speaks of the works of Father, Son, and Spirit (creation, redemption, Church); and it possesses a chronological unity, since it moves from the creation of the world to the second coming on the last day. More compactly and centrally, the unity may be said to be Christological.[5]

Second, however, the idea of development requires a "many" into which this one thing is unfolded or developed or articulated. To illustrate this in a rough and ready way, compare the Apostle's Creed with the *Catechism of the Catholic Church*: while the one Creed is slim and trim and declares a certain original and originating single Christian revelation of the Trinity of persons manifested by Christ, we may say that the *Catechism* is fat and heavy with lots and lots of things, all related to the Creed to be sure, but adding interpretations, explanations, connections, implications, applications, or what we may call "developments."[6] So looking from the Creed to the *Catechism*, there is a "one" revelation that has become a "many"—a manifold collection of many propositions all in some way related to the Creed. As Newman noted:

Creeds and dogma live in the one idea which they are designed to express, and which alone is substantive; and are necessary only because the human mind can-

---

foreword by Ian Ker (Notre Dame, IN: University of Notre Dame Press, 1989 [a reprint of the edition of 1878]), 93. See Terrence Merrigan, *Clear Heads and Holy Hearts: The Religious and Theological Ideal of John Henry Newman*, foreword by Ian Ker (Louvain: Peeters, 1991), 72, and Nicholas Lash, *Newman on Development. The Search for an Explanation in History* (Shepherdstown, WV: Patmos Press, 1975), 98.

3. John Henry Cardinal Newman, "1852 Discourse V. General Knowledge Viewed as One Philosophy," 421–34 in *The Idea of a University*, ed. with introduction by I. T. Ker (Oxford: Clarendon Press, 1976), 423: "An idea [is] a view, an indivisible object, which does not admit of more or less, a form, which cannot coalesce with anything else, an intelligible principle, expanding into a consistent harmonious whole."

4. Newman, *Essay on Development*, 93.

5. Newman, *Essay on Development*, 36. See Avery Dulles, SJ, "From Images to Truth: Newman on Revelation and Faith," *Theological Studies* 51 (1990): 252–67, at 254–55, 259–60.

6. *Catechism of the Catholic Church*, 2nd ed., rev. (Vatican City: Libreria Editrice Vaticana, 1997).

8   CHAPTER 1

not reflect upon that idea, except piecemeal, cannot use it in its oneness and entireness, nor without resolving it into a series of aspects and relations.[7]

Evidently and in the third place there must also be a temporal distance of the many from the one in which the many are formulated and articulated. It is a long time between the composition of the Apostles' Creed in the late second century and the *Catechism* in the twentieth. Fourth, furthermore, we must somehow be able, with a properly Christian exercise of reason illumined by faith, to recognize that it really is the one, integral cognitive whole that is exfoliated into the many subsequent doctrinal propositions. All the four things mentioned are necessary for the phenomenon of "development of doctrine." Without the first thing, the one whole of revelation that stays what it is, that stays the same in the manyness it becomes, we do not have development but transformation, a self-contradictory plurification of Christian discourse where one age says one thing and another something substantially different. Without the second thing, the many articulations of the one, there is no development but only repetition. There is stasis, but no progress. Without the third thing, temporal expanse, development of the one into the many poses no problem to faith. If in the apostolic age there is both the one (summarized by the Creed) *and* the many (to be found in the *Catechism*), then there is apostolic authority—divine authority—for both that is immediately historically evident, and the question does not then arise as to the maintenance of the apostolicity of the Church for us, the maintenance of the truth across time. But of course, the *Catechism* does not exist in the first century, and so the question does arise for us.

As to the fourth thing, without the ability of reason to recognize that the one really is truly and rightly unfolded in the many, our faith in the apostolicity of the Church turns into fideism, a sort of blind trust. We would be in the position of sort of naturally hoping that the *Catechism* preserves the Creed, but we would not know it. So, it is a condition of the possibility of genuine development of doctrine that it be able to be recognized as such, as a plurification in many that does not destroy but only

---

7. John Henry Cardinal Newman, "Sermon 15: The Theory of Developments in Religious Doctrine," in *Fifteen Sermons Preached Before the University of Oxford Between A.D. 1826 and 1843* (London: Longmans, Green, 1896), 331–32.

explicates the one. Christian revelation, as Cardinal Newman says, meets us *as* revelation, up front and recognizably as God speaking, and not as some undeclared revelation of an anonymous inspiration or the voice of conscience.[8] So, if the development cannot be recognized as keeping the sense of what is developed, then the original revelation has ceased to be recognizable in the development. For Catholics, this recognition is magisterial, that is to say, a matter of what popes and bishops teach, but it also engages the *sensus fidei* of all the faithful.

Let us stick with the Christology of the Creed and the Christology of the *Catechism* to illustrate. The Apostles' Creed pretty much just repeats what we find, even as to wording, in the New Testament when it says that Jesus is God's Son and our Lord. But the Creed we recite on Sunday, the Nicene Creed, says that Jesus is "one in substance with the Father," and that he is "God from God," "true God from true God." So there is a change from the second-century statement of who Jesus is (the original form of the Apostles' Creed was formulated in Rome in the late second century) to a fourth-century statement of who—and what—Jesus is (the councils of Nicaea and Constantinople whence we have our Sunday Creed met in the fourth century). So, is the fourth-century statement in continuity with the first-century statement? We had better to be able to figure out that it is, else we cannot be sure we remain in the apostolic faith and are confessing it on Sundays.

Figuring this out can take short and sweet forms as well as long and very detailed forms. In every form, it requires faith. It is a matter of seeing, but a seeing illustrated by faith.[9] But in the long and detailed forms, figuring this out requires also certain aids in coming to a theological judgment of the continuity of the Nicene Creed with the New Testament. These two helps, or *auxilia*, are metaphysical skill and historical learning. The express role of philosophy in the discernment of doctrinal continuity is at least as old as the fifth century, if we think of the scholasticism that

---

8. Newman, *Essay on Development*, 79–80.

9. See Vatican I, *Dei Filius*, chap. 4, in Heinrich Denzinger, *Enchiridion symbolorum definitionum et declarationum de rebus fidei et morum/Compendium of Creeds, Definitions, and Declarations on Matters of Faith and Morals*, ed. Peter Hünermann, and by Robert Fastiggi and Anne Englund Nash for the English edition, 43rd ed. (San Francisco: Ignatius Press, 2012), no. 3016, hereafter cited as DH, and in J. Neuner and J. Dupuis, *The Christian Faith in the Doctrinal Documents of the Catholic Church*, 7th ed. (New York: Alba House, 2001), no. 135, hereafter cited as ND.

set in after the Council of Chalcedon with people like Leontius of Byzantium and which is obviously in play in the sixth century with Maximus Confessor. In fact, it is already in play in the fourth century, since the response to Arianism in that century is philosophically fecund, as we will see in the next chapter. The role of history, while implicitly operating in the Church's assurance of continuity in every age, came more expressly to be recognized in the eighteenth and nineteenth centuries with the emergence of modern historical sciences. Seeing how the *auxilia* of history and metaphysics relate to theological assessment of continuity is therefore an issue just all in itself, lest theories of development embrace some form of rationalism in using philosophy or historicism in calling on historical studies, and whether this occurs either expressly or implicitly.[10]

So there are four things in the idea of development: a "one," a "many," the temporal distance of the many from the one, and the necessity of a reasoned recognition in faith of the one in the many. There is also, however, a fifth thing ordinarily contained in the idea of the development of doctrine, a function especially of the third and fourth things above—an extended temporal course in which the many appear, and our ability to affirm them as expressing the one revelation. Together, they imply that the different expressions of some one revealed truth, different expressions and precisions that come later, enable us to apprehend and appreciate the revealed truth more fully, at least in that we see it from a different angle, so to speak, and find new and different words to articulate it. When we see things from different angles, we see them better, more fully. This implies, however, that if the fourth thing is the ability to recognize the one in the many, it brings with it *also* the ability to see the many in the one. This is very important, for it entails that we can judge the adequacy of *earlier* expressions and the theological success of *earlier* exponents of faith by the measure of the *later* expressions. Or as Cardinal Newman says,

a great idea … is elicited and expanded by trial, and battles into perfection and supremacy. Nor does it escape the collision of opinion even in its earliest years, nor does it remain truer to itself, and with a better claim to be considered one and the same, though externally protected from vicissitude and change. It is in-

---

10. Theology as *sacra doctrina* is rather judge of the auxiliary sciences it uses. See *Summa theologiae* I, Q. 1, a. 6.

deed sometimes said that the stream is clearest near the spring. Whatever use may fairly be made of this image, it does not apply to the history of a philosophy or belief, which on the contrary is more equable, and purer, and stronger, when its bed has become deep, and broad, and full.[11]

The trial of Christian truth in conflict with pagan opinion and heresy, its "collision" with other views of the world and with heterodox opinions about Christ, this "expands" it and "perfects" it in the clarity of its self-possession and expression. This is to say that the future preserves the past in changing it, and therefore for us to know the past as well as we can, we have to know what it becomes in the future.

So much for an initial attempt to fix what we are speaking of when we say "development of doctrine." As it has thus far been presented, development may seem to be a subsidiary or peripheral theological topic. In fact, it is at the center of theology, and it will be worthwhile to close this chapter with a brief word about that.

First, development has been presented already as something an intrinsic part of which is the act of faith, faith in the truth of the original, one revelation, and including the recognition by a perhaps more learned faith of the identity of the subsequent many with the original one. Considered in this way, it just is Catholic Tradition understood as the handing on across time of the one faith. Insofar as the traditioning of faith is inspired by and governed by the Holy Spirit, however, to speak of the development of doctrine is just a way of speaking of the mission of the Spirit to the Church. Second, insofar as the core of what is handed on in the Tradition of the Church is Christ himself, the Word made flesh, who hands himself over to us in the flesh so that we can hand him over in word and sacrament to those we love, then it follows that to speak of the development of doctrine is to speak of the mission of the Word to the economy of salvation: it is the understanding of Christ that in one way or another is always being "developed." Third, the recipient of revelation—the subject who receives it—the subject who then develops revelation into manifold expressions, the subject who steadfastly remains in apostolic faith, the subject who has the competence to separate real development from bogus developments, from corruptions of the faith, the subject who

11. Newman, *Essay on Development*, 40.

12   CHAPTER 1

contemplates the original givenness of revelation with an appreciation enriched by the many developments—this subject is the Church as a whole and not any individual believer, lay or ordained, whether learned or episcopal or papal.

We should expect a theology of the development of doctrine, therefore, to be at once Pneumatological—a function of the "Pneuma," the Holy Spirit—as well as Christological and Ecclesiological. For the active subject of Tradition is the Spirit, Christ is the meaning of Scripture, and the Spirit is easily and recognizably found only in the Church, which is the Body of but one Head, Christ. This will be made explicit in the following two chapters.

CHAPTER 2

THE INVENTION OF DOGMA

In chapter one, the development of dogma was described as the passage from a one to a many, from God's revelation to us apprehended as a whole—say, in the Apostles' Creed—to the many teachings of the *Catechism of the Catholic Church*. The original and terminal points could be illustrated by comparing the Apostles' Creed (composed from the late second to the seventh century, begun in Rome and finished beyond the Alps)[1] to the profession of faith of the Fourth Lateran Council (1215), *Firmiter*,[2] which has many more statements than the list comprising the Apostles' Creed, or to the Profession of Faith of Pope Paul VI (1968), which at seven pages is also quite lengthy.[3]

On the other hand, relative to the many statements of the Bible bearing on Father, Son, and Spirit and their works in the economy of salvation

---

1. DH 30; ND 5.
2. DH 803; ND 19–21.
3. ND 39/3–39/23.

and our participation therein, the more solemnly defined dogmas of the Church can look like a very slimmed down list of the objects of faith. The list stretches from the pronouncements of the Christological councils of the fourth and fifth and sixth centuries to the Council of Trent in the sixteenth century to the First Vatican Council in the nineteenth century and on to the Dogma of the Assumption of Our Lady in 1950, and we can throw in for good measure the teachings of popes and local councils later accepted as universally authoritative in the West, like Pius V's condemnation of Michael Baius (1567) or the Second Council of Orange (529). Still, the list of dogmatic teachings seems rather to be a consommé or a chef's reduction compared to a stew or the original pot roast. Next to the rich fare and thick sauce of the Bible, the list of the Church's dogmatic teachings is a distillation. Why did the Church want this distillation, and for what purpose, and how did she produce it?

The why and for what purpose questions can be answered by looking to the first production of dogma in the strict sense. Yves Congar, relying on the teaching of the First Vatican Council, gives us a definition of dogma in this strict sense as follows.

By the word "dogma" is meant the assertion of some truth contained in the word of God, either written or handed on (*tradita*), and proposed by the Church in an authentic formulation to be believed as divinely revealed, whether by a solemn judgment or at least by the ordinary and universal magisterium.[4]

Evidently, what a dogma is cannot be understood unless it is seen in its relations to revelation (the word of God), Scripture, Tradition, and the ecclesial Magisterium or teaching authority. These relations are explored in the next chapter. But before that more systematic exposition, it is worthwhile to examine the very origin of dogma in this strict sense, for there the nature of the thing first comes to light—*natura* comes from *nasci*, "to be born." The origin of dogma, the invention of dogma, is the work of the Council of Nicaea.[5]

---

4. Yves Congar, OP, *La Foi et la Théologie* (Tournai: Desclée, 1962), 54. Cf. Vatican I, *Dei Filius*, chap. 3: "All those things are to be believed with divine and Catholic faith which are contained in the word of God, written or handed down, and which by the Church, either in solemn judgement or through her ordinary and universal teaching office, are proposed for belief as divinely revealed" (DH 3033; ND 121).

5. Historians of the *word* "dogma" as referring to teaching of faith officially proposed by the

It is not true that prior to the Council of Nicaea in 325 there was no dogmatic movement in the Church in a large sense. Very importantly, there was movement to a common agreement throughout the Church on the canon or at least parts of the canon of Scripture in the second century.[6] Marcion of Sinope (c. 85–c. 160) wanted to abandon the Old Testament and much of the New, and this was rejected by the Church. Justin Martyr and Irenaeus of Lyons considered him a heretic, and he was excommunicated by the Roman Church. On the other hand, the gnostic gospels were not added to what the Church accepted as scripture inspired of God, and the gnostic reading of the canonical gospels was rejected (by Irenaeus again). The pattern of revelation, the great design stretching from Genesis to the Book of Revelation, was therefore preserved (although the Book of Revelation's canonical status was disputed into the fourth century).

Nonetheless, there is a pronounced novelty to the way in which the Council of Nicaea addressed the Arian controversy, and this novelty consisted in its production of a dogmatic statement that nicely separated Arian goats from orthodox sheep. If we consider Nicaea and its achievement carefully, we will learn much about dogma, what it is, and what its "development" must be like. What it is according to Bernard Lonergan is a reflexive grasp of what is contained in revelation where the scriptural statements in which this revelation is communicated to us are taken as true.[7] Of course, the scriptural statements themselves were already appre-

---

Church will commonly say this sense is not fully formulated until Philipp Neri Chrismann, OFM, in 1792, for whom a dogma is a revealed truth, promulgated by the Church to be received by faith, the denial of which is heresy. For the history, see Paul Schrodt, *The Problem of the Beginning of Dogma in Recent Theology* (Frankfurt am Main: Peter Lang, 1978), 131–246, who picks out Melchior Cano, OP (†1560) and Francis Veron (†1649) much before Chrismann; Michael Seewald, *Dogma im Wandel. Wie Glaubenslehren sich entwickeln* (Freiburg, Herder, 2018), 22–51. But the *notion* of dogma is much older than its association with the word, "dogma," and operative with the Council of Nicaea. For the notion in Sacred Scripture, see Heinrich Schlier, "Kerygma und Sophia. Zur neutestamentlichen Grundlegung des Dogmas," in *Der Zeit der Kirche* (Freiburg: Herder, 1966), 206–32.

6. See Rowan Greer, "The Christian Bible and Its Interpretation," in Roman Greer and James Kugel, *Early Biblical Interpretation*, ed. Wayne Meeks (Philadelphia: Westminster, 1986), 107–208, at 110, and Joseph Lienhard, SJ, *The Bible, the Church, and Authority: The Canon of the Christian Bible in History and Theology* (Collegeville, MN: Liturgical Press, 1995), 27–28.

7. Bernard J. F. Lonergan, *Collected Works of Bernard Lonergan*, vol. 11, *The Triune God: Doctrines*, trans. Michael G. Shields, ed. Robert M. Doran and H. Daniel Monsour (Toronto: University of Toronto Press, 2009), 31–33, 43–45 (hereafter, *The Triune God: Doctrines*). See Jeremy D. Wilkins, *Before Truth: Lonergan, Aquinas, and the Problem of Wisdom* (Washington, DC: The Catholic University of America Press, 2018), esp. chap. 7, "Doctrine and Meaning."

hended as authoritative and true. But a reflexive grasp of scriptural truth expressed in extra-scriptural words is something else. In the first place, we want to see why dogma in this sense was produced at Nicaea. Second, we want to see how the Nicene dogma can be recognized as a true rendering of core New Testament teachings on Christ. Here, there is indeed a great boiling down of Scriptural statements into the one statement of Nicaea that the Son of God is one in substance with the Father. Third, in addition to what Nicaea implicitly teaches about dogmatic statements, there is also what it implies about bishops and their authority. It is not just dogma that is invented at Nicaea, but there is first realized at Nicaea a council of bishops that is ecumenical. In defining its teaching and, as it were, inventing "dogma," Nicaea is also claiming and implicitly defining its own authority, the authority of the bishops taken as a whole. Fourth, this authority is strictly bound to an ability to declare in human language expressing propositions what is the case about divine reality, such declarations being "dogmas." Last, Nicaea also reveals something about the providential ordering of history in that it begins a kind of thinking that has come to be called Christian philosophy.

Arius and the condemnation of his teaching at Nicaea

In the second decade of the fourth century, the presbyter Arius of Alexandria stirred controversy by his teaching on the Son of God. In explaining his views to his bishop, Alexander, Arius acknowledges God as alone unbegotten and eternal, who begets a Son, through whom he makes all things. The Son does not "emanate" from the Father, for Arius takes such language to imply a divisible and material divinity whereas he understands divinity correctly enough to be transcendent to matter. The Father begets the Son for Arius, but he makes no distinction between begetting and creating; the Son is created. He is the created instrument of God's creation of all other things. He is therefore before all other created things, but not eternal as is God himself. Like the other things that are made, he proceeds from the will of God.[8]

---

8. John Behr, *Formation of Christian Theology*, vol. 2, *The Nicene Faith*, Part 1: *True God of True God* (Crestwood, NY: St. Vladimir's Seminary Press, 2004), 136–37.

Arius's problem

Khaled Anatolios thinks the Arian controversy was inevitable. The problem is how to integrate a divine Christ into a heightened sense of divine transcendence. This heightened sense is produced by the newly found clarity of Christians about creation, namely that it is *ex nihilo* and that creation proceeds absolutely freely from God according to his will.[9] But there is a primacy of Christ as well as a primacy of the Creator. For Christ is the firstborn of creation (Col 1:15), is the paradigm of creation (Col 1:16), and has primacy in all things (Col 1:17–18). How are these primacies to be fit together?[10] In one way, the primacy of a preexistent Christ can be thought of as part of or within the divine primacy, which means that Father and Son are interior to the divine transcendence as such. But Arius's solution is to locate Christ's primacy as something strictly subordinate to that of the transcendent God. Like creation, he proceeds from the will of God, and though he is the instrument of creation, he is likewise *ex nihilo*.[11]

Two very different readings of Sacred Scripture

If we turn to the subsequent controversial literature of St. Athanasius, who holds that the Son is of the same nature as the Father, the difference between him and Arius appears first of all to be a matter of how they read Scripture. According to John 6:37, "Everything the Father gave me will come to me." If then he receives something from the Father, Arius asks, how can he be one in nature with him?[12] According to Matthew 26:39, Jesus was troubled in spirit at his approaching passion and death. If so, Arius concludes that he cannot be the power of God and so of the same nature as God. Again, according to Luke 2:52, Jesus grows in wisdom, and

---

9. Khaled Anatolios, *Retrieving Nicaea. The Development and Meaning of Trinitarian Doctrine* (Grand Rapids, MI: Baker Academic, 2011), 36, 39. For the emergence of this clarity, see Gerhard May, *Creatio Ex Nihilo. The Doctrine of 'Creation out of Nothing' in Early Christian Thought*, trans. A. S. Worrall (London: T&T Clark, 1994).

10. Anatolios, *Retrieving Nicaea*, 39, 41.

11. Anatolios, *Retrieving Nicaea*, 44–45.

12. Athanasius, "Against the Arians," trans. J. H. Newman and revised by A. Robinson, in *Nicene and Post-Nicene Fathers*, vol. 4: *Athanasius: Select Works and Letters*, 2nd ser., ed. Philip Schaff and Henry Wace (Peabody, MA: Hendrickson Publishers, 1994), 303–447, discourse 3, chap. 26, no. 26, p. 408.

according to Matthew 16:13, he asks his disciples a question. So he cannot be the wisdom of God and of the same nature as God.[13] And there are many such passages that are put in play. In answering, Athanasius holds that when the Word becomes flesh (Jn 1:14), he does not enter into a man but becomes a man.[14] So, "the things proper to the flesh are said to belong to him [the Son of God, the Logos] because he was in it—such things as being hungry, being thirsty, suffering, getting tired, and the like.... But the proper works of the Logos himself, such as raising the dead and making the blind see ... he accomplished through [the instrumentality] of his own body."[15] Christ therefore suffers and is afraid in the flesh, not in his divine nature,[16] and he is ignorant only according to the flesh.[17] As to the Lord Jesus "receiving" from his Father, Athanasius takes John 6:37 to suppose the distinction of Father and Son and to mean that Christ receives what he does from the Father eternally.[18]

Arius and his partisans take the incarnate Son as one who in his single and simple nature is needy, receptive, troubled, and unglorified. Such does not befit the nature of God; therefore, the Son is not truly divine. Athanasius replies by distinguishing the natures, divine and human. What the Lord Jesus says as man and in virtue of his assumed human nature does not, indeed, befit the divine nature he shares with his Father. But that does not mean he is not truly divine, sharing also the divine nature, a nature that he indeed receives from the Father. Athanasius divides or "parts" the sayings and distributes what is said in the Scriptures; some things befit Christ as man, some are suited to him as divine. So, as John Behr has it, we find two kinds of exegesis operative in the fourth century and earlier. He styles these exegetical practices as either "univocal" or "partitive" when it comes to interpreting passages that speak of Christ. "The non-Nicenes ... insisted on an absolutely univocal exegesis, which applied all scriptural affirmations in a unitary fashion to one subject, who thus turns out to be a demi-god, neither fully divine nor fully human."

---

13. Athanasius "Against the Arians," discourse 3, chap. 26, no. 26, p. 408.

14. Athanasius, "Against the Arians," discourse 3, chap. 26, no. 30, p. 410.

15. Athanasius, "Against the Arians," discourse 3, chap. 26, no. 31, p. 410.

16. Athanasius, "Against the Arians," discourse 3, chap. 26, no. 34, pp. 412–13.

17. Athanasius "Against the Arians," discourse 3, chap. 27, no. 38, p. 414.

18. Athanasius, "Against the Arians," discourse 3, chap. 27, no. 35, p. 413.

The Nicene theologians, however, take Scripture to speak of Christ "in a two-fold fashion, demanding in turn a 'partitive' exegesis: some things are said of him as divine and other things are said of him as human—yet referring to the same Christ throughout."[19] Arians will say that God himself is impassible, and cannot suffer as did Jesus. For in God there is no alteration or shadow of decay or possibility thereof. Athanasius will say Christ suffered as a man, not as divine. The two conditions or ways of being of the incarnate Christ are to be respected in what we say belongs to him.

Arius and the frame within which he reads Scripture

It is tempting to suppose that Arius is doing nothing more than assimilating Christian belief in Father and Son and Spirit to the hierarchical metaphysics of some form of neo-Platonism, where Nous, the divine mind and the first emanation from the ultimate One, is thought of in terms apparently within hailing distance of the Bible—Wisdom, Logos—and the third hypostasis, the world Soul, is in turn matched with the Holy Spirit.[20] Origen has used the Platonist language of participation before Arius to describe the relation of Son to Father,[21] and Arius is certainly acquainted with Origen. If the Son only participates in divinity, however, then he is not divine as is the Father. He cannot be equal to the Father. And if divinity itself in its transcendent reality admits of no degrees, then to say the Son participates is to say he is created like the other things that share in God.[22]

However we adjudicate any neo-Platonic influence, direct or indirect, it is clear that Arius has abandoned the frame within which the Church reads Scripture. This frame is embedded in the New Testament itself. So in Philippians, Christ is in the form of both God and man (2:6–7), and invites the partitive exegesis Athanasius practices. Again, the Son of God

19. John Behr, *The Nicene Faith*, Part 1, 14.

20. For brief discussion, see Anatolios, *Retrieving Nicaea*, 45, and Brian E. Daley, SJ, *God Visible: Patristic Christology Reconsidered* (Oxford: Oxford University Press, 2018), 95–96.

21. Origen, *Commentary on the Gospel According to John, Books 1–10*, vol. 80 of *Fathers of the Church*, trans. Ronald E. Heine (Washington, DC: The Catholic University of America Press, 1989), at John 1:1; Book 2, pp. 98–99, nos. 16–18.

22. For discussion, see Lonergan, *The Triune God: Doctrines*, 127–33; John Behr, *Formation of Christian Theology*, vol. 1: *The Way to Nicaea* (Crestwood, NY: St. Vladimir's Seminary Press, 2001), 188–91.

is descended from David according to the flesh, but is designated and manifested as Son of God by his resurrection (Rom 1:3–4). Again, the Word's dwelling among us is according to the flesh, not according to what he is as eternally unto God (Jn 1:1, 14).

Nor does Arius read within the framework of the Church's liturgy. Baptism is into the name of Father, and Son, and Spirit (cf. Mt 28:19), and there is no distinction made to the saving effect of being baptized into one rather than another of the Three. If the saving effect is such, the saving cause is the same. The identity of soteriological-baptismal effect implies an identity of metaphysical status of the persons in themselves.[23]

The teaching of Nicaea

Arius's gift to fourth-century Christian thought was twofold. First, he dismissed the materialist images of Tertullian and others, comparing the relation of Father and Son to that of spring to a stream, or a root to a shoot, as useless for understanding the relation of Son to Father. Second, he posed the question of the Son's status in an unmistakable way: Is the Son created or not?[24] This question was not to be ignored, since it asks about the status of the Son, biblically revealed, in *biblical* categories. He uses the category of "creation," what is made out of nothing by the almighty Creator, to ask of the Son: created or not?[25] This is not a question the Church could refuse. Because of his exegesis, Arius answers the question affirmatively: the Son is created, since in the Incarnation he changes, suffers, and in general is seen to share in creaturely limitation. The council, reading Scripture in accord with the Rule of Faith and according to prior and "partitive" exegetical practice, answers negatively.

According to J. N. D. Kelly, the creed that Nicaea produces is based on an unknown Syro-Palestinian baptismal creed.[26] Conciliar additions to the base text are written in italics.

---

23. See Anatolios, *Retrieving Nicaea*, 145–48.

24. Lonergan, *The Triune God: Doctrines*, 251–253

25. Arius is certainly aware of the second-century clarification of the notion of creation to mean *creatio ex nihilo*; see Anatolios, *Retrieving Nicaea*, 44–45.

26. J. N. D. Kelly, *Early Christian Creeds*, 3rd ed. (New York: Longmans, 1972), 229. According to John Behr, *The Nicene Faith*, Part 1, 155, it is based on the creed of Basil of Caesarea that he presented to the council, itself based on the Creed of Antioch of 324.

We believe in one God, the Father almighty,
    maker of all things visible and invisible;
And in one Lord Jesus Christ, the Son of God,
begotten from the Father, only-begotten,
    (1) *that is, from the substance of the Father,*
God from God, light from light,
    (2) *true God from true God,*
    (3) *begotten, not made,*
    (4) *of one substance with the Father,*
through Whom all things came into being,
    things in heaven and things on earth,
Who because of us men and because of our salvation
    came down and became incarnate, becoming man,
    suffered and rose again on the third day,
    ascended to the heavens,
    will come again to judge the living and the dead;
And in the Holy Spirit.
    (5) *But as for those who say,*
        (a) *There was when He was not, and,*
        (b) *Before being born He was not,*
        (c) *and that He came into existence out of nothing,*
        (d) *or who assert that the Son of God is of a different hypostasis or
            substance,*
        (e) *or is subject to alteration or change*
        —*these the Catholic and apostolic Church anathematizes.*[27]

The text the council starts with did not in its wording expressly exclude
Arianism. It states that Christ is "begotten" and "only-begotten" of the Father. But this scriptural language does not make any distinction between
Arians and orthodox Christians, as long as being begotten is not distinguished from the equally scriptural notion of being created. So we turn to
the additions.

(1) "From the substance of the Father" contradicts Arius's profession
of faith to Alexander of Alexandria of 318. Arius could say the Son was

---

27. This is the translation in Kelly, *Early Christian Creeds*, 215–16, 218 (additions). I have added the formatting.

22   CHAPTER 2

"from the Father," for all things are "from God" (1 Cor 8:6),[28] but he would not say "from the substance of the Father," since that meant for him materialism and change in the godhead. The intention of the council is to say the Son is "*not* out of nothing," that is, not like creatures. Evidently, "from the substance of the Father" implies that the Son is "one in substance" or consubstantial with the Father—*homoousios tô patri.*

(2) "True God from true God." This is a very firm denial of Arianism, and a rejection of its appeal to John 17:3, "the only true God." The Son could be divine by grace, by participation in God, and so, "God," but a lesser god and thus not "true God" or "God himself"—the *theos alêthinos,* the *autotheos.* If what the Son is is true God, then everything truly predicated of the Father as God is to be truly predicated of the Son as God. And that is just what Nicaea means: the Son is God in whatever sense the Father is. It follows that if the Father is the unique God, then so is the Son.

(3) "Begotten, not made." The council distinguishes where Arius did not. The Son is on God's side of the Creator-creature distinction. It is not enough to say that he is simply the first created, the greatest created thing. Of Mary the Mother of God we might say this. But the Son is not created at all. The council simply supposes that what is generated, or begotten, is of the same nature as what generates, begets. Human fathers *generate* human sons—they are of the same status and level of reality. Carpenters *make* chairs; chairs are not human beings. As John Behr puts it, that the Son is begotten and not created "implies that the Son is internal, as it were, to the being of God as Father, rather than a product of a deliberately undertaken action."[29]

(4) "*Homoousios tô patri*"— "of one substance with the Father." This, too, is a certain denial of Arianism. It was inserted because while Arius could find a way to make the biblical language say what he wanted, he could not find a way to make "*homoousios*" say what he wanted. The term was attractive also because its meaning was not yet really fixed in any prior theology of the time except as connoting material reality (which makes Arius reject it).[30] Father and Son are really distinct, but each is the one,

28. Athanasius, "Defense of the Nicene Creed" (*De Decretis*), trans. J. H. Newman, in *Nicene and Post-Nicene Fathers,* 2nd ser., vol. 4, 149–72; no. 19, pp. 162–63.

29. Behr, *The Nicene Faith,* Part 1, 156.

30. Behr, *The Nicene Faith,* Part 1, 157.

unique substance of God. Personal distinction does not divide the God-head into many gods, and both Father and Son are each the one God.[31]

Ousia—substance or being—certainly might suggest to us the working of some philosophical mind. It is not a scriptural term for speaking the relation of Son to Father. But neither is it always a technical philo-sophical term, just as "being" is not always used with some explicit philosophical twist in English. For Athanasius, two men are of the same nature (*homophyês*), or of the same substance (*homoousios*), while a man and a dog are not. Nor of things that are *homoousios* can one of them be so by participation; that would mean likeness, not sameness of substance; the Son is not divine by participation.[32] According to G.L. Prestige, the term *homoousios* is not used in a technical philosophical sense already to hand in Greek metaphysics.[33] In ordinary language, of two copper coins, it could be said on the street that they are "*homoousios*"— "of the same stuff," "of a common stuff." *Ousia* could mean "that which is"—it is, after all, just a participle of the verb "to be"; or more popularly, it could mean bodily stuff, matter.[34] The materialism of Tertullian, however, is excluded in two ways.

First, the relationship of generator to generated qualifies the sense of the "stuff" in question. God is the generator, and the stuff is therefore not material stuff. It will therefore not be a material generation, and the *ousia* common to both will not be a material substance. Second, and more

---

31. See J.N.D. Kelly, *Early Christian Doctrines* (New York: Harper and Row, 1960), 234–35. Here is how Lonergan puts it in *The Triune God: Doctrines*, 183: "[T]his affirmation of the one sub-stance is logically contained in the Nicene decree. For *first*, those who were present at the Council were monotheists; but then if God is one, and the Father is truly God, and the Son also is truly God, it necessarily follows that the divinity of the Father and that of the Son are numerically the same. *Next*, according to the testimony of Athanasius, the Fathers assembled in the Council first thought it would be good to add to the decree that the Son is the true image of the Father, most similar to the Father in all things without any variance; but then, when they realized that this could give a handle to the Arians, ... 'they were forced to go back to the scripture again and express in clearer terms what they had said earlier, and finally to write that the Son is consubstantial with the Father, so as to signify that the Son is not only similar to the Father but is the same as the Father by similitude from the Father....'" He is quoting Athanasius, *De Decretis*.

32. Athanasius, "On the Councils of Ariminum and Seleucia" (*De Synodis*), trans. J.H. New-man, rev. A. Robertson, in Nicene and Post-Nicene Fathers, 2nd series, vol. 4, 448–480; see esp. 478–79.

33. See G.L. Prestige, *God in Patristic Thought* (London: SPCK, 1952), 197ff.

34. Lonergan, *The Triune God: Doctrines*, 173–75.

importantly, the term is explicated by the "true God of true God." We cannot say that only the Father is *autotheos* and that the Son merely participates in him. Whatever it is that is divine belongs equally to Father and to Son. This certainly includes transcendence to the material world and every materially limited being.[35]

The last point indicates another way to explicate the *homoousios*, one taken up explicitly by St. Athanasius. If whatever belongs to the Father belongs to the Son, then we might as well say the following: Whatever you say of the Father say of the Son, and vice versa, as long as you are not denying the distinction between them. This is the "Rule of Athanasius." It is what he formulated in explaining the council. The meaning of the *homoousios* is grasped when one understands a rule about how to make true predications of Father and Son.[36] It means that we are to predicate (assert, affirm, and hold as *true*) the same things of the Son as of the Father: "the same things are said of the Son as of the Father except the name Father."[37] Whatever you say of the Father, therefore, you must say of the Son (and of the Holy Spirit): if you hold it to be true that the Father is good, goodness itself, then you must say the same of the Son; if you say and hold it true that the Father is wise, is wisdom, then you must say the same and hold it to be true of the Son. If the Father is the *autotheos*—the true God, God in the fullest sense, and not by participation—then the same is true of the Son. The exception of the "name of the Father" in the rule of Athanasius is the exception of the term of a relation; it upholds the real distinction between Father and Son. That is, you must not say that the Father is the Son, or the Son the Father—the generator is not the generated, and vice versa. The distinction of Father and Son is predicated only according to a relation, but if the relation is real, then the distinction is real. There are two persons, then, not one, within divine reality.

Here we find what Lonergan calls the "openness" of Nicaea.[38] Nicaea

---

35. Bernard Lonergan, "The Dehellenization of Dogma," in *A Second Collection* (Philadelphia: Westminster, 1974), 23.

36. Lonergan, "Dehellenization," 23.

37. Athanasius, "Against the Arians," discourse 3, no. 4, p. 395. Or, as the Roman Liturgy has it in the Preface for Trinity Sunday (now used throughout the year): "for what we believe of your glory, through your revelation, this we confess of your Son, this we confess of the Holy Spirit, without difference or distinction."

38. Lonergan, "Dehellenization," 23.

does not tie itself to a Greek philosophical conception of God or of the divine in using "*ousia*." And when the *homoousios* is unpacked according to the Rule of Athanasius, we do not learn *what* to predicate of the Son and of the Father; the Rule says only that whatever you predicate of the Father, you must predicate of the Son. But if we want to find out what to predicate, we must read the Scriptures, or read some philosophical theology congruent with the Scriptures. All Nicaea says to us is that if you think of the Father in those categories, you should think of the Son in the same categories.

(5) Last, as to the anathematisms. Note first of all that it is a question of what you "say." It is a question of what one asserts, just as with the Rule of Athanasius. The body of the text speaks of what we *believe*. The anathematisms speak of what someone *says*, for we do not embrace any falsehood with divine and Catholic faith. In either case, however, it is a question of statement, of affirmation. We return to this below and in chapter 4.

The first line (a) means to deny Arius's catchphrase, "there was [a time] when he [the Son] was not." The second line (b) has about the same sense as the first. The third line (c) expressly distinguishes the Son from creatures, and thus fulfills the intent of the first insertion. The fourth line (d) supposes that hypostasis means the same as substance, which was common in the West and Egypt and for the orthodox until 362 (Council of Alexandria). What is being denied is that the Son is a different kind of being than the Father. The last line (e) denies that the Son is changeable, something that is an implication of Arius's position that the Son is created, though one that he did not admit. He held that the Son was morally unchanged, unchanging.

To Arius's question, therefore, the Church answers, "uncreated," while maintaining the real distinction of persons in the Trinity. Identity of substance (or nature) and distinction of persons (or "hypostases," as this word came to be used in the fifth century)—that is the Church's doctrine.

The logic of Nicaea

It remains that there is a verbal gap between the generally scriptural language of the council's creed and its assertion that the Son is *homoousios tô patri*—one in being, or one in substance with the Father. How do we know this verbal gap is not a real gap—the assertion of a different teaching than the teaching of the New Testament? We know it is not a real gap by the force of logic. And this is what we need to see more closely in understanding Nicaea as a development and not a corruption of the deposit of faith.

We may paraphrase the teaching of Nicaea as follows. God the Father does not create the Son from nothing, nor does he make him from some preexistent stuff, but he begets him as consubstantial with himself.[39] In order to understand the teaching, then, we need to distinguish creating, begetting, and making, and say a word about how we shall understand "substance."[40]

Begetting, making, and creating, all three, name the action by which one thing proceeds into existence from another. To make something is to bring something forth from some already existing material. The carpenter brings the table forth from the lumber. To beget something is to bring something forth from oneself. Father and mother bring forth a child from themselves. To create is to bring something forth, neither from oneself nor from some already existing material, but from nothing. This is the production of the entire being of something. It is proper to God alone.

As to substance and consubstantial. One dog is consubstantial with another dog, and one tiger with another tiger, and one eagle with another eagle. Of things consubstantial with one another, all the properties of one are predicated of the other, and all the properties of the other are predicated of the first.

A property is something that flows from the nature of the thing, and so a thing has its properties by necessity of nature. Dogs are white or black or brown; such qualifications are not properties but accidents, things that "happen" to belong to some dog. But that a dog has teeth, paws, a sensitive nose—these are properties, things that belong to all dogs by the nature of what it is to be a dog.

What has the same essence or nature must have the same properties. So, the properties of Fido are also properties of Rex, the properties of John are also properties of Sally, and so on. Where one discovers of two

---

39. A paraphrase of the first thesis of Lonergan's *The Triune God: Doctrines*, 247.

40. Lonergan, *The Triune God: Doctrines*, 257–59.

things that all the properties of one in fact belong to the other, then one knows that the two things are consubstantial.

Now God does not have properties in the way some finite created nature does; he has no properties really distinct from his essence. Nonetheless, the analysis of the divine nature shows us attributes that must be predicated of God—attributes that follow necessarily (with a necessity like unto that of properties) from his transcendence. So, the divine nature is immutable, eternal, all knowing, all powerful, provident. These are attributes verified of the God of Abraham and Moses in the Old Testament.[41]

Evidently, we are dealing with the existence of the Son apart from and independently of his Incarnation, the "preexistent" Son. This is not to say that in the order of our knowledge, we know the Son, the Second Person of the Trinity, apart from and independently of his Incarnation. But we are dealing here with the object known, in himself, the Son who is eternally begotten, and would be begotten by his Father, even if there were no creation, and even if there were no Incarnation. This preexistence is asserted in such texts as John 1:1–3, John 8:58 ("Before Abraham was, I am"), 1 Corinthians 8:6 ("through whom are all things"), Philippians 2:6ff. (where an already existing Christ takes the form of humanity—the form of a servant), Colossians 1:15 ("the first born of all creation"), and Hebrews 1:2 ("through whom also he created the world"). There are also those sayings in the Synoptic gospels where Jesus says of himself that he "has come," where the implication is that he has come into the world from outside the world (from outside the created order), and those sayings where he says he has "been sent"—into the world from outside the world.[42]

Given this clarification of terms, the teaching of Nicaea can be demonstrated part by part, in four parts.

41. The Old Testament mostly gives us God who comes to be known in the immediacy of his personal and historical action engaging the patriarchs, prophets, and kings of Israel. The short form of the demonstration of his transcendence from this engagement is as follows: absolute control of history and human freedom implies absolute control of nature and being which in turn implies that God is creator. Once it is clear that he is not a part of the world that he creates, then one denies of him all limits that are intrinsic to such worldly parts: composition out of parts, operative imperfection or the possibility thereof, finitude, local or temporal circumscription, mutability, ignorance, malice, and limited power.

42. Lonergan, *The Triune God: Doctrines*, 273–75.

First, God the Father does not create the Son from nothing. The Bible speaks of "creation from nothing" in so many terms only once, in 2 Maccabees 7: "God did not make them [heaven and earth and the things in them—all things] out of things that existed" (RSV), or "Dieu les a fait de rien" (Jerusalem Bible). Exegetes, however, do not understand the "nothing" as conceptually distinct from philosophically conceived matter. On the other hand, God makes all things by his word: "He spoke and it [the earth] came to be" (Psalm 32:9; also 32:6). This making by "saying" alone indicates a freedom from any other condition of making, even the conditions of having to have some preexistent material on hand. See also Genesis 1:3, 6, 9, 11, 14, 20, 24, 26, according to which God speaks, and things are made. In Genesis 1, the repeated report that God creates by his "saying" is comprehensive with respect to all formed things. And the "waters" of 1:2? Are the "waters" some preexistent material? No. The deep and the waters are an imaginative way of saying that nothing with any reality is presupposed to creation. Moreover, God does not make the sun and stars out of the waters of the deep.[43]

Now of Christ, 1 Corinthians 8:6 says that he is the one "through whom are all things." Colossians 1:16 says also that "all things were created through him." According to Hebrews 1:2, the Son is the one "through whom God created the world," and of course John 1:3 has it that "all things were made through him [the Word]." But if all things were made through him, he evidently is not one of the things made. If all created things are through him, he cannot be included in the "all." He is not created.

If there is a screwdriver by which all screws are driven, then there are no screws in the screwdriver. If there were, the screwdriver would be a cause of itself. So, if Christ is also one of the things made through himself, he is *causa sui*. This idea was indeed defended by Arians: Christ is created and creator. It is a self-contradictory idea.[44] The scope of what is created is universal, and creation is the production of the entire being of something. Thus, if things are, are beings, and are not God, they are created. If Christ, too, is created, then his power must extend also to himself. But there is no such possible thing.

---

43. See May, *Creatio Ex Nihilo*, for the articulation of creation *ex nihilo* in the second century by Tatian, Theophilus of Antioch, and Irenaeus.

44. Anatolios, *Retrieving Nicaea*, 184.

Second, God the Father does not make the Son from any preexisting created thing. For if God did, then the preexisting thing (matter) was not made through the Son. To the contrary, all things were made through him, and the citations for the first part extend to this.

Third, God the Father begets the Son as Son from himself as Father. For in the first place, the Son receives all from the Father. See Matthew 11:27, "all things have been delivered to me by my Father," and John 5:19, "the Son can do nothing of his own accord, but only what he sees the Father doing; for whatever he does, that the Son does likewise." As for Matthew, "all things" includes divinity itself, and so it, too, has been delivered to the Son. As for John, the Son has no independent agency; he is an agent, but all that he does, he does as something first done by his Father; what he does is received. See also John 5:26, "as the Father has life in himself, so he has granted the Son also to have life in himself." It is a question of the same "life in itself" that the Father has, and that the Son receives, since it is granted him. This declaration is very telling, for the God of Abraham and Moses is preeminently the God of life, who gives life to us and other created living things. But it is not "life in itself" we possess. These few authorities are not all that can be adduced, but they are enough for the demonstration of this part of the thesis.

In the second place, the Son receives what he does from the Father as *Son*, as one begotten as Son. "Son" is said in many ways in the Scriptures, but of Christ in a unique sense. Yes, David is God's son, and the faithful in John 1:13 are "born" of God. These many are born, indeed, of "the will of God," by God's good pleasure. But Christ is born as the "only Son from the Father," according to John 1:14. The same sense of uniqueness is indicated in Matthew 11:27, where "no one knows the Father except the Son." These indications of uniqueness, moreover, push the meaning of the predication in the direction of being properly predicated; that is, the Son is not a son metaphorically, the way David is a son of God. And if we know the Father by the grace of revelation (Mt 11:27), this grace, this revelation, is from Christ, who is himself full of grace and truth (Jn 1:14, 18). The same exclusivity and propriety of predication is indicated in Matthew 21:33–41, the parable of the vineyard: the son whom the owner sends to tenants who leased the vineyard is distinguished just as such, as son, from the servants and envoys previously sent. See the distinction of the Son from prophets in Hebrews 1:1–2.[45] See also John 20:30–33, where, as Lonergan points out for us, "Son of God" is used in an especially solemn declaration of the point of the gospel.

But if he is Son really and truly, then he is "begotten" from the Father, with all due analogizing because of the nonbodily, nonmaterial, nontemporal "begetting" in question.

Fourth, God the Father begets a Son consubstantial to him. In Lonergan's proof of this part of the thesis, he appeals seriatim to eleven predications common to God the Father and God the Son: (1) exclusive knowledge of each other (Mt 11:27); (2) the title "Lord"; (3) the title "God"; (4) the titles "Lord of Lords" and "King of Kings"; (5) the title "Alpha and Omega"; (6) the "I Am"; (7) the glory of God; (8) power; (9) life "in himself"; (10) same knowability—that is, if one knows one, the other is known, too (Jn 14:6–11; 8:19; 12:45); (11) having all things in common (Jn 16:15; 17:10).[46]

So, for instance, Father and Son share the title "Lord." "The day of the Lord" of Joel 3:4 is quoted in Acts 2:20, and we read of the "day of the Lord" who is Christ in 1 Corinthians 1:9 and 5:5; 2 Corinthians 1:14; 1 Thessalonians 5:2; and so on. "The name of the Lord," that is to say, the name of the Lord God whom Jesus later addressed as "Father," is invoked in Joel 3:5, is quoted in Acts 2:21, but refers to Christ in Romans 10:9 and 13, and Christ's "name" is called on even as was God's in the Old Testament (see 1 Cor 1:2, Acts 9:14, Jas 2:7, etc.).

Just as God is the Alpha and Omega in Revelation 1:8 and 21:6, so also is this phrase applied to Christ at 1:17 ("the first and the last"), 2:8, and 22:13. As God is the I AM in Exodus 3:14 and Isaiah 43:10, so is Christ in John 8:24, 8:28, and 13:19. As the Father has Life "in himself," so also does the Son (Jn 5:26). See John 14:6—"I am the Life." They have also the same power: God is the one through whom are all things (Rom 11:36), and so is Christ (1 Cor 8:6, etc.).[47]

From the consubstantiality of the Son, it follows that Father and Son are alike at least specifically, by nature. That is, they are alike at least in the

---

45. Lonergan, *The Triune God: Doctrines*, 281ff.

46. Lonergan, *The Triune God: Doctrines*, 287–89.

47. For the same kind of argumentation in Athanasius, see Anatolios, *Retrieving Nicaea*, 110–12, 112–14, and in Gregory of Nyssa, *Retrieving Nicaea*, 185–86.

way that Tom and Harry are alike, in both being men. But the humanity of Tom, while specifically the same as that of Harry's, is not numerically the same. If it were, Tom and Harry would be one man, not two men. Father and Son are rather alike in being the one numerically unique divine nature.

The Son is therefore "not just similar," but "the same thing" as the Father, and yet, the Son is distinct from the Father, as an image from what it images, and as something "out of" the Father. The one God is one thing; the persons are distinct from one another, but each person is one and the same thing, divinity, God.[48] In this way, the council simply upholds the mystery of the identity of God as revealed in Scripture. The divinity of God, as including difference within its one substance, its one and undivided being, is shown to us by the career of Jesus and the subsequent mission of the Holy Spirit at Pentecost. In this way, the council upholds Christian hope for salvation and deification. Beyond the Arian sequestration of true divinity behind a created Son, divinity is understood as in itself shareable, in itself perfectly communicable. The Father begets the Son—shares his divinity with another. And this is the ground also of our confidence that the divinity is shareable, communicable, outside God, extending also to us. The grace by which we are saved really does introduce us into the life of God, not the life of a created intermediary, but the life of God, so that we can be *consors divinae naturae* (2 Pt 2:4, and cf. 1 Pt 1:23).[49]

These pages have been devoted to the logic and the *scriptural* logic of Nicaea because this is how one comes to recognize that as a development, Nicaea is a genuine development; this is how one comes to recognize the identity in plurality of the sense of Christ expressed in Scripture and the sense of Christ expressed by the council. *There is no other way to do it.* The discernment of the loving heart, which has yet to be addressed, the connatural knowledge of the truth of some proposition bearing on divine things, delivers only that to us: a judgment of truth. It does not deliver the very way to see the identity in plurality that the above logical exercises do. Affirming the identity is a requirement of divine and Catholic faith; seeing the identity is a part of *fides quaerens intellectum*, a theological task.

48. See especially Athanasius, "Against the Arians," discourse 3, no. 4, p. 395.
49. See Anatolios on Gregory of Nyssa, *Retrieving Nicaea*, 185–90, 194, 203–4.

This section, then, does nothing more than partially illustrate the program of Newman's *Essay on the Development of Doctrine*. The fourth and the sixth "marks" of developments taken together indicate the prominent role logical continuity plays in our ability to recognize them as genuine: "logical sequence" and "conservative action on its past." The Nicene teaching is logically related to the teaching of Scripture, tightly so, and thus conserves in the fourth century (and beyond) what was taught in the first century in the New Testament. According to Reinhard Hütter, all these marks, but especially the marks that engage the discursive, logical mind, are the very way in which Newman expresses the principle of Vincent of Lérins, that developments are genuine developments only according as they maintain the same sense and meaning of what they are developments of.[50] Newman brings the marks of development touching on logic to an acute point in *The Idea of a University* (1852).

Induction is the instrument of Physics, and deduction only is the instrument of Theology. There the simple question is, What is revealed? all doctrinal knowledge flows from one fountain head. If we are able to enlarge our view and multiply our propositions, it must be merely by the comparison and adjustment of the original truths; if we would solve new questions, it must be by consulting old answers. The notion of doctrinal knowledge absolutely novel, and of simple addition from without, is intolerable to Catholic ears, and never was entertained by any one who was even approaching to an understanding of our creed. *Revelation is all in all in doctrine*; the Apostles its sole depository, the inferential method its sole instrument, and ecclesiastical authority its sole sanction. The Divine Voice has spoken once for all, and the only question is about its meaning.[51]

We are not done with speaking about the role of logic and the varieties thereof in the development of dogma and recognizing developments as genuine. But this role is already prominent in understanding the Nicene

---

50. Reinhard Hütter, "Progress, Not Alteration of the Faith: Beyond Antiquarianism and Presentism. John Henry Newman, Vincent of Lérins, and the Criterion of Identity of the Development of Doctrine," *Nova et Vetera* (English) 19 (2021): 333–91, at 370–71 and 380–81. For Vincent, see the "Comminatory" (*Commonitorium*), trans. C. A. Heurtley, in *Nicene and Post-Nicene Fathers*, 2nd ser., vol. 11, *Sulpitius Severus, Vincent of Lérins, John Cassian*, 123–59, edited by Philip Schaff and Henry Wace (Peabody, MA: Hendrickson, 1994), chap. 23, no. 54, p. 148, where progress in the understanding of faith is to be "in the same doctrine, in the same sense, and in the same meaning."

51. John Henry Newman, *The Idea of a University*, ed. I. T. Ker (Oxford: Clarendon Press, 1976), 190 (223 in the 1852 edition). Emphasis added.

achievement. This is not to say that dogma is purely the product of logic, which would usurp the sovereign role of revelation itself, but it is to say that when the Church was delivered of the first of her dogmatic pronouncements, dialectics attended the laying in and maintained the health of the child.

An ecumenical council

The authority of Nicene dogma derives from the authority of those who, with the assistance of the Holy Spirit, composed it, and from the authority of Scripture, also divine, which it summarizes and interprets. As to that first root of its authority, Nicaea was the first of what Catholics recognize as ecumenical councils, where the whole Church exercises the authority with which she herself determines doctrine in the persons of the assembled bishops and with the participation of the Roman Church. It is the ecumenical or universal character of the council that is the guarantor of its authority. An individual bishop may err in matters of faith and morals. Local councils may err in such matters, too. It is only to the whole Church that the promise that Christ's words will not pass away is made (Mt 24:34–35), and the promise is realized in the exercise of the whole company of bishops standing for and acting on behalf of the whole Church (Matthew 18) or by the bishop who presides over all bishops, the bishop of Rome (Matthew 16).

Of course, first times and first things are not always recognized in their true nature at their first appearance, and so it was with the Council of Nicaea. It took rather the rest of the fourth century for the authority of the council and so the authority of its teaching to be recognized.[52] Even the very name "ecumenical" comes late to the council. That name is first applied to the Council of Constantinople in 381 by the attending bishops in the letter that accompanies their creed.[53] The creed of Constantinople itself reexpresses the Nicene Creed and teaches the divinity of the Holy Spirit. It expressly ratifies the dogmatic teaching of Nicaea.[54] Between Ni-

52. See Anatolios, *Retrieving Nicaea*, 15–31.
53. See "A letter of the bishops gathered in Constantinople," in *Decrees of the Ecumenical Councils*, vol. 1, ed. Norman P. Tanner, SJ (London: Sheed & Ward and Georgetown University Press, 1990), 25–30, at 29.
54. "A letter of the bishops," Tanner, *Decrees*, 1:29, and Canon 1, 1:31.

34 CHAPTER 2

caea and Constantinople in 381, however, there was a long series of councils seeking to settle the disagreements of various theological parties by any way except that of the Nicene doctrine. The inability to find a solution to these difficulties except by reappropriating the denial that the Son is created and in terms of the *homoousios* proved rather a sort of inductive test of the truth of Nicaea and its effectiveness in providing a standard for the faith and for the unity of the Church. The Nicene settlement was expressly the standard of Ephesus in 431, and Nestorius and Cyril of Alexandria were judged solely on the question of who was and who was not in accord with the creed of Nicaea (Cyril, yes; Nestorius, no).[55] Ephesus, too, styles itself "ecumenical,"[56] and provides that no other creed be accepted except that of Nicaea.[57]

While the authority of an ecumenical council in defining dogma comes to light in the fourth century, the role of the *sensus fidelium* also appears at the same time. The bishops at Nicaea exercised their ability to teach authoritatively. But the laity of the fourth century, as Newman pointed out, exercised a correlative power of doctrinal discernment. Even in the absence of episcopal leadership, many Christians rejected the Arian and semi-Arian teaching. They provided, as it were, an index of how the truths of the faith could be discerned.[58]

Dogma

The novelty of a first ecumenical council and the novelty of dogma are coeval, and together with the *sensus fidelium*, they are not understood apart from one another: they are related as teacher, teaching, and taught. Still, another word about the novelty of dogma is in order.

The novelty of dogma has first to do with its attention to the truth of the Scriptures interpreted according to an equally true statement that recapitulates the sense of the Scriptures. This is evident in St. Athanasius's account in the early 350s of why an extrabiblical term, the *homoousios*, was adopted to express biblical teaching. In chapter 5 of the *De Decretis*, or

---

55. Introduction to Ephesus, 37–39 in Tanner, *Decrees*, 1:37.

56. Ephesus, "Synodical letter about the eastern bishops," 62–64 in Tanner, *Decress*, 1:62.

57. Ephesus, "Definition of the faith at Nicaea," 64–66 in Tanner, *Decrees*, 1:65.

58. See John Henry Newman, Appendix 5, "Orthodoxy of the Faithful during Arianism," in *Arians of the Fourth Century* (London: Longmans, Green, 1901), 445–68.

Defense of the Nicene Council, he explained that the fathers wanted to express the Son's relation to the Father by saying that the Son was "from God." But, Athanasius continues, those sympathetic to Arius, like Eusebius of Caesarea and others, could say that all things—all created things—are "from God." So, the fathers added that the Son is "from the essence [*ousia*] of the Father," and therefore not merely from the creative power of the Father.[59] Again, the fathers wished to say that the Son is the power and image of the Father, like the Father, in the Father, always with him, inalterable. But the Arian party could say that men are in the image of God and like God, that we are in him, always with him (as long as we exist), "in him" as St. Paul told the Athenians (Acts 17:28), inseparable from God's love (Rom 8:35) and in that sense inalterable, and that there are many (created) "powers" of God. So, the fathers said that the Son is "one in essence," *homoousios*, with the Father.[60] This the Arians could not do and preserve their own way of interpreting the Scriptures. Athanasius points out, however, that, for all that, the new phrases introduced by the fathers declare the true sense of Scripture.

[I]f a person is interested in the question, let him know, that, even if the expressions are not in so many words in the Scriptures, yet, as was said before, *they contain the sense of the Scriptures*, and expressing it, they convey it to those who have their hearing unimpaired for religious doctrine. Now this circumstance it is for you to consider, and for those ill-instructed men to give ear to. It has been shown above, *and must be believed as true*, that the Word is from the Father, and the only Offspring proper to Him and natural.[61]

Note the attention of Athanasius to the sense of Scripture taken as true. Lonergan emphasizes that the way forward at Nicaea consisted merely but essentially in taking the lowly propositions of Scripture as able to deliver the truth, where what the predicate expresses truly belongs to the subject it is referred to. This is not something peculiar to the statements of Scripture just insofar as they belong to Scripture, of course, but something true of these statements just as propositions. We assumed such

---

59. Athanasius, "Defense of the Nicene Council" (*De Decretis*), chap. 5, no. 19, pp. 162–63.

60. Athanasius, "Defense of the Nicene Council" (*De Decretis*), no. 20, pp. 163–64.

61. Athanasius, "Defense of the Nicene Council" (*De Decretis*), no. 21, p. 164. Emphasis added. Athanasius subsequently proceeds to explain that *homoousios* cannot be taken in a bodily, corporeal sense (nos. 22–24, pp. 164–66).

above in demonstrating Nicaea's teaching: from what was *said*, in the same way, in the same sense, of Father and Son, there was concluded the consubstantiality of Son to Father. From what was *predicated*—in the Bible, in Scripture—we arrive at the reality of the relation of Son to Father, of their equality, of their common true divinity. Scripture is taken as making true, informative predications, and that was the way forward beyond Arius. This attention to the truth and cognitive force of human language, this "realism" of Athanasius, is a presupposition of revelation and will be visited again in chapter 4.

It is also true, of course, that beyond this attention to the truth of biblical (and conciliar) statement, the Nicene teaching, its doctrine or "dogma," also introduces an extrabiblical statement of faith that is binding on faith. This is indeed a novelty. The nonbiblical *homoousios* moves us beyond a restrictive Biblicism, where in explaining Scripture all we can do is repeat the very words already used by Scripture. It moves us, in fact, to what can be called Christian philosophy.

Nicaea and Christian philosophy

Sometimes Nicaea is presented as if it were the wholesale adoption of Greek philosophy, Greek metaphysics. This is not quite right, but one understands what is being gotten at. It is rather an emerging philosophical context, not a fully blown one, that is elaborated at Nicaea. All that is actually going on is logic. What is going on is a reflection on propositions. This, it may be admitted, is characteristically Hellenic.[62] And what was first discovered by the Greeks was bequeathed to the rest of the West. Language can reflect on itself, and it is an abiding human possibility to control our language with language. That is what is going on at Nicaea. The meaning of the *homoousios* as unpacked by Athanasius is the assertion of a proposition about propositions; it is, as Lonergan says, the assertion of a second-order proposition, the employment of typically Greek technique in the effort to say what one means with precision, rigor, clarity. "The Son is consubstantial with the Father, if and only if what is true of

---

62. Lonergan, "Dehellenization of Dogma," 23.

the Father is true of the Son, except that only the Father is Father."[63] There are other and similar "Greek" techniques to make language rigorous, as for instance, an attention to definition—a Greek technique we see inaugurated with Socrates in the early dialogues like the *Euthyphro* and *Lysis*: X is a definition of Y iff (1) for every p that is X, p is also Y, and (2) for every p that is Y, p is also X. This technique is in play in controlling the sense of "divinity" asserted of Father and of Son: what is true of the divinity of one will be true of the divinity of the other.

Beyond the brief foray into logic that Athanasius makes in explicating the *homoousios*, however, there is no adoption of any Greek theory of being. The holy 318 fathers were not thinking of Aristotle's *Metaphysics* when they reproved Arius, nor were they reading Plato's *Statesman* or *Parmenides*. They picked up some tools that would lead to a fully developed Christian metaphysics, but they adopt no already extant Greek metaphysics.

Nonetheless, there are metaphysical implications in the Nicene teaching. First, there is an implied criticism of Platonism as a fit instrument for Trinitarian thinking. Neither Neo-Platonism nor Middle Platonism can provide a comprehensive frame into which the gospel will fit. The sliding scale of divinity in Origen is implicitly rejected, and the projection of some middle being between the Creator and creation is likewise rejected.[64] Similarly, Nicaea constitutes an implied rejection of materialism. You cannot be a Nicene Christian and embrace some form of contemporary materialism, or positivism, or philosophical naturalism. We will return to this in chapter 4.

Nicaea also prepares the way for an introduction of other terms more expressly capable of philosophical elaboration in further dogmatic teaching: nature, essence, person, relation.[65] We will return to this in chapter 6.

---

63. Lonergan, "Dehellenization of Dogma," 23.

64. See Khaled Anatolios on Gregory Nyssa, *Retrieving Nicaea*, 185, 206, 216.

65. For "Christian philosophy," see Leo XIII, *Aeterni Patris* (1879), DH 3135–40; John Paul II, *Fides et ratio*, in *Restoring Faith in Reason: A New Translation of the Encyclical Letter* Faith and Reason *of Pope John Paul II*, trans. Anthony Meredith, SJ, and Laurence Paul Hemming, with commentary (Notre Dame, IN: University of Notre Dame Press, 2002), no. 76, pp. 123–25. And see Gregory B. Sadler, trans. and ed., *Reason Fulfilled by Revelation: The 1930's Christian Philosophy Debates in France*, (Washington, DC: The Catholic University of America Press, 2011).

Conclusion

The long analysis of Nicaea we have undertaken is very worthwhile for a consideration of the theology of dogmatic development, because, to reason illuminated by faith, it discloses the causes of dogmatic development, here lined up from the most evident to the least evident.

(1) First, there is the shock of heresy. Arius's denial of the divinity of Christ is a cause of the Church's assertion of it.

(2) Second, there is the deliberation and decision and declaration of the council itself: the ecumenical council or the equivalent thereof is the author of dogmatic statements, the author of dogmas. This is to advert to the "teaching Church," the Church represented by and finding personal agency in the bishops as the maker of doctrinal statements.

(3) Third, there is the work of the mind illumined by faith reading Scripture to contemplate Christ and thinking how to formulate the truth of Scripture in a way to exclude the heresy of Arius and manifest its falsity. This cause we discern in reading the controversial literature of the time, Athanasius and Hilary of Poitiers, the Cappadocian Fathers, Chrysostom and Augustine. This material, though much of it follows the council, is very much a part of the conciliar "moment" itself, which does not end in 325. This work of the mind can fairly be characterized as discerning the logic of Scripture where the Scripture is taken as true and as a coherent whole. The logical aspect has been emphasized because it tends to be ignored or shuffled away today. In historical reconstructions of dogmatic development, there will be reports of past logical and exegetical moves. But also, without making the same moves ourselves, we cannot intelligently settle the issue of Nicaea for ourselves in communion with the Church.

(4) Fourth, in addition to the "teaching Church," there is the indispensable role of the "learning Church." The reception of the teaching of Nicaea by the Church, and by the laity in despite of episcopal prevaricating, is also a cause of the Nicene development of dogma.

(5) Fifth, there is also to be discerned the context in which Arius said what he did and in which the council responded to him. This context was a culture in which philosophical ways of thinking were not foreign. This context included a sophisticated political peace and order in the Medi-

terranean basin. It is impossible to suppose that the teaching of Nicaea would have looked like it does without these factors. History, as Andrew Meszaros says, explains not only why the Church says something, but how it says it.[66]

These five things, of course, are but penultimate things. For Catholic faith supposes that the Holy Spirit inspires bishops with the charism of truth and laymen with the gift of wisdom to recognize it, and an illumination of faith that gives the peace and courage to study the Scriptures in the confidence of hearing the word of God. The transcendent and supernatural cause of the second, third, and fourth things is therefore the Holy Spirit given to the Church at Pentecost. But history, ecclesiastical and cultural, philosophical and political, does not take place apart from the God whose wisdom orders all things mightily and sweetly. Therefore also the first and fifth things are to be reduced to the Providence of God as their ultimate cause.[67]

---

66. Andrew Meszaros, *The Prophetic Church: History and Doctrinal Development in John Henry Newman and Yves Congar* (Oxford: Oxford University Press, 2016), 162, 182.

67. For a like listing of the cause of development, see Congar, *La Foi et la Théologie*, 107–12.

CHAPTER 3

FRAMING THE DEVELOPMENT OF DOGMA THEOLOGICALLY

The theology of the development of dogma is a part of what is called "fundamental theology," and it is hard to think about development rightly without looking directly at some of the other parts. Fundamental theology is the theology of the foundations of theology; it involves looking at the things theology uses to do theology, especially Scripture and Tradition. When a theologian says what he says about Christ, the Church, or the sacraments, and so on, he says what he says only as warranted by Scripture and Tradition. An integral part of Tradition, moreover, are the dogmas proposed to Christian faith by bishops and popes. The fundamental theological consideration of Scripture and Tradition, however, is an examination of how revelation is accomplished and communicated to us in the Church, and so presupposes a consideration of the nature of revelation itself.

However, fundamental theology is *theology*, so it is like a craftsman using his tools to examine their capacities and maintain them, or like using a microscope to examine the microscope. In other words, fundamental theology means using Scripture and Tradition to understand Scripture and Tradition; it means using revelation to understand revelation—not the content so much, which is examined in Christology, Ecclesiology, and so on, as the ways and means of the revealing itself. In a theology of dogmatic development, this will entail using Scripture, Tradition, and dogma itself to understand dogma and the nature, prospects, and limits of its development.

So it will be good to speak in order about: revelation; Scripture and Tradition; magisterium and dogma; and finally, the idea of dogmatic development as itself a development of scriptural data.

Revelation

In chapter 1, the development of dogma was described as the unfolding of a "many" from a "one," where the "many" are many dogmas and the "one" was identified simply as "revelation." As was noted, "revelation" is a way to refer to what Cardinal Newman called the "idea" of Christianity, which originally is *God's* idea. The chapter then proceeded on the assumption that this one revelation can be summed up in the creed, whose unity was emphasized. From the first article of the creed that speaks of the Father's creation of the world to the last which speaks of resurrection and everlasting life in the Holy Spirit, just as from Genesis to the Book of Revelation, there is a chronological unity. But since the center of the creed is Christ, just as the climax of revelation is the gospel, and just as Christ is begotten by the Father and promises the Spirit, its unity can also be characterized as Trinitarian, set forth in the three articles of the creed that declare Father, Son, and Holy Spirit and the works especially associated with each. This one, unified revelation is as it were the point of departure for the development of doctrine, and we therefore need to think about it more closely. What is it? Also, is it "cognitive"? Is it "communal"? And is it "closed"?

What is revelation and how is it accomplished?

Revelation is the manifestation of something not previously in the light, something not previously cognitively available. Divine revelation is God's manifestation of himself and of his mind about us and of his will for us to us. In some fashion, the very work of creation manifests the existence of God and his power and deity to us, as St. Paul points out (Rom 1:19–20). This raises the question as to whether God could ever be absolutely hidden from us, something whose reality could never have been available to us.[1] But beyond such natural revelation of God from the things that have been made, there is also a more than natural revelation of God and his plans for us, a revelation by the act of God over and above calling things into being, an act that invites us into a personal relation with him, one demanding a response of faith and obedience.

When the First Vatican Council addressed itself to the topic of revelation, it appealed to the first two verses of the Letter to the Hebrews: "In many and various ways God spoke of old to our fathers by the prophets; but in these last days he has spoken to us by a Son" (1:1–2).[2] The council thus conceives of this supernatural revelation as a matter of God speaking to us in the words of the prophets and of Christ. This is quite distinct from creation, which ought not be counted strictly as a "speaking" of God; creation "expresses" him, but does not "manifest" him the way proper speech does as addressed directly from one person to another person.[3] Christ speaks to us evidently in his parables and sermons and discourses, even as he did to the disciples and the crowds and the Pharisees. Ought the Incarnation itself, the very assumption of flesh and the entire living of his life—ought that to be counted as a speaking, also? When the Second Vatican Council takes up the topic of revelation, it takes things in this fuller direction.[4] It embraces a more capacious idea of how revelation is accomplished than the spoken word alone. With the First Vatican Council, the

---

1. Pope Pius XII raises this question in *Humani generis* (1950); DH 3875–76, ND 144–45.

2. Vatican I, *Dei Filius*, chap. 2; DH 3004.

3. St. Thomas, *Commentary on the Epistle to the Hebrews*, trans. and ed. Chrysostom Baer, O. Praem. (South Bend, IN: St. Augustine's Press, 2006), chap. 1, lecture 1, no. 15.

4. *Dei Verbum*, no. 4; DH 4204, ND 151. We read here that God reveals himself to us in Christ "by the whole presence and manifestation of himself, by word and works, by signs and miracles, but especially by his death and glorious resurrection from the dead" (my translation).

THE DEVELOPMENT OF DOGMA THEOLOGICALLY   43

Second says that God reveals both himself and his will for the salvation of man.[5] But it specifies that this revelation is by way of constructing a "pattern" in history, a pattern that "unfolds through deeds and words bound together by an inner dynamism."[6] This inner dynamism bespeaks the connection between the deeds and the words: the words indicate the meaning of the deeds (as, say, Jesus's words at the Last Supper indicate the intelligibility of his death on Calvary), and the deeds corroborate the truth of the words (as, preeminently, the resurrection corroborates Jesus's claim to be the Son of God). Christ himself then, in his whole reality, "is at once both the mediator and the fullness of revelation."[7]

The pattern of revelation, the economy of salvation—this is the entire course of what is given to us in the words and deeds of the patriarchs, the prophets, the kings, the people of Israel, and given to us in the New Testament in the words and deeds of Christ and the apostles and the first Christians. This is to say that revelation is accomplished narratively. The story of the Old Testament leads up to Christ; the story of the Church, whose fundamental structure is displayed in the Acts of the Apostles and the letters of Paul and Peter and John, follows from Christ; and Christ himself is given to us first in the gospels, in the story of his life, death, and resurrection.

Revelation in its finished form and looked at as a whole turns out to be a great and complex but unified pattern. It stretches from the foundation of the world and the creation of man to an anticipation of the end of time; within it there is a host of people, from Adam and Eve to Abraham and Isaac and on to Moses and Joshua, from Gideon and Samson to the first king, Saul, and the great king, David. There are also prophets and priests. In the New Testament, there are disciples of Christ and Peter and Paul and ordinary people, too, who are by no means bit players because they are the people for whom the main figures do what they do, teach what they teach, and suffer what they suffer. There is a succession of covenants in which

5. *Dei Filius*, chap. 2: *aeterna voluntatis suae decreta* (DH 3004); *Dei Verbum*, no. 2: *sacramentum voluntatis suae* (DH 4202; ND 149).

6. *Dei Verbum*, no. 2; DH 4202, ND 149.

7. *Dei Verbum*, no. 2; DH 4204, ND 149. See further Gregory Vall, "Word and Event: A Reappraisal," in his *Ecclesial Exegesis: A Synthesis of Ancient and Modern Approaches to Scripture* (Washington, DC: The Catholic University of America Press, 2022), 193–226.

God comes close to man, stretching from Adam and Noah to Moses and David and to the last and everlasting covenant sealed by Christ at the Last Supper. Besides the covenants, the succession of which proceeds to an ever more interior union of God and men who have the law written on their hearts and who eat the Bread of Heaven, there are other, correlative unifying threads that stretch from Genesis to the Book of Revelation. The Bible opens with the marriage of Adam and Eve and closes with the Wedding of the Lamb, and both Israel and the Church are importantly figured as brides, Israel of the Lord God and the Church of Christ. There is also from first to last a temple where God dwells with men, from the temple of the created cosmos to the New Jerusalem descending from heaven, with the Tent of Meeting and the Temple of Solomon and the Church in between. This pattern, this design of God arranged by the providence of God and including the free actions of those whom God addresses by the word of prophet and apostle, this pattern is a unified whole, and speaks a large, multifaceted, dense, word to the human race. Beholding the pattern and hearing this one "word" and responding to it in faith and charity is something that calls on all the resources a human being can muster, and rightly so, for God wants to save all of us, our whole reality.

Constructing the pattern is the course of revelation, and it is like weaving a great tapestry—think of the Bayeaux Tapestry—or like painting the Battle of Atlanta for the Cyclorama in Atlanta. But even more than the Tapestry or the Cyclorama, the pattern of revelation is inexhaustible in its detail, and in the way one can link the details together, from beginning to end, and taking in the architectonic Midpoint. This gives us a good way to think of the development of doctrine. Revelation is the weaving of the tapestry. But development is now looking at the completed whole, seeing how the details in the completed picture are intelligibly related to other details and speak in a way not yet noticed before. Revelation is adding bits of glass and foil to the box of the kaleidoscope. Development is turning it to see the further and further juxtapositions and reflections of the colored bits. But we know that the bits and pieces are already related to one another, once we notice that revelation itself is a development. It is not just one thing after another, but one thing building on an earlier one, later things subsuming and adding to earlier things, later prophecies filling out earlier ones—once we see this we understand why Cardinal Newman thinks we should expect there to be doctrinal development.[8]

There are two ways to look at the great tapestry of revelation, to see the "more" that a detailed study will deliver. The first way is to look back and forth from Old to New Testament, and from New to Old. This kind of engagement with the pattern of revelation fixes for us in ever greater detail and depth what theologians call "the economy of salvation." It is an "economy"—originally in Greek the management of a household with all its people and servants and slaves and all its goods and tools and services. But here, the manager is God, his stewards are the prophets and apostles, and the management is unto salvation, and not just the bodily and moral health of the members of the household. Looking at the entire economy, we see things like the fulfillment of all sacrifice in the sacrifice of Christ, and we see it as at once the sacrifice of perfect atonement and perfect communion, both made present at mass. These things are touched on by the Council of Trent. Looking at the entire economy, we see the Church stand out in her continuity with and difference from Israel. This is touched on by the Second Vatican Council. Looking at the entire economy, we see why the Virgin Mary ought to be virginal, why she ought to be the Mother of God, and why she ought to be conceived without being touched by the sin of Adam.

Looking at the pattern of revelation in this way, taking our lead from *Dei Verbum*, we are also taking our lead from Yves Congar, who before the council had already shaped things up in this way. He thought that in discerning Christ as the center and culmination of revelation, we could infer things from their relation to Christ. So, he thought the Marian doctrines were intelligible in this way, because of the relation of the Second Eve to the Second Adam. Again, he noted that some things in the pattern of revelation are promises, the entire sense of which is not apparent until they are fulfilled, and in this way, he thought Catholic doctrine on the successor of Peter was intelligible.[9]

But there is a second way to take the economy of salvation, and that is to take it as telling us about God. In the first way, so to speak, we make

8. Newman, *Essay on Development*, 64–66.
9. Congar, *La Foi et la Théologie*, 102, and more generally, 99–103.

horizontal moves. But in this second way, we make a vertical move. So for instance, when we focus on the reality of the incarnate Son as Arius provided occasion for the Church to do in the fourth century, we see that the Son of God, the Word of whom John speaks in the first chapter of his gospel, must be consubstantial, one in essence, with his Father. In this way, we enter into what "theology" originally named for the Fathers of the Church, the doctrine of what God is in himself, and even independently of the economy of salvation.[10]

Both ways of viewing the design or pattern or tapestry of revelation amounts to putting two and two together. I have spoken of "seeing" things, or "focusing" on things, or "moving around" in the completed picture. But we should make no mistake. When a theologian comes to explaining how some development is related to the deposit of revelation, the explanation will be by way of logic, the various forms of which serving the explication of development have yet to be detailed.

Is revelation cognitive?

We have now to note some key aspects of divine revelation. First of all, is it cognitive? That is to say, is it informative, and do the revealed statements really inform us about what they purport to be speaking of, even when what they purport to be speaking of is the nature of God (transcendent to the world, all-powerful, all-good), or the Trinitarian persons (undivided in agency, coeternal, one proceeding from another, etc.) or the human soul (not annihilated at death), or angels (agents of God's providence)? The answer has of course to be yes. And it may be wondered what the point of the question is. But it has to be explicitly posed because of certain denials of it in the history of western thought, and in particular because of its connection to how the development of dogma was thought about at the turn of the nineteenth century at the time of Modernism.

Scripture certainly presents revelation as cognitive. Christ, after all, was a rabbi, a teacher (cf. Mk 6:30). He tells us about his Father, the Holy Spirit, about the Kingdom of Heaven, about the final judgment. The "good news," after all is in the first place *news*, and according to St. Paul, faith comes from what is heard, from hearing the gospel, the news (Rom 10:5–21). In the Old

---

10. See Meszaros, *The Prophetic Church*, 98.

Testament a prophet is a prophet because the word of the Lord comes to him. He speaks what he hears, and the message is a message—something addressed in the first place to the mind. When a prophet introduces his message with "Thus says the Lord," if he is telling the truth, then the Lord is saying something. Nicaea, as is clear from chapter 2, supposes the revelation recorded in the Scriptures is informative about the relation of the Son to the Father, and does itself purport to be informative about the same thing. When the Church has turned explicitly to the issue of revelation in the Vatican Councils (*Dei Filius* and *Dei Verbum*), it is supposed that revelation is informative: God informs us about himself and our divine destiny and how it is realized. The teaching of St. Thomas also supposes this: revelation is necessary so that we know what our end is and how to get there—it *tells* us, informs us, of these things.[11]

Of course, the prophets, Christ, and the apostles have to say what they say in human words. But what they say is spoken on the authority of God. In the Old Testament, human actors in the drama speak and so persuade, threaten, praise, and inform, just as the Lord God also speaks, and so persuades, threatens, praises, and also *informs*, which makes no sense if revelation is not cognitive. Or again, when the Lord Jesus tells us that the Father knows the Son and the Son knows the Father (Mt 11:27), he is telling us something or not. When he says that the Kingdom of God is at hand, thus, that God is at hand, meaning that God is now active in the world in a new and final way, that is either informative or not. If it is informative, then revelation is cognitive. St. Paul evidently supposes the informative, cognitive nature of revelation (Rom 10:14–18).

Sometimes the cognitive nature of revelation is played off against the personal nature of revelation, as if cognitivity impeded or got in the way of this personal nature. So, it has sometimes been the fashion to insist that revelation is not a list of propositions (statements), or "not merely" propositional.[12] It is rather supposed to be a personal event, an encounter of persons, divine and human. Of course, to say revelation is not "merely" propositional is not to deny it is propositional. But sometimes this

11. *Summa theologiae* I, Q. 1, a. 1.

12. Cf. Avery Dulles, SJ, *Models of Revelation* (Garden City, NY: Doubleday, 1983), for whom the "propositional" is merely one of five "models" of revelation, and see 8–14 for discussion of a Christianity without revelation.

alleged opposition is drawn very strongly. The scriptural or traditional or dogmatic statements of faith that seem to be telling us about God or the Trinity have no real reference to God; they are better understood, not as informing us about God, but as directive of action whose utility is proved by the authenticity of the moral practice they govern.[13] Moreover, to insist that the statements of faith function like ordinary statements, and inform us of the reference of their grammatical subjects, invites the Christian to a prideful knowing that puffs up and is opposed to charity; it invites the rigidity and defensiveness that are said to be characteristic of the theology of the nineteenth and first half of the twentieth century (that is, generally, scholastic theology before the Second Vatican Council). This idea that, contrary to first appearances, the statements of faith do their work noncognitively is hard to distinguish from the Kantian agnosticism embraced by Modernism at the turn of the twentieth century. In this light, what we call revelation turns out to be not what God says to us, but what *we* say about God based on our experience of ourselves and our spiritual and moral aspirations.

What is to be said here? Revelation is completed by our hearing a message from the God who creates us, but it is not in the first place our witness to him. Christian life subsequent to revelation can be said to bear witness to God, to be sure. But it is a derived, dependent witness based on what we have heard. What we have heard—from God in Christ through the Church—this message *founds* the practical pattern of Christian morality and communal responsibilities and liturgical practice, but it is distinct from it. It is after all because the Lord said "do this" on the night before he died that the Church continues to celebrate Mass. The knowledge that the consecrated elements are the Body and Blood precedes the command. It is because we now know what love is, because one man has died for us while we were still in our sins (Rom 5:6–8), that we can love one another as Christ did (Jn 13:34). Here again, knowledge, the knowledge of revelation, precedes our response to it in life and liturgy. Christ was a rabbi, a teacher, and teaching is preeminently both personal and cognitive.

Of course, nothing could be further from the truth than to maintain

---

13. This was the position of Edouard Le Roy at the time of Modernism.

THE DEVELOPMENT OF DOGMA THEOLOGICALLY   49

that the propositional and the personal are at odds with one another. We know this from the briefest examination of our own life and love. When human love is personal, it absolutely depends on shared knowledge: when love rises above the automatic directedness and immediacy of animal affection, then it is informed by shared knowledge and shared responses to the intelligible and intellectually known good. The flowering of the personal thus depends on the propositional. And the propositional, often enough, depends on the persons—we want to know things just in order to share our knowledge with our friends.[14]

The unity of the propositional and the personal is indicated by the Lord Jesus when he tells his disciples: "I have called you friends, for all that I have heard from my Father I have made known to you" (Jn 15:15). What he has heard from his Father—the revelation of the Father and of the Spirit, the revelation of the Eucharist, and the revelation of the victory over sin in the humiliation of the cross—all these most personal communications of the Lord to his disciples, propositionally delivered as they are, these are what his friendship with them in the charity of the Holy Spirit is founded on. Their truth is corroborated by his action, to be sure. But what is corroborated is known in words, in propositions.

This is continued in apostolic times, and it is just as 1 John says: "that which ... we have heard, which we have seen with our eyes ... concerning the word of life, we proclaim also to you, so that you may have fellowship with us" (1 Jn 1:1–3). The telling of the truth of the gospel is first—what was heard from and seen in Christ about the word of eternal life—but its end is fellowship, the union of charity which is the Church.[15] The Word becomes incarnate (Jn 1:14) just so he can speak the words to us that are "spirit and life" (Jn 6:63). If we think of the Lord's practice of teaching, of telling us true propositions, say, in the Sermon on the Mount or the discourses in John, then it is evident that these propositions are about persons—the persons of Father and Son and Spirit and us—and that they

---

14. For an extended defense of the necessity of both "persons and propositions" in thinking about revelation apropos of *Dei Verbum*, see Matthew Levering, *An Introduction to Vatican II as Ongoing Theological Event* (Washington DC: The Catholic University of America Press, 2017), 20–49. See also Mats Wahlberg, *Revelation as Testimony: A Philosophical-Theological Study* (Grand Rapids, MI: Eerdmans, 2014), 25–42.

15. It is just this passage that opens the Dogmatic Constitution on Divine Revelation, *Dei Verbum*.

50   CHAPTER 3

manifest the Person who speaks them, Christ, disclosing his personal reality as Son and Word, and that their end is to establish communion of persons, gathering us into fellowship with Christ in the Spirit unto the praise of his Father.

Is it communal?

Evidently, revelation is communally received; it is addressed to the community of those who are being saved. But also, revelation is communally established: the deeds and words that reveal God and his covenanted promise to the Israelites unto their salvation as recorded in the Old Testament are indeed recorded by individual prophets and inspired historians and commented on by wisdom writers. These individuals are not to be overlooked. But it is Israel as a whole who constitutes the covenant partner of God, and it is Israel as a whole who proves obedient and faithful or disobedient and idolatrous. The responses of Israel as a whole, just like the responses of key individuals like Abraham and Moses, Samuel and Saul and David, are free. This is to say that things—events, saving events, divine punishment—could have been different. And the oracles and reactions of prophets and kings themselves are conditioned by the whole community addressed and governed. So, the pattern of words and deeds we see in the Old Testament is in part established by the community of Israel, later the communities of Judah and Israel, as wholes. Revelation is established communally.

The same is true in the New Testament. Christ longed to gather the children of Israel as a hen her chicks, and to save Jerusalem. But they would not (cf. Mt 23:37). It could have been that the Jews received the word Paul first addressed to them in faith; but they did not, and so he turned to the gentiles. The Corinthian community need not have divided into factions and been so contentious. The joy with which the Philippians received the gospel was a function of their free reception of it. These things condition Paul's relation to these communities as expressed in the letters. Once again, therefore, and notwithstanding the preeminent position of people like Peter and Paul and John, the deeds and words are communally conditioned, communally established. But the conversational relation of prophet and apostle to the communities they address bespeak

THE DEVELOPMENT OF DOGMA THEOLOGICALLY 51

a deeper dialogical relation, that between these communities and God. Revelation is in the end a conversation between God and Israel, between Christ and his contemporaries, Christ and his disciples.[16] But these conversations lead to and are also embodied in conversations between Moses and the people of Israel, and between Paul and John and the communities they lead and write to.

Now, this is important to notice, because it predicts that the development of doctrine will also be something communally executed. It may be easy to pick out the role of Duns Scotus for the theology of Mary's Immaculate Conception. We can think of the special role Maximus Confessor played in the Church's acknowledgement of the human will and freedom of Christ. Evidently, certain bishops and popes stand out in the history of the development of doctrine—St. Athanasius, Pope Innocent I, Pius IX, and so on. Still, these people do not exist independently of the Church as a whole. And still more, as has already been noted with the faith of Nicaea, there is the role of the sense of faith of the whole Church for the development of doctrine.

Is it "closed"?

That revelation is "closed" or finished is understood to mean that we should expect no new public revelation bearing on the Christian gospel and Christian faith.[17] This idea is contained in the description of what has been entrusted to Timothy and Titus as a *depositum* in St. Paul's Pastoral Letters. The gospel, what Timothy and Titus are to teach, is something that is to be guarded as a complete and integral whole; nothing is to be taken away from it, but also, nothing is to be added to it, for an addition would amount to an adulteration. As St. Paul puts the matter elsewhere, there is no other, no different gospel than the one he preaches (Gal 1:6–9).

A firm purchase on the fact of revelation's closure is very important for a theology of the development of dogma. Without it, it is all too easy to understand the development of doctrine as the continuation of revela-

16. For Scripture as the product of the dialogue of God and human beings, see Joseph Ratzinger's comments on the draft schema on the sources of revelation at the time of the council, text 4 in Jared Wicks, SJ, "Six Texts by Prof. Joseph Ratzinger as *Peritus* before and during Vatican Council II," *Gregorianum* 89 (2008): 233–411.

17. See *Dei Verbum*, no. 7; DH 4207. The council appeals to 2 Cor 1:20 and 3:13–4:6. Jude 3 is also often invoked for the closure of revelation.

tion. The failure easily to see some dogma in revelation such as Scripture and Tradition mediate it to us then poses no problem: God continues the dialogue with man begun with Israel, continued in the Church, and he says new things to us, things not previously said. Such solutions invite the Church as she now exists to think of herself as contributing to revelation in the way the Church of the New Testament did. They make of the Church now an instrument not only of the teaching of what has been revealed, but an instrument of further revelation.

And what would be the problem with that? Why not a Church as continuing the constitutive role in revelation of the Jews and the first Christians? The trouble is Christological. We would not be able to think of the Lord Jesus as completing the work of revelation as Christians have been wont to do (e.g. Mt 5:17; Jn 1:14; 2 Cor 3:13–4:6). We would not be able to think of the Lord as being the incarnation of that Word of God in which all things are said for our salvation, the Word unto which all things in the prior history of Israel led up, the Word from which all ecclesial words follow, not as additions, but as explanations, or implications or commentaries or … developments. Having spoken his Word to us in the Incarnation, God has nothing more to say to us, as John of the Cross put it.[18] Another way of putting the point is that the "New Covenant" would not be "everlasting" were revelation not closed (Lk 22:20; 1 Cor 11:25; Heb 10:12–16).

It is noteworthy that the closure of revelation is taught in the condemnation of Modernism.[19] This is because the modernist view of revelation as a wordless experience or consciousness of God does not make of the act of God's revelation something in principle finished with the age of the apostles. Modernists like George Tyrrell acknowledged a normative role of the first, apostolic formulations of the gospel.[20] Still, even these words are derivative and secondary to the original and wordless revelato-

18. St. John of the Cross, *The Ascent of Mount Carmel*, book 2, chap. 22.

19. *Lamentabili* 21; DH 3421. Of course there are other denials of the closure of revelation, some of them very early, with the Montanists of the third century, who claimed a revelation from the Spirit distinct from and in addition to that of the gospel, and some medieval, like that of Abbot Joachim of Fiore, whose "eternal gospel" would similarly complete revelation with a final outpouring of the Holy Spirit. In this light, see also the condemnation of an order of salvation and revelation of the Spirit that is independent of Christ by the Congregation of the Doctrine of the Faith, *Dominus Iesus* (2000); DH 5085, 5086, 5089.

20. George Tyrrell, "Revelation," in *Through Scylla and Charybdis*, 264–307 (London: Longmans, Green, 1907), 292.

ry experience of God. Revelation, Tyrrell insists, "is a vision or showing, but not a statement."[21]

Closure means that Christ delivered his message and himself completely and without reserve to the apostolic Church. The witness to him and his preaching and his deed as recorded in the New Testament has therefore an unsurpassable character that is normative for all subsequent ages of the Church. This is what it means to say, in the imagery of St. Paul, that the household of God, the Church, is "built upon the foundation of the apostles and prophets, Christ Jesus himself being the cornerstone" (Eph 2:20). The implication of the image is clear: if there is something not built on the apostolic and prophetic foundation, then it is unfounded, and does not belong to the faith on which the Church is erected. The apostolic age, however, is over, and we expect no new apostle to appear upon whose witness we can build another wing of the house of God. Revelation is in this sense closed.

On the other hand, there is perfectly good sense in which revelation continues to occur, if we advert to the correlatively necessary role of the hearer of the word in any real speaking of a word. If no one hears anything, nothing has been spoken, just as if nothing was learned, nothing was taught, and if nothing was seen, nothing was unveiled. This is the important insight of Joseph Ratzinger in his *Habilitation* thesis.[22] For St. Bonaventure, furthermore, inspiration and revelation are not to be distinguished, and revelation just is the spiritual understanding of Scripture, itself not to be separated from the scientific exegesis of Scripture.[23] This is how he sums things up in *Milestones*:

"[R]evelation" is always a concept denoting an act…. By definition, revelation requires a someone who apprehends it…. [I]f Bonaventure is right, then reve-

---

21. George Tyrrell, "Revelation," 303; or again, 285, revelation is "not statement but experience." This is, as it were, the DNA of the position, faithful to Friedrich Schleiermacher, for whom revelation is "God-consciousness." It seems ineluctably to sever revelation from history and put us on the road to transcendental, idealist determinations of what God's relation to us is.

22. Joseph Ratzinger, *Das Offenbarungsverständnis und die Geschichtstheologie Bonaventuras: Habilitationsschrift und Bonaventura-Studien*, in *Joseph Ratzinger: Gesammelte Schriften*, vol. 2, ed. Gerhard Ludwig Müller (Freiburg: Herder, 2009), 91–92, 101–2, 221, 239–41. The second half of this study was published in English translation in Joseph Ratzinger, *The Theology of History in St. Bonaventure*, trans. Zachary Hayes, OFM (Chicago: Franciscan Herald Press, 1971).

23. Joseph Ratzinger, *The Theology of History in St. Bonaventure*, 62–69.

54 CHAPTER 3

lation precedes Scripture and becomes deposited in Scripture but is not simply identical with it. This in turn means that revelation is always something greater than what is merely written down.[24]

In this light, it makes sense to say that the event of revelation is consummated every time someone hears the word of God, not just in the age of Isaiah or of John the Evangelist, but in the age of Augustine, Bonaventure, Bossuet, or Balthasar. Faithfully reading Scripture, faithfully hearing the word of God, is therefore also to discover oneself within the history of which the text speaks.[25] It is to discover Tradition as a necessary companion to Scripture.

Scripture and Tradition

The closure of revelation seems at first glance incompatible with the development of doctrine. If revelation is finished, because the apostolic witness to the incarnate Word is finished, what place is there for development? If development is not ongoing revelation and cannot be given the comprehensive character of revelation in Christ, then can it be anything other than an icing the finished cake does not need? This question of the place of development relative to a closed revelation emerges more clearly, however, when we examine more closely how the closed revelation is communicated to us past the generation in which it is completed, that generation, namely, that had living memory of apostolic witness and preaching, apostolic mores and moral practice, apostolic worship, apostolic institution and governance.

Revelation is passed on very obviously in the Scriptures. Just because of the fixity and immutability of the written word, moreover, Scripture enjoys a preeminence in the communication of revelation to us that all Christians recognize. Those Christians who recognize no other way in which the gospel is communicated, however, suppose that Scripture alone

24. Joseph Ratzinger, *Milestones: Memoirs 1927–1977*, trans. Erasmo Leiva-Merikakis (San Francisco: Ignatius Press, 1998), 108–9; see also 127. See also Joshua R. Brotherton, "Development(s) in the Theology of Revelation: From Francisco Marín-Sola to Joseph Ratzinger," *New Blackfriars* 97 (2016): 661–76, esp. 671–73.

25. Alasdair MacIntyre, *Three Rival Versions of Moral Enquiry: Encyclopaedia, Genealogy, and Tradition* (Notre Dame, IN: University of Notre Dame Press, 1990), 83.

is sufficient for the presentation of the now closed revelation, age to age. Thus the Protestant principle of *sola scriptura*.

Moreover, Scripture seems to witness to its own self-sufficiency. When St. Paul says that the Church is built on the foundation of the apostles and prophets (Eph 2:20), we have what will later be taken as a sort of first sketch of the canon of the Bible, indicating its two great wings, the Old Testament and the New.[26] But if "the apostles and prophets" just are the Scriptures, then the Church is built on the Scriptures. The whole Church is founded thereon; there cannot be any other foundation. So, *sola scriptura*. Can the Church herself and apart from Scripture be involved in giving us the one and only revelation of God? No; the Church is built *on* the Scriptures, not on itself. Nor can it be "Scripture and *Tradition*." Tradition seems too loose, too uncontrollable, next to the fixed and easily determinate shape of Scripture. If Scripture is inspired of God (2 Tm 3:15–16) because written by inspired men (2 Pt 1:21), if it contains and is the word of God,[27] if it is "inerrant,"[28] if the canon is closed the way revelation is closed because all has been said by and in the incarnate Word, then why is it not self-sufficient, and why do we need "tradition"? The Church, however, insists that revelation does not meet us except through all three things—Scripture, Tradition, Church—working together.[29]

In the first place, it is obvious that Tradition is something temporally prior to Scripture. The tradition of apostolic preaching evidently preceded the writing of the New Testament. The "deposit" that Timothy received from Paul he presumably received orally (1 Tm 6:20; 2 Tm 1:12–14). But once the New Testament is written, does the Christian still need an extrascriptural, unwritten traditioning of the gospel? Once the Church has

---

26. What we think of as the prophetical books of the Old Testament, Isaiah, Jeremiah, Hosea, Amos and so on, are originally only the "latter prophets." The "earlier prophets" give us what we commonly think of as the historical books of Samuel, Kings, and so on. And when we remember that Moses is the greatest prophet (cf. Dt 18:18), the books ascribed to him, the Law or Pentateuch, are also prophetical. As to the New Testament, if some book of the New Testament is not apostolic in the sense of being written by an apostle, it is apostolic as giving us apostolic witness, as Mark gives us the witness of Peter, and Luke of Paul. See Denis Farkasfalvy, O. Cist., *A Theology of the Christian Bible: Revelation – Inspiration – Canon* (Washington, DC: The Catholic University of America Press, 2018), 168–69.

27. *Dei Verbum* nos. 9 and 13; DH 4212 and 4220; ND 247 and 251.

28. *Dei Verbum* no. 11; DH 4216, ND 249.

29. *Dei Verbum* no. 10; DH 4214; ND 248.

recognized the canon of Scripture, can it do any more by way of imparting the gospel, conveying the once-and-for-all closed revelation of God completed in Christ?[30] Yes, for in the second place, as Yves Congar says, "It seems beyond serious question that the teaching of the apostles entrusted to the churches was a totality beside which what is formulated in their writings represents mere fragments."[31] Is *everything* contained in Scripture in one way or another? This is the question of the so-called "material sufficiency" of Scripture. Rather than saying yes or no, it seems best to observe with Congar that the Church proposes no doctrine to be believed by divine and Catholic faith solely on the basis of either Scripture or Tradition. Both are always involved.[32] Furthermore, the invocation of Tradition is more prominent for some doctrines than for others. Of the "Marian mystery," and so of Christian veneration of Mary, of monachism and the religious life, of consecrated virginity, of the presence of Christ in the Eucharist, Congar says, "their biblical foundations are very solid but are revealed only in tradition."[33]

In the third place, and as the most decisive consideration, no text is self-interpreting.[34] No text, no written word, is heard except within some anticipation of what and what kind of thing it will say, and without some sympathy for the author of the text. This is true whether we are reading the newspaper or an article in a scientific journal. We have to inhabit the same world in whole or in part, really or at least imaginatively, as the writer does, for the words to do their work. The sympathies and anticipations needed to read human texts can be humanly acquired. But in addition to

30. For this question of Oscar Cullman, see Yves Congar, OP, *The Meaning of Tradition*, trans. A. N. Woodrow (San Francisco: Ignatius Press, 2004), 35–36.

31. Congar, *Meaning*, 103.

32. Congar, *Meaning*, 39–40, 106. See the extended discussion in Yves Congar, OP, *Tradition and Traditions: An Historical Essay and a Theological Essay*, trans. Michael Naseby and Thomas Rainborough (New York: Macmillan, 1967), 409–422. For Joseph Ratzinger, it is difficult to maintain the material sufficiency of Scripture in any straightforward sense; see his *God's Word: Scripture – Tradition – Office*, trans. Henry Taylor (San Francisco: Ignatius Press, 2008), 49–50. And see the very helpful study of Joshua Brotherton, "Revisiting the Sola Scriptura Debate: Yves Congar and Joseph Ratzinger on Tradition," *Pro Ecclesia* 25 (2015): 85–114, esp. 106–7.

33. Congar, *Meaning*, 126.

34. Newman, *Essay on Development*, 56: "[I]deas are in the writer and reader of the revelation, not the inspired text itself: and the question is whether those ideas which the letter conveys from writer to reader, reach the reader at once in their completeness and accuracy on his first perception of them, or whether they open out in his intellect and grow to perfection in the course of time."

the many human authors Scripture has, it has also a divine author telling us things reason cannot establish and that are, so to speak, beyond the natural world. The sympathy that puts us in tune with the authors of Scripture, human and divine, is for that reason established by the theological virtues of faith, hope, and especially the charity that makes the Holy Spirit dwell in our hearts. The anticipation of what the text will say is framed capaciously and comprehensively by the creed, an extrascriptural Rule of Faith and, as a "rule," authoritative.[35] But faith and charity and the indwelling Spirit are instilled in us by the sacraments and strengthened in us by prayer and the works of love, corporal and spiritual.

The sacraments, the creed, the forms of Christian prayer, especially the Mass, and the forms of Christian spiritual and moral life are all things we receive in Tradition, whose created agent is the Church and whose ultimate agent is the Holy Spirit himself.[36] This Spirit presides transcendently over the things "handed down" historically from the apostles. And without them, without the frame of mind they give us, we are not in the right frame to hear what the written word of God, the Scriptures, say. The divine speaker may speak a word in Scripture, and all the words may be his, but the auditory space, the "auditorium," is not established by that word all by itself. The auditorium is the Church, and it is established by all the other things in addition to Scripture the Church contains. So *Dei Verbum* says summarily, "the Church's certainty about all the things that are revealed is not drawn from Scripture alone" but from Scripture and Tradition.[37]

We can put the point this way. Every text requires the right readers, the right interpreters. An article in a scientific journal cannot be received intelligently unless the right education, a scientific education, has already been received.[38] Thus, the text of the New Testament cannot be received in such a way as to be read truly without other things being received with it. Prebaptismal catechesis, instruction in how to pray, introduction to the Eucharist (the premier place where Scripture is read), the moral con-

---

35. Guy Mansini, OSB, *Fundamental Theology* (Washington, DC: The Catholic University of America Press, 2018), 47–50.

36. Congar, *Meaning*, 47–81.

37. *Dei Verbum* no. 9; DH 4212; ND 247.

38. That is how Congar puts it, *Meaning*, 22.

text of a virtuous Christian life—all these things compose the framework within which the New Testament is apprehended as the sense of the Old and renders up its own sense for Christian belief and practice and worship. Without these things, and without the Rule of Faith, the New Testament disintegrates into the pieces that, according to St. Irenaeus, the gnostics rearranged to form the picture not of Christ the King, but of some beast.[39] An education in Christian things, the adoption of the entire *institutio vitae christianae*[40]—this alone provides the auditorium in which Scripture can be heard, and the scriptorium where it renders up its sense in the commentaries of the Fathers of the Church.

However one comes down on the question of the material sufficiency of Scripture, it is certainly not formally sufficient as if nothing else is needed to hear the word of God except Scripture alone. Notwithstanding the preeminence of Scripture as a sure container of what God has revealed, and as a supremely accessible norm of what God has revealed simply because it all fits within one handy volume, it does not stand alone. It is a powerful engine of the presence of revelation in the world. But it is a machine that needs the owner's manual directing us how to use it. That manual is Tradition.

Granted that Scripture is the privileged witness to the words and deeds of Jesus (Gospels), both prophetically (Old Testament) and memoratively (Acts and Epistles), the Tradition that accompanies it can be taken in three ways. First, it is the frame within which to read Scripture, the interpretive key, especially in the form of the Rule of Faith, but also as to subsequent sedimentations of authoritative readings in the form of creeds and doctrines.[41] Second, since this frame bespeaks the intelligibility of the Church, embedded in her profession of faith and also embodied in her structures and sacraments and moral practices, the Church herself can be styled as "tradition"—the subject who hands on, and reads, the Scripture she hands on. Just as Louis XIV was the principle of the reality of the state of France in the sixteenth century, so the Church is the created principle of the authority of reading and hearing the Scriptures and

39. St. Irenaeus, *Adversus Haereses*, book 1, chap. 9, no. 4.
40. Ratzinger, *God's Word*, 76–82, 84, explaining the Tridentine decree.
41. See Congar, *Meaning*, 127–28.

THE DEVELOPMENT OF DOGMA THEOLOGICALLY   59

can say, *"tradition—c'est moi."* Return to the text of St. Paul according to which the Church is built on the apostles and prophets (Eph 2:20). True as this is, the stones that are placed on this unique foundation are still *other* stones, the Church is not just its foundation (1 Pt 3:4–6), and it is "through the church that the manifold wisdom of God" is known. Third, Tradition is not only the frame of the interpretation of Scripture but is the interpretation itself.[42] In this sense, Tradition as reading is the consummation of revelation as event in that speaking is speaking only if it is heard.[43] Even if we wish to speak of the material sufficiency of Scripture, this does not say all that is necessary. Rather, as Ratzinger puts it,

[revelation] is present and remains present in terms of its reality.... We are indeed faced with a concept according to which revelation does indeed have its *ephapax* ["once for all" character], insofar as it took place in historical facts, but also has its constant "today," insofar as what once happened remains forever living and effective in the faith of the Church, and Christian faith refers equally to what is present and what is to come.[44]

It is revelation as heard today that is then the womb of "developments," and, as the gathering up of all these "hearings," Tradition serves as the conscience of the Church relative to the discrimination of genuine developments from erroneous and novel opinion.[45]

---

42. See again Congar, *Meaning*, 127–28.

43. Of course, not everyone wants to conceive tradition in this way. In his arrestingly entitled *Interrupting Tradition: An Essay on Christian Faith in a Postmodern Context* (Leuven: Peeters, 2003), Lieven Boeve tells us that postmodern wisdom rejects every "master" narrative, every narrative that aspires to a totalizing view of history. Such closed, master narratives are not only totalizing but "totalitarian" (110). They prevent the narrators from recognizing who is "other" to this tradition precisely in his otherness (91). Only open narratives, traditions that recognize their "specificity," particularity, and limited context (176) are ethically permissible. For Christianity, this means that all a Christian may do is "witness" to the incomprehensible, hidden, and absent God (152–59) and hold himself open to interruption by the differing witness of non-Christian religions (171–74). What is constant in Christian tradition is ethical praxis, therefore, not some "content" (99) of which the contradictions of Christian dogmatic history show the contrary (103–5). So on this view, tradition is not the continual handing on of a revealed word. But then, neither could it ever be, since revelation itself is "inexpressible" (177). Postmodern tradition is, then, a return to the "tradition" of the Catholic modernists.

44. Ratzinger, *God's Word*, 86–87.

45. See Meszaros, *The Prophetic Church*, 88–89, 216.

Magisterium and dogma

Magisterium means teaching authority, and the word comes from *magister*—teacher. Revelation itself is not unfittingly described as a teaching, as was already noted; it is God's teaching us about himself and his plans for us. The communal constitution of revelation does not count against this; lots of good teachers entertain questions. Teaching may be more impersonal when it is about impersonal things—say, geology or chemistry. But when it is about personal things, it is itself very personal, and involves an element of witnessing. To the extent personal realties are a function of freedom and choice, our knowledge of them depends on the testimony of the one who has chosen. So Christ is a witness to the proximity of the Kingdom for this depends on his agency.[46] Still, Jesus's working title is rabbi—he is a teacher.

Christ, to be sure, is more than a teacher in the way the scribes and Pharisees were teachers. They were bound to expounding an already given Law, whose understanding is already extended in the later prophets. Christ, on the other hand, teaches "with authority," not like a scribe, as the crowds notice (Mt 7:29). Teaching with divine authority, he modifies and fulfills and does not just explain the Law. But now, on the other side of Christ, Christian teachers are once again more like the scribes. Their charge is to teach in the sense of expounding an already given truth, the truth of the gospel. They are not to change but to "guard" the deposit, in St. Paul's words. Nonetheless, they teach with authority, an authority received from the apostles, and so from Christ. It is precisely the people Paul is addressing in the Pastoral Letters, Timothy and Titus, who are charged to do this. They are overseers and governors of the first Christian communities. They are bishops.[47]

The first duty of the bishop is to teach the gospel. It is first, because his sanctifying function in the sacraments presupposes the faith of those who receive them, and the faith is elicited by episcopal teaching. It is first because his ruling function presupposes the charity that binds the ruled community together, and charity is given in the sacraments, which can be

---

46. Levering, *An Introduction to Vatican II*, 31–32.

47. Ceslas Spicq, OP, *Saint Paul Les Épîtres Pastorals*, 2 vols. (Paris: Gabalda, 1947), 1:84–97, esp. 93–96.

received only by faith. The teaching authority of the Church, then, is by the Lord's institution first of all exercised by the bishops; to them belongs the ecclesial "magisterium."[48]

Perhaps it is unfortunate that this Latinate and foreign-sounding term has become a technical term in Catholic theology, because it makes the exercise of the bishop's office sound foreign and technical. If we let things sink back into the New Testament, of course, it turns out otherwise. St. Paul compares himself to a nurse taking care of her children (1 Thes 2:7). He recalls the gentleness with which he taught them and the affection and charity with which he cared for them. For the best care of a person, after all, is to teach them what saves them from the greatest misery and fits them for the greatest happiness, and this makes those who do so most of all our friends.[49]

In the ongoing traditioning of the truth of the gospel, the ongoing traditioning of the words of Scripture in catechesis, homily, and commentary, questions arise that the catechist, priest, and theologian cannot answer, or cannot answer with certitude. Where these questions are important, the teaching of authority of the Church answers them. That is to say, the pope and bishops answer them. Sometimes they do this scattered throughout the world, yet speaking in harmony on some issue of faith and morals, as they have done and do relative, say, to the evil of abortion. This is called the "ordinary universal magisterium of the Church." Sometimes they do this solemnly as gathered in council. And sometimes the pope alone, "strengthening his brothers" (Lk 22:32), solemnly determines some matter of faith and morals as president of the college of bishops.[50] Whether ordinarily or solemnly, when pope and bishop do this, they articulate what is called "dogma" in the strict sense.

---

48. On the office of bishops, see Robert Sokolowski, "The Identity of the Bishop: A Study in the Theology of Disclosure," in Robert Sokolowski, *Christian Faith & Understanding: Studies on the Eucharist, Trinity, and the Human Person*, 113–30 (Washington, DC: The Catholic University of America Press, 2006), 117: "Apostolic teaching establishes the possibility of sanctifying and governing and it gives these other two tasks their sense."

49. See Jean Pierre Torrell, OP, *Saint Thomas Aquinas*, vol. 2, *Spiritual Master*, trans. Robert Royal (Washington, DC: The Catholic University of America Press, 2003), 381–82: "To announce what one has understood of the Gospel truth to someone deprived of it is to come to the aid of the worst poverty and to participate in the highest act of divine mercy." See St. Thomas, *Summa theologiae* I-II, Q. 108, a. 4, *sed contra*, where Christ as teacher of the New Law "maxime est sapiens et amicus."

50. For these forms of magisterial teaching, see *Lumen gentium*, no. 25; DH 4149.

62 CHAPTER 3

Just as the title of the foregoing section of this chapter was "Scripture and Tradition," since neither can be understood without its relation to the other, the title of this section is "Magisterium and dogma" and for the same reason. Magisterium and dogma are, so to speak, coeval realities. This was evident in chapter 2, where the authority of the first ecumenical council and the binding character of its formulation of faith, its "dogma," came to be realized in the course of the fourth century. But now we must attain some insight into why this is so, and Cardinal Newman supplies it to us. He offers us the intelligible connection between magisterium and dogma.

Newman begins the *Essay on Development* by showing that every great idea "develops"; once introduced into history and the mind of man, it shows its reality, its intelligibility, its parts, its aspects only slowly over the course of time (chapter 1). Now, Christianity is a great idea, and therefore we should expect developments (chapter 2, section 1). This amounts to maintaining, in part, that Scripture, for all its finality, inspiration, and inerrancy, requires interpretation: "[I]deas are in the writer and reader of the revelation, not the inspired text itself."[51] But which of these ideas conceived by the reader, himself not inspired, are accurate readings of the text? What developments of the idea of Christianity are truly so and not corruptions? Thinking of revelation and its reception in the Christian mind, thinking of possible developments and various interpretations of Scripture, the antecedent probability of the establishment of an authoritative judge of these matters impresses itself on us (chapter 2, section 2). Is this authoritative judge Scripture itself, or is it not likely that there will be an appointment of an "external authority"—an authority external to the progress of the putative developments?[52] How to decide between Protestantism and the Catholic Church, between Scripture alone and ecclesial magisterium?

Just at this point Newman makes an important distinction that provides the key to the answer of the question. "There are various revelations," he grants, "all over the earth ... inward suggestions and secret illuminations granted to so many individuals," including "traditionary doctrines

51. Newman, *Essay on Development*, 56.
52. Newman, *Essay on Development*, 78.

which are found among the heathen." However, these various and numerous revelations of God "do not carry with them the evidence of their divinity." He continues, "But Christianity is not of this nature: it is a revelation which comes to us as a revelation, as a whole, objectively, and with a profession of infallibility."[53] Supposing such a revelation were introduced into history, its continuance must also be given, else it ceases to be identifiable for subsequent generations.[54] The maintenance through time of revelation *as* revelation—the reduplication here is key—requires that there be a present guide, a present judge, that discerns genuine developments among all that are proposed as such, true interpretations among all proposed interpretations of Scripture. That there be such a present judge of developments is evidently a condition of the possibility of a theological science.[55] And that the Catholic Church alone makes this claim to be the authentic guardian and interpreter of the idea of Christianity once it unfolds into its many consequences, aspects, parts, and implications is itself a manifestation of its truth.[56]

That the Church so decide, that the Church so declare Athanasius's rather than Arius's interpretation of Scripture to be authentic, is the production of "dogma." Does the existence of a public magisterial authority and published dogmas follow from the idea of revelation alone? They do not. They follow from the idea of a revelation that meets us *as* revelation.

This way of arguing that Newman deploys in the *Essay* is efficacious for bringing to light the internal intelligibility of the establishment of both magisterium and dogma. They are not, as it were, afterthoughts nor additions to the idea of Christianity itself. And their articulation in Newman is not only itself an instance of discerning the correctness of developments within the Church, but is also an example of argument—from antecedent probability to its historical corroboration—that accounts for the justification of other developments of doctrine, as will be seen in chapter 5, where this kind of logic will be explored in more detail.

53. Newman, *Essay on Development*, 79.
54. Newman, *Essay on Development*, 85.
55. See Thomas Joseph White, OP, *The Light of Christ: An Introduction to Catholicism* (Washington, DC: The Catholic University of America Press, 2017), 36–39.
56. Newman, *Essay on Development*, 87–88.

"Dogma" in Scripture

Let us close this chapter by delimiting the notion of dogma more carefully and looking for an anticipation of its development in Scripture. I repeat the definition from Yves Congar's *Foi et théologie*:

> By the word "dogma" is meant the assertion of some truth contained in the word of God, either written or handed on (*tradita*), and proposed by the Church in an authentic formulation to be believed as divinely revealed, whether by a solemn judgment or at least by the ordinary and universal magisterium.[57]

This definition is parasitic on *Dei Filius* of the First Vatican Council which, without using the word dogma, teaches:

> All those things are to be believed by divine and Catholic faith which are contained in the word of God, written or handed on, and which are proposed by the Church to be believed as divinely revealed whether by a solemn judgment or by the ordinary and universal magisterium.[58]

This is, as it were, to fix the idea of dogma dogmatically. The notion emerges in the fourth century, as was seen in chapter 2; the ecclesial definition is proposed in the nineteenth century.[59]

According to Newman, one of the notes of a genuine development is that there be an "anticipation of its future … at an early period in the history of the idea to which it belongs."[60] We have seen the development of doctrine take place factually in the practice of the Church in the fourth century. But we may also ask whether the development of doctrine itself is, *in globo*, anticipated in Sacred Scripture. Surely it is.

Certain pieces of Scripture seem to have development already in mind when we look back at them with that idea. So in the Parabolic Discourse in Matthew, Jesus concludes by saying that "every scribe who has been trained in the kingdom of heaven is like a householder who brings out of his treasure what is new and what is old" (13:52). Cannot we see developments as the "new" the householder brings forth? Of course, this requires us to identify the householder with subsequent popes and bishops and to

---

57. Congar, *La Foi et la Théologie*, 54.
58. *Dei Filius*, chap. 3; DH 3011; ND 121.
59. For the history of the word and idea, see the resources noted in chapter 2, note 5.
60. Newman, *Essay on Development*, 199.

ask how the "new" can already be in the treasure, and to specify the relation of the new to the old. The saying all by itself can be taken as a foreshadowing, but it does not get us very far on its own. When the Lord tells Peter that whatever he binds on earth will be bound in heaven, and this in the context of indicating that his faith is the rock on which the Church is built (Mt 16:18), should we not see here the prospect of developments of doctrine ratified and proposed to faith by the pope? Every Catholic will answer yes. But the verse just in itself tells us nothing about how Peter and his successors will have the occasion for, and why they will have, the duty of binding authoritatively, or how what they bindingly teach is related to the faith on which the Church is built. Matthew 16 is a promise, but it is only the fulfillment in the history of the Church that lets us appreciate the scope of the promise.[61]

One might appeal to Acts 10, where Peter baptizes Cornelius without first circumcising him, and to Acts 15, where the question of keeping the Law for gentile Christians is determined more expressly. But it may be more useful to look to places where a postapostolic time is directly envisaged. We can interrogate the New Testament on the issue of development by putting ourselves in the place of apostles, evangelists, and pastors in the latter part of the first century. By this time, the Church has had some experience of those who do not teach in accord with the gospel originally delivered by Christ and the apostles. So, we might well expect Paul to warn Timothy against those who do not agree "with the sound words of our Lord Jesus Christ and the teaching which accords with godliness" (1 Tim 6:3). We might well expect whoever of the apostles are still alive and the elders and overseers (*presbyteroi* and *episcopoi*) to take more watchful care of the integrity and authenticity of the gospel. And so it is not surprising that Paul ends this letter with a sort of solemn charge: "O Timothy, guard what has been entrusted to you. Avoid the godless chatter and contradictions of what is falsely called knowledge" (1 Tim 6:20). "What is falsely called knowledge [*gnôsis*]" is perhaps already some form of the Gnosticism that afflicted the Church in the second century. Avoiding it is part of the duty of guarding "what has been entrusted to you." What has

---

61. See Newman, *Essay on Development*, chap. 4, section 3, and Congar, *La Foi et la Théologie*, 102–103.

66   CHAPTER 3

been entrusted is here conceived as something "deposited" for safe keeping, like money or valuables, to one who is legally bound to keep it safe according to the customary law of Rome.[62] The custodian of the deposit does not own it but is only its safe keeper. He is bound to render it back to its owner in its integrity upon demand. In the Pastorals, what is this *depositum* or *parathêkê* more exactly? It certainly has to do with the contrary of "false knowledge," and so means "true knowledge." It is associated with "the pattern of sound words" (2 Tm 1:13; see Ti 1:9) and so perhaps involves an already fixed confession of apostolic faith. Here, we have one of the foundations of the Church's understanding of the duty enjoined on all Christians but especially on office holders—bishops and priests—to maintain the purity of the gospel. And that is how the *depositum*, the treasure of Gospel truth, is rendered back to the Depositary: the Lord receives it back on the last day when he returns to judge the living and the dead.

The letters to Timothy and to Titus therefore prescribe a policy that is rightly described as conservative. Timothy is to maintain "sound doctrine" (1 Tm 1:10), healthy or saving teaching (*hygiainousa didaskalia*); references to teaching and sound teaching abound (1 Tm 1:3, 4:6; 6:3; 2 Tm 4:3; Ti 1:9; 2:1); and the teaching is to be fairly strictly handed on: "[F]ollow the pattern of the sound words which you have heard from me" (2 Tm 1:13). This is precisely how the "good deposit," the good teaching, is to be guarded (2 Tm 1:14). Paul is a teacher (1 Tm 2:7; 2 Tm 1:11), and so also are Timothy and Titus teachers (1 Tm 4:13, 16; 6:1; Ti 2:10), and they are to appoint teachers (1 Tm 3:2; 2 Tm 2:2; Ti 1:9). "Myths and endless genealogies" are to be avoided (1 Tm 1:5); "empty talkers" who want Christians to be circumcised are to be silenced (Ti 1:10–11). On the other hand, Paul himself intimates that guarding the deposit is not simply a matter of saying the same thing. When he mentions the false teaching according to which Christians are to abstain from certain foods, he answers with an argument: "[E]verything created by God is good, and nothing is to be rejected if it is received with thanksgiving" (1 Tm 4:4). The *depositum* is singular, one thing. But as expounded and defended by Timothy and Titus it becomes, across time, as needs be, many teachings. We have the same structure described in chapter 1 and so, "development."

62. See Spicq, *Les Épîtres Pastorales*, 1:331–335.

THE DEVELOPMENT OF DOGMA THEOLOGICALLY   67

There is therefore also a second reasonable expectation the Church might have at the end of the first century. It may not be enough to guard the deposit of faith simply by avoiding false teaching. It may not be enough to guard the deposit simply by repeating the same things in the same words over and over again. It may be necessary also to engage false teaching in order to refute it. It may be necessary to show how the deposit of faith functions in new circumstances and times. And then, besides the capacity to remember and repeat, there is the necessity to paraphrase, recapitulate, and, in short, say the same old thing in a new way. This is anticipated in the Lord's promise of the Holy Spirit in the Gospel according to John. "I have yet many things to say to you, but you cannot bear them now. When the Spirit of truth comes, he will guide you into all truth" (Jn 16:12–13a). This saying takes up, but differently, what the Lord had said earlier: "[T]he Counselor, the Holy Spirit, whom the Father will send in my name, he will teach you all things, and bring to your remembrance all that I have said to you" (14:26). Putting the two together, the Lord Jesus has in some way said, and in another way has not said, "all truth." What the disciples cannot bear to hear is somehow already present in the whole truth Jesus has taught them. Moreover, in the time of the Church, when the Holy Spirit has been sent, "all truth," the truth Christ came to reveal, will be in the Spirit's charge.[63] He has an indispensable role in making that truth available to the remembrance of the Church. Both novelty and continuity are therefore asserted. The Spirit brings to mind what Jesus taught in new situations, and so the truth he guides us into is not other than what Jesus first said. There is continuity. But also, in this remembering, the Spirit guides the Church into saying things the Lord did not quite "say" because the disciples could not bear them at the time. The one whole becomes many teachings. It is just this anticipation of saying the one same thing in saying different things that is the idea of

63. The reader will observe that this reading of John takes the "you" whom Jesus addresses as including the postapostolic Church as represented by the apostles themselves. See Gregory Nazianzen, Oration 31, the Fifth Theological Oration, 27. For this kind of a reading, see the notes by Scott Hahn and Curtis Mitch in the *Ignatius Study Bible* at the cited passages. It is possible to understand that the "many things" the Spirit has to tell the apostles is told them, completely and without remainder, at Pentecost. So for instance Charles Journet, *The Church of the Word Incarnate*, vol. 1, *The Apostolic Hierarchy*, trans A. H. C. Downes (London: Sheed and Ward, 1955), 132–36. He is following St. Thomas here.

development. The Holy Spirit that Paul says will help Timothy guard the truth entrusted to him (2 Tm 1:14) will help him guard it by teaching aptly (cf. 1 Tm 3:2), which is to say he will teach by bringing forth both old and new things from the deposit of faith (cf. Mt 13:52). As Vincent of Lérins put it, "Do not say new things but say old things newly (*dicas nove, non dicas nova*)."[64]

64. Vincent of Lérins, *Commonitorium*, chap. 22.

CHAPTER 4

PHILOSOPHICAL PRESUPPOSITIONS OF DOGMA AND DEVELOPMENT

Just after Yves Congar introduces his definition of dogma, which we reproduced in chapter 2 and again in chapter 3, he notes that there are three presuppositions to it. The first is "the existence of a magisterium." The second is "the validity of conceptual affirmations bearing on meta-empirical reality." The third is a little longer:

[T]he continuity of the connection (a) from the historical facts which are imbued with revelation, (b) to the testimonies to these facts, (c) to the sense given to these testimonies once the generation of those who testified to them has passed away, and (d) to the formulation of this sense in dogmas, dogmas that the Church, many centuries after this formulation, still imposes on the judgment of the faithful.

We have already seen that binding statements of faith contained in revelation but claiming to unpack it presuppose an authority that can declare them to the Church. They presuppose a teaching authority. What Congar is talking about in the second presupposition are statements that bear on realities that cannot be sensed and that do not fall within the subject matter of any of the modern empirical sciences, statements that inform us about God, angels, the spiritual soul. The "historical facts" of which the third presupposition speaks are preeminently things like the death and resurrection and ascension of Christ. These facts—these deeds—are meaningful; the meaning is declared in the witness of Christ and the apostles; this meaning is recorded in the New Testament; this meaning finds subsequent expression in the dogmas of the Church. This third presupposition involves not only the existence of a continuity of meaning from saving events to ecclesial teaching but our ability to know that continuity, to affirm it reasonably.

Congar points out that the first presupposition is denied by the Reformers of the sixteenth century. All the Reformers rejected papal authority, and Protestantism generally rejects episcopal authority and power, including the authority to teach in a way that binds the faithful, as it has come to be understood in the Church. The second presupposition is denied by Emmanuel Kant (†1804). He held that our knowledge in the strict sense extends only to what we can sense. If we speak about God and the immortal soul, then we do so only according as we must hope there is a God and the soul immortal if we are to make sense of our moral life. It is because of this that Christianity has to become a religion of the experience or consciousness, but not of the knowledge, of God. This inaugurates the line that runs from F. Schleiermacher (†1834) to the liberal Protestants to the Catholic Modernists (and beyond). Revelation is strictly only experiential; turning it into communicable language is a human work, and the conceptual expression of the experience will vary from age to age according to cultural and especially philosophical change.

The third presupposition, too, was contested by the Modernists. As to the second, they were certainly influenced, directly or indirectly, by the agnosticism of Kant, if only through such liberal Protestants as Auguste Sabatier (†1901). But in addition, they observed that modern historical studies not only offered no demonstration of the continuity required for the idea of Church dogma such that it remain an intelligibly unified thing, but that these studies seemed rather to demonstrate discontinuities between what our Lord claimed about himself, what the first Christians said about him, what was recorded in the later parts of the New Testament, especially John's Gospel, and the dogmas that bear on Christ such as we find them in the Councils of Nicaea, Ephesus, and Chalcedon. Alfred Loisy thought that whatever Jesus said about himself, it nowhere supported the idea that he is the Word of God, such as he is said to be in the first chapter of John.[1] George Tyrrell denied the coherence over time of Church doctrine.[2] So, for the Modernists, dogma, like revelation itself, does not really inform us about God or the soul, and can have but a symbolic or practical value.

The three presuppositions are also contested today, and some note of this will be taken further along. The existence and nature of teaching authority in the Church is something expressly taken up in fundamental theology and ecclesiology and was touched on in the last chapter. But we need to say a word in defense of the other presuppositions of dogma because they and what they themselves presuppose are often not clearly recognized today in discussions of dogmatic development. We will do so under six heads: knowing; the cognitive as conceptual; revelation and dogma as conceptual and propositional; the analogical knowledge of nonempirical things; epistemological realism; the historicity of man and of human truth.

Knowing

Congar framed his second presupposition as "the validity of conceptual affirmation of meta-empirical reality." "Meta-empirical" knowledge is addressed more particularly in the section on analogical knowledge. But

---

1. See Alfred Loisy, *Autour d'un petit livre*, 2nd ed. (Paris: Picard et Fils, 1903), part 4.

2. George Tyrrell, "Semper Eadem II," in George Tyrrell, *Through Scylla and Charybdis: or, the Old Theology and the New*, 133–54 (London: Longmans, Green, 1907), 153; "'Theologism'—A Reply," in *Through Scylla and Charybdis*, 308–54; see 346–49. A good description of Tyrrell's position is to be found in Jan H. Walgrave, *Unfolding Revelation: The Nature of Doctrinal Development* (Philadelphia: Westminster, 1972), 178.

72   CHAPTER 4

what are "conceptual affirmations"? They are instruments of knowing, instruments by which a knower knows what he knows. Since they are instruments of knowing, perhaps it is best to start with what they are ordered to, namely, knowing itself. What is knowing? St. Thomas and Thomists like Congar are at this point thoroughly Aristotelian. Knowing is the identity in act of knower and known.[3] The identity is established by a common possession of the same "form": the form that makes the horse a horse is also possessed by the human knower, but in an immaterial way; the common possession of the same form makes them "one in act."[4]

The definition of knowing as identity in act of subject and known object, as formal identity, can be arrived at by way of elimination, on the supposition that knowing is realistic. Here is a statement of epistemological realism:

(1) There are beings which are, and are what they are, independently of anyone's knowledge of them.

(2) These beings are capable of being known in human cognition, more or less adequately, and often with great difficulty, but still known, and known as they really are in themselves and not merely as they are relative to some knower.[5]

This statement of realism is by no means without interest to a Catholic theologian of development, and the reason is simple. Insofar as he is committed to the truth of the dogmas defined by the Church, he is also committed to what Bernard Lonergan calls "dogmatic realism," touched on but not so named in chapter 2.[6] That is, in defining the dogmas of Nicaea, Ephesus, Chalcedon, and so on, the conciliar fathers supposed that they were talking about real things—God, Christ, the salvation of human beings—and that these things could be known "as they really are and not simply as they are relative to some knower." That is, epistemological realism is the tacit presupposition of the dogmatic statements of the Church. It would, of course, be double-minded, schizophrenic, to suppose that we can be epistemological realists in religion but idealists or Kantians or something else in the rest of our thinking.

---

3. Aristotle, *De Anima*, book 3, chap. 4, 429a16–16, 429b31, 430a3–4; c.5, 430a20; c. 7, 431a1.
4. Aristotle, *De Anima*, book 3, chap. 8, 431b28–30.
5. Henry Babcock Veatch, *Intentional Logic* (New Haven, CT: Yale University Press, 1952), 7.
6. Bernard Lonergan, *The Triune God: Doctrines*, 240–47.

There is a vivid witness to realism and "dogmatic realism" in the conversion of Jacques Maritain. It turned in part on his realization that God reveals himself in truths accessible to human reason. Maritain once thought that our ideas are merely practically valuable, in the way that H. Bergson supposed, and do not close on the real. But Christian revelation implies realism, and so the trustworthiness of human concepts across the board (see the next section). Our mind is therefore naturally oriented to the real, to being.[7]

Even prior to accepting revelation by faith, however, we can come to epistemological realism from the knowledge God gives us of himself from the things that have been made (Rom 1:19). For if they are made, they proceed from Mind. Their truth is measured by their conformity to the divine intellect, as St. Thomas says, and this conformity is prior to their rendering this truth to our mind.[8] According to St. Thomas, truth is first of all in the intellect: in the divine mind creatively measuring things, in created things as measured by God, and as measuring our mind when we know them. This truth about the created truth of things implies also that things want to be known. They want to be named, and the poet's original expression of his friendliness to things just by naming them corroborates the realism of which we are speaking. Things want to appear as they are, and the poet responds to this desire.[9] It is precisely in this light that

7. Jacques Maritain, *Bergsonian Philosophy and Thomism*, trans. Mabelle L. Andison (New York: Philosophical Library, 1955), 17: "Since God gives us, in concepts and conceptual propositions (which reach us dripping with the blood of martyrs—in the days of Arianism men knew how to die for the sake of an iota) truths transcendent and inaccessible to our reason, the very truth of his divine life, that abyss which is His, it is because the concept is not a mere practical instrument incapable in itself of transmitting the real to our mind whose only use is in artificially [nominalistically] breaking up ineffable [Bergsonian] continuities, leaving the absolute to escape like water through a sieve. Thanks to analogical intellection, that natural marvel of lightness and strength which, thrown across the abyss, makes it possible for our knowledge to attain the infinite, the concept, divinely elaborated in the dogmatic formula, contains but does not limit, and causes to descend to us, in an enigmatic and mirrored but altogether true manner the very mystery of the Deity which pronounces Itself eternally in the Uncreated Word, and which has been told in time and in human language by the Incarnate Word."

8. St. Thomas, *Quaestiones Disputatae de Veritate*, ed. R. Spiazzi (Rome: Marietti, 1949), Q. 1, a. 2. See Josef Pieper, "The Negative Element in the Philosophy of St. Thomas," in *The Silence of St. Thomas*, 45–71, trans. John Murray, SJ, and Daniel O'Connor (New York: Pantheon, 1957 [German, 1953]), at 50–57.

9. Truth does not, then, come late to things; see Robert Sokolowski, *Presence and Absence* (Bloomington, IN: Indiana University Press, 1978), 170. And from the other side, "we are the kind

George Steiner speaks of the "covenant" between word and world: they want, as it were, to be faithful to one another.[10] It is easy to see already how Christian revelation confirms the epistemological realism natural theology demonstrates. God is infinitely intelligible, and he makes intelligible things. Man, the rational animal, the *logikos* animal, confronts no meaningless world, but a *logikos* world, because God makes it through his Logos, his Reason-Logic-Word, as John 1:3 tell us. We return to this below in a further discussion of realism.[11]

If we are realists, however, what sort of analysis can we invoke to speak of knowing in an insightful way?[12] Knower and known become "one" in some fashion or other. An identity is established. But what is the nature of this identity, and what is its cause? Efficient causality will not help: if to know the known means the knower changes it, then the objectivity of knowledge presupposed by realism is destroyed. Could it be the other way around, that the known object exercises agency on the knower? This seems to be a condition of sense knowledge. The held object conforms my hand to its shape and temperature. But this can be but a condition, otherwise we would say that every exercise of agency makes the patient a knower. It would be strange to say, however, that the log comes to know the logger. Nor can material causality help to explain things: when George knows a stone, he does not share the material extension of the stone nor does the stone become fleshy.

The identity in question is rather, as Aristotle indicates, a *formal* identity. That is, the known object and the knower are identical in that in each there is the same "form" (or "essence" or "nature" or "quiddity"). However, this form does not exist in the same way in knower and known (and it almost certainly does not exist in its fullness and all its detail in the

---

of thing to whom being is exposed," Robert Sokolowski, *Phenomenology of the Human Person* (Cambridge: Cambridge University Press, 2008), 310.

10. George Steiner, *Real Presences* (London: Faber and Faber, 1989), 90: "[T]he relationship between word and world, inner and outer, has been held 'in trust.' This is to say that it has been conceived of and existentially enacted as a relation of responsibility"; and "The covenant between word and object, the presumption that being is, to a workable degree, 'sayable', and that the raw material of existentiality has its analogue in the structure of narrative—we recount life, we recount life to ourselves—have been variously expressed." Steiner then evokes Adam in Genesis, Plato's dialectical grasp of the archetypes, and Descartes's *Third Meditation*.

11. See Gregory Vall, *Ecclesial Exegesis*, 205.

12. For the following, see Veatch, *Intentional Logic*, 8–10.

knower). When I know the dog, I do not acquire an appetite for chasing rabbits. Doginess—caninitude—exists in the dog as actually constituting an individual dog. The dog-essence as existing in me exists in me without the matter of the dog, but in such a way that I understand the dog, what the dog is; I possess some at least of its intelligibility and truth.

We should be careful not to think we have explained much when we say that knowing is the identity in act of knower and known, and that this identity is a formal identity and means sharing a common form.[13] Have we really explained knowing? Or have we just described it more elaborately? It may be the course of truthful humility to take the latter course. And what, after all, could "explaining" knowing be? It would be like explaining being, or truth. Still, even if our description is simply a more complicated way of naming it, it protects us from making materialist and positivist and scientistic mistakes—for instance, identifying knowing with neural activity, its immediate substrate. Moreover, it connects us with the original apprehension of knowing articulated by Aristotle and the Greeks. In this light, we have not explained so much as simply indicated the magical fact of knowing. For knowledge *is* magical; it makes present what is absent; it conquers spatial distances; it annihilates temporal passing and anticipation and makes the past and the future present.

The cognitive as the conceptual

It is in asking how this identity in act is established and exercised in knowing that we get to the concept. The formal identity of knower and known is produced by the reception of the form of the known in the knower. St. Thomas distinguishes (1) the intellect, in potency to knowing or understanding the object, (2) the act of understanding the object; and (3) the "species" or form by which the intellect is made actually to understand the object.[14] The species or form which grounds the intellect's actually understanding the object reduces the intellect from potentially understanding the object to actually understanding it. The species or form is a

13. We should be careful also not to think that knowing the intelligibility of material things is simple and easy; see Benjamin M. Block, "Thomas Aquinas on Knowing the Essences of Material Substances," *The Thomist* 87 (2023): 87–130.

14. *Summa theologiae* I, Q. 79, aa. 2 and 3.

product of the agent intellect, the power to make what can be understood actually understood. It is a result of what St. Thomas called "abstraction" from sense data.[15] This is not some occult procedure, but a matter of questioning, of asking the sensorily present object what it is and whether it is, conformable to the givens of sense knowledge. Asking questions is a conscious endeavor, and (in the original metaphor) is the very shining of the light of being on the object to be known. It is the light of *being*, for we ask whether something *is*, and what it *is*. We ask of the object to be known, already present to us in the data of sense, about its parts and integrity, about what is essential to it and what is not. If we are lucky, we have an insight (something conscious—we "get it"). We "see in" the data an intelligibility: the intellect is reduced to act, which is to say there is a further actualization of intellect by way of the species or form it receives, and which form is the immediate principle by which we understand.

But there is more. The cognitive relation understood as a relation of formal identity in which we know things as they are in themselves requires us to speak also of *concepts* as the conscious instruments of knowing the known object. Why is this? According to St. Thomas, the exterior word, spoken or written, can be taken to refer to none of the three things enumerated above. "Dog" does not name the intellect, the power that understands. It does not name the act of understanding the dog. And it does not name the species or form received in the intellect, for that is known only as a deduction within the metaphysics of knowing, in that reduction of potency to act requires a formal principle in act, the species. This "species" does not itself enter into consciousness, modifying the mind unto intending what we understand of dogs. There is, however, needed some consciously available specification of the act of understanding, making it an act of understanding of dogs. And that is what the name "dog" is first related to for St. Thomas. "Dog," the word, names something that St. Thomas says is "formed," that is, made or constructed by the act of understanding,[16] and that is what he calls, following Augustine, the interior word or word of the heart, and what is more generally called the concept. This he calls the species "in which" the intellect understands the known

15. *Summa theologiae* I, Q. 85, aa. 1 and 2.
16. *Summa theologiae* I, Q. 85, a. 2, ad 3.

PHILOSOPHICAL PRESUPPOSITIONS   77

object.[17] Really distinct from the object known, it is the object known as consciously present in the mind.[18]

The covenant relation between word and world of which G. Steiner speaks is also a nuptial relation, and a fruitful one, and hence the felicity of speaking of what the mind conceives in this embrace, a *conceptus*.[19]

Let us take a longer way around to the concept.[20] Could it be that what we know is the very principle by which we know it, that the *quod* of knowledge is the instrument of knowledge, the *id a quo*? In some sense, that must be true. But it cannot be supposed that knowing is like eating. Can we maintain that "just as the thing to be eaten becomes the thing being eaten by entering into the body of the eater, so the thing to be known becomes the thing being known by entering into the mind of the knower"?[21] But the object known does not itself enter into the mind of the knower. When I know fire, I do not get burned. When I know some property of an object, I am not conditioned by that property; when I know the grass as green I do not become green.

17. The great texts are *Summa contra gentiles* I, c. 53; IV, c. 11; *Summa theologiae* I, Q. 34, a. 1; *Commentary on John*, chap. 1, lecture 1, nos. 25–33. From the enormous literature on the interior word in Aquinas, I recommend Bernard Lonergan, *Verbum: Word and Idea in Aquinas* (Notre Dame, IN: University of Notre Dame Press, 1967), which situates it systematically in St. Thomas's theory of mind. For careful discussion of how to think about concepts, see Jacques Maritain, *Distinguish to Unite or the Degrees of Knowledge*, trans. under the supervision of Gerald Phelan (New York: Charles Scribner's Sons, 1959), appendix 1: The Concept, 387–417, and note the convenient collection of texts from St. Thomas on the concept, 399–417. Henry Babcock Veatch argues vigorously for the need to speak of concepts in *Intentional Logic*, chap. 4, 81–115, and also treats of classes as substitutes for concepts in mathematical logic (115–53). In an expressly logical context, see Robert W. Schmidt, *The Domain of Logic According to Saint Thomas Aquinas* (The Hague: Martinus Nijhoff, 1966), 94–122, 127–201. For an introductory discussion of the interior word in St. Thomas's Trinitarian theology, one can begin with Gilles Emery, OP, *The Trinitarian Theology of St. Thomas Aquinas*, trans. Francesca Aran Murphy (Oxford: Oxford University Press, 2006), 57–62, 180–85. There is a very fine discussion of the mental word or concept in Olivier-Thomas Venard, OP, *A Poetic Christ: Thomist Reflections on Scripture, Language and Reality*, trans. Kenneth Oakes and Francesca Aran Murphy (London: T&T Clark, 2019), 260–301.

18. See for this way of speaking Robert Sokolowski, *Phenomenology of the Human Person*, 178–79, 301–3.

19. See Maritain's suggestive remarks in *The Degrees of Knowledge*, 407, commenting on the *Summa contra gentiles*, book 4, chap. 11: "St. Thomas is defining *intentio intellectus*; it is that which the intellect *conceives* or gives birth to within itself through the thing intellectually grasped. It is the concept in the fullest etymological force of the term, the *fruit conceived* by and in the intellect and *conceived of the thing*."

20. For much of the following, see Mortimer Adler, *The Difference of Man and the Difference It Makes* (New York: Holt, Rinehart and Winston, 1967), 340–47.

21. Adler, *The Difference of Man*, 341.

Could we suppose, second, that knowing involves nothing more than the knower's turning his attention to the object known? Perhaps knowing is like illumination. The object is illumined when the light shines on it; the object is known when I attend to it. But if knowing were such a simple affair, in which the known object was known by simple presence to the knower, how could I ever be in error about objects? In fact, I often make mistakes. (There are perceptual errors, e.g. "the bent oar in the water"; there are conceptual errors—I can be mistaken about the properties of gold). If, however, we supposed that there were an instrument of knowing interior to the knower, then I can explain error in the following way: the instrument of knowing, by which I intend the known object, may not always be exactly suited to the object known.

Suppose, third—a very attractive suggestion—that words (the words of our natural languages) were the adequate instruments of properly intellectual knowledge. But how does a meaningless mark on a page, or a meaningless vocable, acquire meaning? Does the word "dog" become meaningful by repeated association with particular dogs, or pictures of dogs? This will not do. Association does not get us to names, otherwise animals would speak. Furthermore, I have many words to designate the selfsame perceptible object: "poodle," "quadruped," "mammal," and so on. If words gained their meaning through simple association with the perceptible objects they are able to name, why do not "poodle," "quadruped," and "mammal" mean the same thing? In fact, these words have different connotations (i.e. they comprise different intelligible contents or senses) and denotations (i.e. they refer to different groups or classes of objects).

Hence, the meaning of words cannot be derived from simple association with perceptible objects (otherwise "poodle" and "dog" and "mammal" would have the same connotations and denotations). Do we want to say that the meaning of words must be derived from association with the appropriate *classes* of objects? Yes, we do. But classes are not objects of perception; the objects of perception are individual members *of* classes. How do I know classes? This is to ask how words can gain the connotative and denotative significance they acquire. There must be some other instrument of knowledge, in addition to words, by which the words have the connotative and denotative significance they have. Call these instruments "concepts."

PHILOSOPHICAL PRESUPPOSITIONS   79

There is also the very simple demonstration of the necessity of concepts from the fact that our natural languages have words for the same thing. "Chien" and "Hund" and "dog" have the same meaning. Without this same meaning, which is distinct from the many names, translation would be impossible. Is this meaning embodied in the rules that determine when we use "chien" and when we use "dog," such that if the rules are the same, then the meaning is the same, and the meaning then turns out to be indistinct from the rules? This is an illuminating move by which to say what "meaning" means. But it is incomplete. Knowing does not lose us in language, the newer form of idealism. To be sure, we meet reality only within language and not apart from it. But it is reality we meet, and not simply more and more language. The rule-theory of meaning does not measure up to the statement of realism at the beginning of this section. What therefore is this same meaning that "chien" and "dog" have? They evoke the same concept.

The concept, or "interior word," just is the meaning the name has, without which it is a dead name, opaque and thinglike. St. Thomas spoke of interior words as *similitudines*, for it seems that concepts must in some sense be genuine likenesses of what they are of, formally identical, else whence could we know the object through them?[22] This instrument of knowing, on the other hand, while representative of the known, does not present itself in itself *as* a representative, as a copy. Then we would find ourselves lost in the subjectivist dilemma, we would find ourselves lost in John Locke, for whom words first and last refer to ideas. But if we had to know the idea, or concept, first in itself before knowing the object, how should we ever know the object in itself in order to check on the adequacy of the representation? Rather, concepts must have the character of formal signs; they are pure signs, self-effacing, purely donative of the content of the object.[23]

22. See Robert Sokolowski, *Phenomenology of the Human Person* (Cambridge: Cambridge University Press, 2008), chap. 18, for a careful assessment of the dangers of speaking of *similitudines*. And see below, note 24.

23. It is by recourse to John of St. Thomas that the concept is here defined as a formal sign. This elegant development of Thomist thought, defended and explored in the last years by John Deely, is not always welcomed by Thomists today. For an introduction to the literature, one might begin with the sympathetic account of Thomas Osborne, "The Concept as a Formal Sign," *Semiotica* 179 (2010): 1–21. For an accessible statement of the scholastic division of signs, see John Oesterle, *Logic: The Art of Defining and Reasoning* (New York: Prentice-Hall, 1963), chap. 1.

These signs *express* the object known, and so express the identity achieved by the form (*species*) received in the intellect. However,

[they] could not have definite, determinate natures of their own—at least not in the usual sense. If they did, then they could represent other things only as being similar to themselves, or as causes of themselves, or as effects of themselves, or as in some way or another related to themselves. But a formal sign does not signify or represent other things in this way: it does not present them as they are in relation to it, but rather as they are in themselves. The real object, in short, which the formal sign signifies is itself that sign's very content.[24]

In this light, it may be useful to characterize them simply as the presence or presencing of the intelligibility of the object to the mind, as already suggested. "Presence" adds something to "intelligibility," but it does not invite us to take the concept as a medium standing between the knower and the known that has first to be known in itself and independently of the object.

It is important to note that the content of a concept is the very intelligibility of the thing of which it is the concept—more or less complete, more or less detailed, the intelligibility at least anticipated and intended where names serve only as placeholders for the results of inquiry.[25] It was noted above that it is this conceptual identity across languages that enables translation from one language to another. For ordinary things, ordinary concepts, and well-worn languages, it is evident that the same intelligibility, the same concept, the same meaning, is evoked by *chien* as by *Hund* as by *dog*. This innocent fact, however, will play an important role later in this chapter and in chapter 6.

Conceptual epistemological exclusivity and the upshot for revelation and doctrine

Exclusivity

Concepts and the propositions they make up, when we assert or deny some predicate of a subject, are the way of knowing that is proper to man,

---

24. Veatch, *Intentional Logic*, 13–14, and on formal signs generally, 12–15.

25. Veatch, *Intentional Logic*, 10: "[T]o say that a concept is *of* something does not mean that the concept resembles what it is of, or is similar to it, or copies it, or anything of the sort. What the concept is of is or becomes the very content of the concept itself."

and this conceptual knowing is the only way of rational knowing that we have, which is to say, the way of knowing commensurate with language, and without which language cannot do its cognitive work.[26]

It is proper to man. God and the angels do not know discursively, by asserting or denying predicates of a subject. God simply is an unrestricted act of understanding himself and all the things that participate or can participate in him.[27] Angelic understanding is founded in the intelligible species with which they are created, and their knowledge of what they know does not pass from subject to predicate or from premises to conclusion but is simple, like the simple act of understanding we experience when we know the truth of first principles.[28]

Very importantly for our understanding of revelation and the development of dogma, human knowing just is the assertion and denial of propositions. I do not actually know anything about the tree in the garden until I can speak about it. I may sense its color and smell its bark and so know it the way animals know things. But until I can say the tree is a black oak, is large, is dark green, is 40 feet tall, and so on, all of which things are formulated in propositions and affirm some concept of the subject, then I do not know it the way human beings know things. Is there another way for us to know things? I may have an insight into the health or disease of the tree from examining its leaves and the dead branches in the crown (which things I first see and can report propositionally—"the branches are dead"). What I observe is indeed grist for the mill, but the mill is the production of a proposition: "The tree seems to be unhealthy."

The upshot

Words, spoken or written, do two things for us that nothing else does.[29] They do these things, they accomplish this their cognitive work for us, by the concepts and propositions they call to consciousness. Both of these

---

26. The following stipulation can be useful: names are to concepts as declarative sentences are to (mental) propositions as syllogisms on the page are to (interior) arguments.

27. *Summa theologiae* I, Q. 14, a. 4.

28. *Summa theologiae* I, Q. 55, aa. 2–3.

29. For much of the following, see Robert Sokolowski, *Presence and Absence: A Philosophical Investigation of Language and Being* (Washington, DC: The Catholic University of America Press, 2017), especially chap. 3.

things, moreover, are extremely relevant to the work words do in theology, doctrine, and revelation itself.

First, words let us master absences by making things present to us by the concepts they evoke. The written or recorded word gives us the presence of someone's narrative or analysis in the absence of the speaker or writer. The speaker or writer may be dead; they may be so absent that we do not know who they are or were. Concomitantly, words make *things* present to us, to our mind, even if they are bodily absent. "Chicago," I say. And the Windy City is present to us—or we are present to Chicago—though it is many hundreds of miles away from sunny Florida. The senses also make absent things present, but not in the same way, not with the same surety, not with the same absoluteness. Smell makes the dead rat present to us. But only within a certain olfactory envelope. I can see things very distant from me, the stars, for instance, or mountains at the end of the Colorado plain. But the distance is not infinite. The senses do not master infinities. But words do. Think of the infinite series of adding 1 to 1, and 1 to 2, and 1 to 3, and so on. There is nothing like that "and so on" for the senses.[30]

Words make absent speakers or writers and absent objects present. They also allow us to make present things absent, hidden, as when I nominalize some complex state of affairs. "Thomas Aquinas flourished in an age of increasing urbanization, increasing institutionalization of learning, increasing legal regulation of institutions, both ecclesial and temporal. That is a fact about his situation." And then I can refer to "that fact," in two words, and the complex articulation of reality disappears into those words.[31] Of course, I can rearticulate it, bring it out from hiding. But my words master both the absent historical reality of Thomas's situation and the presence of that situation to our minds.

We can say, correlatively, that words let us negotiate identity and difference. This is another way of getting at the mastery of presence and absence. "George was at the store this morning. He is at the beach now." But it is the same George, identified in two different places. The words let me

30. For another way of getting at this, see Bernard Lonergan, *Method in Theology*, 2nd ed. (New York: Herder and Herder, 1973), chap. 3, on linguistic meaning and the world mediated by meaning.

31. See Sokolowski, *Presence and Absence*, 50–62, on the nominalization of facts.

capture an identity across differences. And according to the direction of my interest, I can make to differ the same thing, a single identity by my words. "George is quite another man at the beach—playful and relaxed—than he is in the store—serious and sober." It is still the same George, but across more intimate, more personal differences.

A second thing that words do is make present for us things in their intelligibility.[32] This was already noted in the original description of what concepts are, for words evoke concepts.[33] But it bears further reflection. For one thing, it is more basic than the first function of words. It explains the first function, that words are instruments that enable us to deal with presence and absence. It is because words present things just and only in their intelligibility that we can detach them from their concrete times and places. We can detach them from existence itself.

"Make me a boat," I say to the boatwright. "I want a shallow draft, five-man boat for getting around the swamp." I have named some properties of the boat—things that do not go without saying them. There are accidental things, too: "I want a yellow boat." Because I like yellow. Or: "I want a yellow-green mottled boat." Because I want to sneak up on alligators. But suppose I also say: "Yes, and I want a boat that floats." But I do not have to say that. Why not? Because that is part of the nonnegotiable intelligibility of any boat. So if I say that—"It should float"—I do nothing but reveal my ignorance of boats, and at that point, of the language. The "essence" of a boat, its boatness, is floatability. And the name "boat" makes the object present to me with just that understanding.[34]

But now let us think of matters theological. In chapter 3, the cognitive character of revelation was established by observing that it is a matter of the words of prophet and apostle as mediating the word of God to us. God reveals himself and his mind to us. How does he do this? Not by smiling. We do not see his face. Not by a statue or picture—though there

32. Robert Sokolowski, "God's Word and Human Speech," *Nova et Vetera* (English) 11 (2013): 187–210, at 199: "This is the magic of words. They capture and carry the intelligibilities of things and weave them syntactically into statements, arguments, narratives, and conversations."

33. Veatch, *Intentional Logic*, 82: "Hence no matter what a given concept may be a concept of, i.e., whether it be the concept of yellow or of tree or of a transitive relation of just a being, such a concept is necessarily the concept of what something is, of a *nature or essence*, in other words." Emphasis added.

34. See Sokolowski, *Presence and Absence*, 130–43, on language and essentials.

is a sense in which we see him in his images, our brothers and sisters. We can tell something about him from his most perfect creature, created persons. And there is a sense in which the plan of salvation constitutes a picture, or better, a drama, as Hans Urs von Balthasar would have it. But that is not given to us without lots and lots of *words*. Here, too, the words do their work once again by way of the concepts they evoke.

The unique capacity of words to master absence and presence is absolutely crucial for the event of revelation, of God speaking to us, and this involves the very identification of the speaker—our ability to identify him. The speaker of revelation, God, is not identified without the use of some very special words. These special words are not "God" or "Lord" or any other natural language equivalents. These special words are "whole" and "not."

To tie down the reference to God, to make reference to God, we need the capacity to affirm all things, to say "all" or "whole." And we need the capacity to deny, to say "not." For we identify God correctly only when we say he is not any of the things of our experience, that he cannot be experienced at all. It is not just that we do not see him; we cannot see him. He cannot be seen. Or touched. If we touch it—it is not God. If we think God can be experienced, we reduce him to a thing of the world; we are not really thinking of him any longer. But see what is required then in order to refer to God: we need a summing up, which can only be a *linguistic* gathering of all that is, of the world, of the universe of universes. Only in language can we gather up not only all material things, the galaxies and modern parallel "universes"—if there are any—but all the souls and all the spirits and demons and angels, too. We have to pick out the whole, the all, of which we are a part. And then we have to add the "not": We have to say, but I am *not* speaking of *that*, of that *whole* of things, when I say "God." Rather, I refer to the one *beyond*.

The indication of the "all" on which reference to God depends cannot be accomplished by a gesture—a gesture of enclosing in the arms, or looking in all directions and nodding, or something like that. We would never know the extent of such gesturing. And the "not"—the *not* lives in language: the "not" is not death, or rejection, or hatred. It is like the false of the true and the false: it is a thing of language. Nor can the transcendence of God—he not being one of the things of the world—nor can this

PHILOSOPHICAL PRESUPPOSITIONS 85

transcendence be indicated by pointing up. Or pointing up and jumping. No gesture of nodding or shaking the head or open hands or smashing fist can on its own accomplish these radical feats of language.

The thing most transcendent to the world, not part of the world, therefore the thing most absent from our minds that are necessarily in the world and ordinarily suited to dealing with things in the world in their presences and absences—that thing, that One, can be identified by language, and precisely as the Most Absent.

God's name makes God present to us. And what of the second thing words do? Does God's name make God's intelligibility present to us? The answer is no, if we mean that "God" functions the way "boat" does, or "democracy," or "Mount Everest." But the answer is yes, if we are careful and know how to speak. "God" makes his intelligibility present to us as the superintelligibility of which all the intelligibilities of the world are shares and imitations. Therefore, he cannot be defined as something is defined within the world. But when we say "God," we are not pointing. We are not "gesturing." We are naming. We are naming that of which it is impossible for any finite intellect to have quidditative knowledge.

Of course, if we think God is one of a kind, then we are thinking of a god, and not God. If we think God has parts, we are thinking of a god, and not God. But there are many ways to think God truly. God is Truth. God is his eternity. God is that than which nothing greater can be thought. God is that in which there is no distinction of essence and being.

It is to be wondered whether these true ways of understanding what cannot be understood the way anything else is understood would be available to us had God not revealed himself. Is not Etienne Gilson right that there is a metaphysics of Exodus?[35] With the help of the name God gives himself, "I am who I am," we make him present precisely in his transcendence. We make the most absent thing, the God transcendent to the word, present to our mind. That is to say, he has found a way with our language to make himself, the most Absent, present to us as He Who Is.[36]

---

35. Etienne Gilson, *The Christian Philosophy of St. Thomas Aquinas* (New York: Random House, 1956), 43–95.

36. The best thing at this point is a careful consideration of Robert Sokolowski, "God's Word and Human Speech." See also Olivier-Thomas Venard, OP, "Scriptural Hermeneutics and the Thomistic Making of a Doctrine of God," *Nova et Vetera* (English) 12 (2014): 1091–123.

If we take the concept as necessary for the constitution and communication of knowledge in language, and if we take it that there is no other way to constitute and communicate knowledge *except* by way of words that signify things *only* by also signifying concepts, then we have established a powerful principle by which to judge certain theories of doctrinal development. For where these theories appeal to an experience of reality, divine reality, that is prior to or works independently of the conceptual, or where these theories appeal to an access to reality, divine reality and the mysteries, that cannot logically, which is to say conceptually, explain the relation of some new doctrine with past (conceptual) expressions of revelation, we will know they are wrong.

It is good at this point to look back to chapter 1 and the "idea of Christianity" with which Newman begins his *Essay on Development*. There is sometimes an uncertainty about how we should think of it. Terrence Merrigan, when he considers the fact that Newman sometimes speaks of it as a "force" and as something not wholly reflexively (Newman says "consciously") possessed, something therefore in some way only "implicit," is reluctant to think of the idea as "strictly propositional."[37] On the other hand, when we recall that the "idea" is not only articulated in doctrines but is conveyed by "enunciation" and "statements of the doctrine,"[38] then there is no real distance between Newman and what has been affirmed in this section. Indeed, the idea of Christianity is a "*living* idea"; it is not "received passively" but becomes an "active principle."[39] But this is to say that the idea of Christianity is of a living, powerful, active *Reality*. Once fully received, therefore, it does not leave the mind at rest, but invites contemplation, comparison, application, and, indeed, developments, which is to say, further articulations of its heights and depths. But this does nothing to gainsay its presence in the mind by way of concept and proposition, and its conveyance thereto by language. The original words of the witness to revelation preserved in Scripture and the Creed establish an intelligibility in our mind that is pregnant with many more explanatory words.

The trouble is not the conceptual and propositional presence of revelation, of the deposit of faith, in our mind, but the underestimation of the

37. Merrigan, *Clear Heads and Holy Hearts*, 94, but see 93–95 as a whole.
38. Newman, *Essay on Development*, 36, 37.
39. Newman, *Essay on Development*, 36.

PHILOSOPHICAL PRESUPPOSITIONS 87

power of the proposition. This underestimation is tied to thinking of concepts as "representations," more or less successful—as pictures that more or less, but mostly less, approximate some photographic standard. But that is not what they are. They are the presence of the real to us precisely in its intelligibility. Because of this, the propositions of faith make the very reality of what they speak of present to us, including the very reality of God. This is exactly what St. Thomas means when he says that the act of one who believes terminates not in the proposition but in the reality. In this way, he continues, the assent of faith is exactly like the assent of science.[40] Sometimes this is badly reported. Indeed, there is a distinction to make between the proposition and the reality it terminates in. And it is true that we can have only the proposition and not the reality. We do this when we wonder whether some speaker's proposition is true or not, whether it deserves assent: when we do that, we are stopping at the proposition, at the proposal, and not going through it, as it were, to land in the reality.[41] But the reverse is not true: we cannot have the reality in its intelligibility *without* the proposition. It is misleading to say then that for St. Thomas, faith gives us the reality "and not just" the propositions. Faith, the propositions of faith, give us the reality, and they do so *just according to the shape and content of the concepts that form them*, no more and no less.

Realism

We can now also better understand what happened at the Council of Nicaea, a sketch of whose achievement was outlined in chapter 2. For Bernard Lonergan, the fathers of Nicaea produced their teaching by attending to the statements of Scripture taken as true, and so implicitly embraced what he calls "dogmatic realism." The "realism" in question is the realism that was characterized by Henry Veatch in the first section of this chapter. It is the position that whatever is real is being, and that being

40. *Summa theologiae* II-II, Q. 1, a. 2, ad 2: "Actus autem credentis non terminatur ad enuntiabile, sed ad rem: non enim formamus enuntiabilia nisi ut per ea de rebus cognitionum habeamus, *sicut in scientia*, ita et in fide." Italics added.

41. Robert Sokolowski, *Presence and Absence*, 146–47, and see the "dis-quotational theory of truth," in Robert Sokolowski, *Introduction to Phenomenology* (Cambridge: Cambridge University Press, 2000), 100–102.

is known through true propositions. But at Nicaea, the position is dogmatic: realism is asserted implicitly in requiring Catholic Christians to confess the creed of Nicaea, that is to say, the very *propositions* that make up the creed. It is only by so assenting to the propositions that the Christian will know the truth that is from God and about God. Remember the anathematisms of the creed of Nicaea reported in chapter 2: those "who *say* there was a time" when the Son was not are excluded from the communion of the Church. The council bears down on the "saying" because saying, affirming a statement and supposing a proposition to be true, is a claim about how *reality* is—here, the reality of the relation of Son to Father. This position is asserted implicitly, but in a way more emphatically, in the Rule of Athanasius, which is a proposition about how to make orthodox propositions about Father and Son. The Rule can be the key to the doctrine of Nicaea, therefore, only if the really important thing is to make the right predications of Son and Father, the right predications found in Scripture.

What is required, according to Lonergan, is that we attend to the word of God contained in Scripture as true.

Dogma emerges from the revealed word of God, carried forward by the tradition of the Church; it does so, however, only to the extent that, prescinding from all other riches contained in that word of God, one concentrates on it precisely *as true*.[42]

Further:

… if one separates the word from the truth, if one rejects propositional truth in favour of some other kind of truth, then one is not attending to the word of God as true.[43]

To be sure, this claim about realism is implicit; the Fathers of Nicaea held no disputation on the critical problem. But they were concerned about propositions, the right propositions to make in answering Arius, the right propositions to use in speaking about Father and Son. For propositions mediate being to us. They are the instruments, indeed the only instruments, of our grasp of being as being. They say what is. And they say it

---

42. Lonergan, *The Triune God: Doctrines*, 41.
43. Lonergan, *The Triune God: Doctrines*, 41.

expressly, for there is no proposition that does not engage the mighty copula.

The thing to note in a fundamental theological context is in the first place the role that Scripture plays. But in the second place, Scripture does not play its role unless it is taken as true. Faith in the New Testament means trust; it means obedience; also, it means holding certain things as true, the true expressed in words. "Let your word be Yes, Yes, or No, No; anything else comes from the evil one" (Mt 5:37). And again, "No one can say Jesus is Lord but in the Holy Spirit" (1 Cor 12:3). Faith surely depends on the Holy Spirit, but it is a matter of what we say.[44]

For the council, the real is known through propositions, propositions dictated by the word of God found in Scripture and interpreted according to the Rule of Faith. This is nicely called "dogmatic realism" by Lonergan. It is realism because it is interested in what is, independently of our feeling or wishing or imagining or thinking. But it is not a realism that is critically established by epistemological argument. Rather, it is a realism inherent in accepting the word of God contained in Scripture as true, and as subsequently expressed in the dogmas of the Church.[45] It is a realism that concern for our salvation in Christ commits us to. It is the realism Nicaea commits us to, according to which the real is being, and we know the being of God and the beings God speaks of through true propositions rationally affirmed. Knowing how God is, that the Son is consubstantial with the Father, enables us to make a true act of faith and so truly insert ourselves into saving reality.

Once we realize that the predicates of Scripture deliver what is true of the subject of which they are said, however, once we realize that the proposition as a whole puts us in possession of the real, and once we realize this is not peculiar to Scripture, then we are ready to generalize and say that whatever is real is known in the act of judgment, in assenting to a proposition. We are ready to see, too, that the scope of human judgment

---

44. See also 1 Tm 1:10; 2 Tm 4:3f.; 2 Pt 2:1. A confidence in the realism of the statements of Scripture is common to the fourth century, for which see Anatolios, *Retrieving Nicaea*, 9, 36.

45. For revelation as presupposing philosophical realism, see John Paul II, *Fides et ratio*, nos. 80–85, esp. 83, *in Restoring Faith in Reason: A New Translation of the Encyclical Letter Faith and Reason of Pope John Paul II*, trans. Anthony Meredith, SJ, and Laurence Paul Hemming, with commentary (Notre Dame, IN: University of Notre Dame Press, 2002), 129–41, esp. 135–37.

is not limited by matter, not limited by space and time. For indeed it is not so limited in thinking about the Trinity. We are ready at that point to affirm that being as such, not being as extended, not being as mutable, is the native object of human intellectual desire, and the ancient hold of materialism is broken, as well as its renewal in post-Kantian positivism.

Could it be that all this talk of realism is an alien imposition on the text of Scripture and has nothing to do with the pure word of God or our understanding of revelation? Or that it is nothing more than a last attempt of a sort of debased Hellenism to view the experience of God and the Christian experience of Christ through the distorting cultural lens of what, after all, must remain a single culture among the many cultures the gospel must be preached to? Could it be, for instance, that the Church rather invents her dogmatic tradition as she comes to flourish in this, that, and another time and culture, and that the measure of the truth of dogma is not whether it truly affirms some intelligibility of the subject it refers to, but rather whether it fosters greater authenticity among those who confess it? This is the proposal of Terrence Tilley.[46] But things cannot fall out so. In the first place, the "realism" in question is not the limiting proposal of a limited culture, but is coeval with the distinction of *nomos* and *physis*, convention and nature, that is one and the same thing as the very discovery of cultural difference over against a reality prior to and independent of it. Tilley's proposal is just one more post-Kantian attempt to confine religious discourse to what we think we already know morally. But moral reality is not the whole of reality. The confession of Catholic dogma does of course conduce to the greater "authenticity" of those who believe. But it does so because it connects them with the source of grace and charity in God and Christ, truly possessed by faith in the affirmation of doctrine, and which possession of reality is the first, formal effect of affirming it.

In the second place, the "realism" in question is no imposition on the

---

46. Terrence Tilley, *Inventing Catholic Tradition* (Maryknoll, NY: Orbis Books, 2000), 164–67. How we know what *Christian* "authenticity" is independently of the truth of the teaching of the Church, creedal and moral, is a problem here. In fact, it is hard to keep Tilley's "authenticity" from collapsing into what we think we already know as postmodern liberals. For discussion of Tilley's view, see Matthew Levering, *Engaging the Doctrine of Revelation: The Mediation of the Gospel through Church and Scripture* (Grand Rapids, MI: Baker Academic, 2014), 146–58.

gospel but is readily read off from the creation accounts in Genesis. This was adverted to in the introduction, but its philosophical consequence is at issue just here. God creates by calling things into being by their names. "God said, 'Let there be light.'"[47] And there was light: the thing that comes into being answers to its name. This is so because created light is nothing more than a participation of uncreated Light, and the truth of created light is a knockoff of subsistent Truth, its intelligibility a partial imitation of infinite Intelligibility.[48] Furthermore, the animals that God calls into being by naming them are named also by Adam. He gets the names right.[49] It is crucial to notice here that the report of God's creating, of his calling things into being is rendered for us in a natural human language—as it happens, Hebrew, but for that matter, also able to be rendered into Latin or Greek or English. The Hebrew of the first eleven chapters of Genesis is not some original and unique and untranslatable language of the angels or even some protohuman *Ursprache*, but one of the existing "natural languages," all of which come into being, according to Genesis, with the confusion of tongues at Babel (Gn 11). The upshot is that the natural languages of man are good to report the language by which God calls things into being.[50] Now, God's calling things to be makes each one what it is, and human language itself indicates the same essential distinctions the divine wisdom installs into created reality: plants yielding seed are not plants yielding fruit, fishes are not birds, creeping things are not cattle. The language of God can be translated into Hebrew, and as translated, names things distinctly and essentially. The creative realism of divine discourse that establishes things that we too can name is a condition of the possibility of revelation, a possibility most excellently realized in the Incarnation itself.[51]

47. The "let there be" in Hebrew is not an imperative, supposing the existence of something addressed, but a third person jussive, bespeaking the mind and intent of the speaker, a volitive.

48. See O. T. Venard, *A Poetic Christ*, 275, 319–22.

49. *Summa theologiae* I, Q. 94, a. 3, sed contra: Adam names the animals and "names ought to agree with the nature of things" (my translation). So also can we get the names right: see *Summa theologiae* I, Q. 84, a. 4, ad 1, and Q. 105, a. 3.

50. For this argument, see Paul Mankowski, SJ, "Language, Truth, and Logos," in *The Oxford Handbook of Christology*, 9–20, ed. Francesca Aran Murphy (Oxford: Oxford University Press, 2015), 15: "That the Bible gives us God's discourse in a language other than God's leads to the distinct theological recognition that translation is not only possible but *permissible*."

51. See again St. Thomas, *De Veritate*, Q. 1, a. 2; Gregory Vall, *Ecclesial Exegesis*, 202–203. More at length, see Benoît Montagnes, OP, "La parole de Dieu dans la creation," *Revue Thomiste* 54 (1954):

Analogical words and ideas and realities

Congar's second presupposition of dogma amounts to saying that our language is really capable of speaking meaningfully and truly about God. Since God speaks meaningfully and truly about himself in our language, it must be so capable. For Karl Barth, it is God who makes it so capable in the event of revelation itself. Philosophically, Barth remains within the limits Kant imposes on man's speculative knowledge, and revelation is a miracle that brings with it the human possibility of hearing it.[52] But for Catholics, this response to Kant is unsatisfactory. It is not just that it presupposes the impossibility of natural theology, whose possibility the Church solemnly asserts.[53] It also seems to imply a sort of miraculous transformation of human language, giving it a capacity it does not natively possess. It goes against the grain of the capacity of human languages to render divine language implied by Genesis, or, if you prefer, of the ability of the divine mind to express itself in human language.[54] At the level of knowledge, it seems to imply a sort of miraculous transformation of the human mind. Barth's position makes the difference between nature and grace too great, such that nature has no antecedent openness to grace, and the mind no antecedent openness to the word of revelation. It seems to imply that we cannot speak of man as created in the image of God, the consequence of which is that images of their nature want to be more and more related to their "exemplar"—man by his nature wants to be more and more related to God.

For St. Thomas, the proper object of man's intellect is the nature of material things, and in that sense, he sounds very Kantian indeed.[55] But this

---

213–41, at 218–22. He picks out three conditions of the possibility for human speech to be the speech of God: "In order that human language be truly the word of God, it is necessary that God himself guarantee the correspondence of the signs at each stage: of the divine reality to 'worldly' reality by creation; of created ontological likeness to its human conceptualization by prophetic illumination; of the thought to its oral and written expression by the charism of prophecy" (241). Venard relies on Montagnes a lot in "The Existence of Language as a Theological Question," *A Poetic Christ*, 302–36.

52. See Trevor Hart, "Revelation," in *The Cambridge Companion to Karl Barth*, ed. John Webster (Cambridge: Cambridge University Press, 2000), 41–44.

53. Vatican Council I, *Dei Filius*, 1st canon of chap. 2; DH 3026, ND 115.

54. See Yves Congar, OP, *La Foi et la théologie*, 33–40, a discussion whose point of departure is Barth.

55. *Summa theologiae* I, Q. 84, a. 7; Q. 85, aa. 1 and 8; Q. 88, a. 3.

proper object is not the adequate object of man's intellect.[56] The adequate object of man's intellect is demonstrated by the questions we are natively given to ask. If we ask what things *are*, and whether they *are*, then it seems that the formal object of man's intellect ought to be described as being, and not material being.[57] The very fact that such a distinction makes sense to us demands that we have a very good reason why it would be senseless to ask whether a God who is responsible for the very existence of the things of our experience himself exists.[58] If there is no good reason, then there is no good reason to deny that revelation, the New Testament, and Catholic dogma, regularly and without breaking any bogus philosophical law, meaningfully speak of God, the angels, and the immortal soul of man.

This topic is usually elaborated in Catholic theology under the title of the doctrine of the "analogy of names"—the names of God—and our understanding of dogma and its scope depends on this elaboration.[59]

We give names to things according as we know them and have a concept of them.[60] But sometimes we use the same name for related and even quite different things. So, names can be predicated of something univocally, equivocally, or analogically. If I say Fido is a dog and Rex is a dog,

56. *Summa theologiae* I, Q. 5, a. 2: "Primo autem in conceptione intellectus cadit ens.... Unde ens est proprium obiectum intellectus."

57. For a careful discussion of the object of the intellect, see Réginald Garrigou-Lagrange, *De Revelatione per Ecclesiam Catholicam Proposita*, 4th ed., vol. 1 (Rome: Fr. Ferrari, 1945), 353–359: the proper object is "*ens intelligibile rerum sensibilium seu essentia rei sensibilis*/the intelligible being of sensible things or the essence of the sensible thing" (354). But the *adequate* object of the intellect is "*ens secundum latitudinem entis, et non solum prout est cognoscibile in speculo sensibilium*/ being according to the whole breadth of being, and not only insofar as it is knowable in the mirror of sensible things" (355). God, *deitas*, does not fall outside this adequate object (357–58). It is very telling, however, that Garrigou-Lagrange grants that the argument that includes God within the adequate object is not apodictic, but merely probable (359). The argument is a sign, but not a demonstration, of the obediential potency of the intellect for grace and glory (359). For a denial that God's "pure actuality" is included in the transcendental reach of the intellect, see Thomas Joseph White, OP, *Wisdom in the Face of Modernity: A Study in Thomistic Natural Theology* (Ave Maria, FL: Sapientia Press, 2009), 164–5.

58. Herbert McCabe, OP, *God Matters* (Springfield, IL: Templegate, 1987), 5.

59. For the teaching of St. Thomas, see White, *Wisdom in the Face of Modernity*, 88–94, 268–74, and Gregory P. Rocca, OP, *Speaking the Incomprehensible God: Thomas Aquinas on the Interplay of Positive and Negative Theology* (Washington, DC: The Catholic University of America Press, 2006), and Steven Long, *Analogia Entis: On the Analogy of Being, Metaphysics, and the Act of Faith* (Note Dame, IN: University of Notre Dame Press, 2011). More recently and very compactly, see Michael J. Dodds, OP, *The One Creator God in Thomas Aquinas & Contemporary Theology* (Washington, DC: The Catholic University of America Press, 2020), 84–92

60. *Summa theologiae* I, Q. 13, a. 1.

"dog" is said univocally, with the exact same meaning in each case, which is to say the same concept is evoked. If I say the pigs were penned and the letter was penned, "penned" is said equivocally—it does not have the same meaning at all across the two cases. The two uses evoke two concepts. But if I say George is smart and Rex is smart, although I do not mean the exact same thing, since Rex cannot do sums or make distinctions in speech, still, there is such a thing as animal intelligence. "Smart" has been said analogically. Two concepts have been evoked, but they are related to one another.

Now, when we speak of God and say such things as that God is good, wise, loving, and merciful, we use those predicates analogically.[61] For God is not wise the way we are wise (if we are), having it as an attribute distinct from himself (the way our wisdom is distinct from us, since we can exist without being wise).[62] God's wisdom is himself, and it is unlimited. So, God is wise (since, after all, he is the ultimate cause of created wisdom),[63] but he is not wise the way we are (limitedly and having wisdom as an attribute distinct from a substance); he is wise supereminently.[64] And so on for all those names that name pure perfections, that is, things not intrinsically limited in some way (the way whiteness or bovinity are).

The doctrine of analogy means that when we speak of God the way we do calling him wise, good, and so on, then our language really does truly inform us of God and does so literally.[65] God is literally wise. Sometimes people say that all our language for God is metaphorical or symbolic. But this is not true. If it were true, then God would be absolutely unknown to us. Analogy is not metaphor. Here is a metaphor: "That car is a lemon; don't buy it." The car is not literally a lemon or lemony—it is not literally sour tasting. The car is such a mess, however, that, if owning a good car is "sweet," then owning this car will be "sour," meaning lots of repairs, lots of lost time. Notice that, for the metaphor to work, we have to have knowledge of both cars and lemons, and to be able to speak of them in ordinary, literal language.[66] If everything we said of lemons, for instance, was metaphorical, then we would know nothing about lemons. So, also, to repeat,

61. *Summa theologiae* I, Q. 13, a. 5.
62. *Summa theologiae* I, Q. 13, a. 1, ad 2, and a.
63. *Summa theologiae* I, Q. 13, a. 1.
64. *Summa theologiae* I, Q. 13, a. 2 and 12.
65. *Summa theologiae* I, Q. 13, a. 3.
66. See William Alston, "Irreducible Metaphors in Theology," in *Experience, Reason and God,*

if all that was said of God were metaphorical (like "God is the rock of your salvation"), then we would know absolutely nothing about him, or even whether he existed.

The fact that our language really can speak of God meaningfully and truly is implied by revelation, as already noted. God speaks to us about himself in the Bible. If the language really misfired, then God would be represented as telling us about himself when, really and truly, he was not telling us about himself because he could not. And think, too, of the Lord Jesus. When he says that God is good in the Sermon on the Mount, he means it. It is literally true. He is not giving us an image, or a figure, or a puzzle, or a paradox, but simple, straightforward affirmation.

Moreover, the fact that the world is created also implies that we can speak of God meaningfully and truly. For effects are in some way, even if not very much, like their causes. Therefore, from the things that have been made, as chapter 1 of Romans tells us, we can know God. But real knowledge enables literal speaking.[67] The very way created things are created, moreover, in that they are created by the word of God, implies that he can speak to us, and we in turn can speak of him and to him.

The historicity of revelation and Church teaching

The third presupposition to dogma Congar lists, it will be recalled, concerns the continuity of meaning embedded in the death and resurrection of Christ, his and the apostles' witness to this meaning, its transcription in the New Testament, and its expression in the dogmas of the Church. There are two issues here, one historical and one theoretical. First, how do we come to recognize this continuity of meaning so as reasonably and responsibly to make the act of faith in the same message that Christ, the New Testament, and the Church deliver to us? Second, does the historicity of man exclude such time-transcending meanings, such that we cannot reasonably and truly say that we believe what St. John the Evangelist, St. Athanasius, St. Augustine, and St. Catherine of Siena believed?

129–48, ed. Eugene Thomas Long (Washington, DC: The Catholic University of America Press, 1980).

67. See St. Thomas, *Summa theologiae* I, Q. 13, a. 3.

The historical issue

The key here is the historical objectivity of the gospels as really delivering the events of Good Friday and Easter Sunday, and the testimony of Jesus and the apostles as to what these events mean. Once that is in place, the continuity of the conciliar teaching of the Church depends on a reasonable account of dogmatic development, the topic of this book.[68]

What impedes a spontaneous acceptance of the gospels as historically reliable sources of the words and deeds of Jesus has largely to do with the form critical approach to Scripture. This approach to the gospels is no longer the exclusive or even always trusted instrument of analysis it seemed to be fifty years ago.[69] But its influence was mighty and lingers on in ways still calculated to provoke skepticism about the reliability of the gospels. Why do many people think the gospels give us myth and legend, but not historical truth? Why, for instance, are we not confident, the way Christians were for close to two thousand years, that when we read the Sermon on the Mount, we are getting the actual teaching of Jesus?

The form critical approach to the gospels can be summarized as follows:

a) The gospels are not biographies

b) and were written by unknown writers,

c) who composed them mostly or exclusively from material passed down orally, where the formulation of Jesus's sayings and the stories about him had already been adapted to community needs,

d) and unknown writers further shaped the whole story of Jesus and its pieces primarily to serve their own disparate and divergent theological and community concerns,

e) and whole stories were chosen from among many candidates for gospel status by a Church unconnected to apostolic memory.

This way of viewing things opposes at every point the traditional view of things:

---

68. This section reproduces what was said in *Fundamental Theology*, 203–205.

69. See John Barton, "Biblical Studies," in *The Blackwell Companion to Modern Theology*, ed. Gareth Jones (Oxford: Blackwell Publishing, 2007), 18–33.

PHILOSOPHICAL PRESUPPOSITIONS 97

a') The gospels are biographies (in the ancient style),

b') were written by the named people the Church has always attributed them to,

c') were composed from eyewitness accounts of Jesus's teaching and actions passed down by people interested in what Jesus himself said and did,

d') were shaped primarily to remember Jesus faithfully and accurately and elicit faith in him,

e') and were received by a Church still connected to the memory of the apostles.

The third point, which touches on the malleability of oral tradition, was supposed to be the basis of form critical analysis, but the analysis of oral traditions has now become so sophisticated and detailed that there is no simple line to be drawn between the Norwegian and German folkloric tradition that so impressed the architects of form criticism (e.g. Rudolf Bultmann) and traditions of historical intent.[70] Evidently, the assessment of the reliability of orally preserved history varies according as one evaluates the importance the accurately remembered facts have for those who pass them on. For Christians, this importance is hard to overestimate, since they believed that their relation to God and their share in eternal life depended on what Jesus had taught and done in the flesh. This concern also governs an assessment of the reliability of the evangelists themselves.

As to the first thing, the nature of the gospels, they fit well within the genre of Greco-Roman *bioi* of the Hellenistic period.[71] As to the fifth thing, this is matter of the temporal overlap, historically plausible if not demonstrable, of the production of the gospels and living apostolic memory.

As to the attribution of the gospels to those to whom the Church has always attributed them, Martin Hengel has observed that there is no evidence whatsoever that the gospels at any time ever circulated anonymously, that had they done so we should expect many attributions for each gospel, and certainly attributions of more authority than to Mark or to Luke, that

70. See Jan Vansina, *Oral Tradition as History* (Madison, Wis.: University of Wisconsin Press, 1985); Birger Gerhardsson, *The Reliability of the Gospel Tradition* (Peabody, Mass.: Hendrickson Publishers, 2001); Richard Bauckham, *Jesus and the Eyewitnesses* (Grand Rapids, MI: Eerdmans, 2006), chapters 10, 12, and 13.

71. Richard Burridge, *What Are the Gospels? A Comparison with Graeco-Roman Biography* (Cambridge: Cambridge University Press, 1992).

98   CHAPTER 4

anonymous gospels would have had no authority either generally or for worship, and that the fragments of Papias reliably take us back to the end of the first century for the attributions of the first and second gospels.[72]

Outside the canon, Papias is concerned with the authenticity of apostolic witness and as contained in the gospels; within the canon, 2 Peter is also concerned with the same issue of the authenticity of apostolic witness in written form.[73] They are concerned at just the same time, the first quarter of the second century. That is when the credentials of the New Testament must be nailed down, the last period of overlap between the gospels as we have them and people who were still in a position to judge their accuracy.

This argument takes us back to the Modernist concerns at the beginning of the twentieth century. Is there a *demonstration* of historical objectivity of the gospels, and so a *demonstration* of the continuity of meaning Congar speaks of as prerequisite for Catholic dogma? Of course not. This is a matter of history, not of mathematics. But contrary to contemporary enlightened prejudice, it is reasonable and responsible to take up the gospels and read them as historically accurate records.[74]

The theoretical issue

The historical issue is a matter of coming to a reasonable judgment about the origins of Christianity—the trustworthiness of a witness, the trustworthiness of the report of this witness, and so on. The theoretical issue has to do with the fact that we who want to know these historical matters are ourselves historical things, situated in a time other than the time of the past thing we want to know. Moreover, our being historically contingent in this way is a necessary aspect of human being—human "historicity" names something essential about us, and, for people like Edmund Husserl and Martin Heidegger, the most fundamental thing about us.

A human being lives in a present out of a past unto a future. The past

---

72. Martin Hengel, "The Titles of the Gospels and the Gospel of Mark," in *Studies in the Gospel of Mark*, trans. John Bowden (Philadelphia: Fortress Press, 1985), 64–84.

73. Farkasfalvy, *A Theology of the Christian Bible*, 168–169; *Inspiration and Interpretation*, 44.

74. For the teaching of the Church, see *Dei Verbum*, no. 7; DH 4207; and the Instruction of the Biblical Commission, *Sancta Mater Ecclesia* (1964), "On the Historical Truth of the Gospels," ND 240–45.

is not irrelevant to our present, but constitutes it and has made us what we are now, and yet it does so only on condition we are looking to a future that is not yet but only anticipated (without which anticipable future we would be dead), and which anticipation controls how much of our past we wish to bring forward into the next approaching present moment. This much is common sense. But so true is it, that consciousness itself cannot be understood except as a now that cannot be except there is always in it a shadow of the just past, and a conscious feeling of the not yet but coming next moment. It is this primordial presence of the past and the future in each flowing present moment that makes memory and imagination, history and planning, possible.[75]

History (*res gestae*/deeds done) is thus not only contingent in itself, but when we want to know it (*historia rerum gestarum*/account of deeds done), it has to be constructed from the contingency of our own present moment. And just as the individual brings forward and fashions his past on the basis of the future he anticipates, so will he construct the history of his family or nation. So will he construct the history of Christian origins; he will construct the history of the meaning embedded in Christ's life and in the original witness thereof remembered and recorded in the gospels and subsequently manifested in dogma. Does the temporality and historicity of our way of existence let us really do this? If our being is time, can we confidently capture a time not our own? This is the question of "historicism."[76]

Theologically, the upshot is that we cannot come to know the original and universal meaning of the events of Christ's life, his passion and death and resurrection. Just as the first statement of their meaning was parochi-

---

75. See Hans-Georg Gadamer, *Truth and Method* (New York: Seabury, 1975), 214–17 (Husserl), 227–28 (Heidegger). And see Gadamer's "Hermeneutics and Historicism," in *Truth and Method*, 460–91.

76. Paul Hamilton, *Historicism* (London: Routledge, 1996), 19: "Our interpretative decisions … will be based on a judgement between different possibilities of the time; and the history of interpretations shows such adjudications to be abundantly and *primarily* expressive of their own period of utterance. Historicism is the name given to this apparent relativizing of the past by getting to know the different interpretations to which it is open and deciding between them on grounds *expressing our own contemporary preoccupations*." Emphasis added. The possibility of such a view is opened up by Kant, for whom only the empirical sciences are objective, and it is realized by Wilhelm Dilthey (†1911), for whose extreme version of historicism see Hamilton, 68–77, and Richard Palmer, *Hermeneutics* (Evanston, IL: Northwestern University Press, 1969), 116–18.

al, so also every attempted New Testament or dogmatic reconstruction will be similarly parochial. Theological meaning is necessarily temporally and historically relative, and so no continuity such as Congar speaks of in his third presupposition of dogma is possible. If historicism is true, then the Modernist account of the history of dogma must be true. If historicism is true, then we could never know that later expressions of the gospel really are expressions of the same gospel. We would never be able to have reasonable assurance that the "one" Christian idea is truly to be found in the "many" developments.

There are two answers to the question historicism poses to the possibility of Catholic doctrine. The first answer is philosophical. It consists in saying that we can be sure that we know how Aristotle or St. Augustine understood some reality, and then can share it, as we like, according as we do our historical excavation of their position carefully and critically. Our historical work is careful according as we interpret the relevant text of Aristotle or Augustine within the context of their work, and within the context of their time, which will tell us how they used the words they did, what they presupposed, what they must have been ignorant of, and so on. Our historical work is critical according as we notice the difference between our antecedent understanding of the reality in question, and theirs. In other words, the philosophical answer is to become hermeneutical. Is philosophical hermeneutical retrieval of past meaning always successful? No. Is it always certain? No. But it is possible. And it is necessary if we want as responsibly as possible to join the conversation of our culture.

This answer seems to suppose the truth of Christianity or some version of Platonism. If all being is time, however, such an answer to the question of historicism is impossible and it is hard to resist the most radical consequences of Heidegger's history of being. On the other hand, if human being is a participation in God's being, then such an answer suffices. Various temporally achieved articulations of the intelligibility of man, the world, and God and the world can be made intelligible to one another because all are embraced by a trans-temporal, eternal and divine moment.

Just in itself, moreover, philosophical historicism skates very close to the thin ice of self-referential incoherence, and it seems to suppose an insurmountable resistance of reality to reason. Historicism maintains that reason, including philosophically deployed reason, is necessarily "pa-

PHILOSOPHICAL PRESUPPOSITIONS 101

rochial"; that is, it is always so limited by the historical circumstance in which it is exercised in what it can understand of human being, nature, and reason itself, that it cannot attain to what Carl Page, following Aristotle, calls "first philosophy," the knowledge of the first causes and principles of things.[77] It is a denial, in other words, that the distinction between *physis* and *nomos* is ever adequate, such that philosophy can come to know *physis* prior to and independently of *nomos*—the real that is prior to and independent of culture, that is to say, the laws and customs of the city where the philosopher abides. The very distinction that founds philosophy is impossible to draw:[78] we thought we were making it, but, if historicism is true, we were not. It rather turns out that cultural, historical baggage always conditions our understanding of first causes and principles, such that we can have no necessary knowledge of them. As Carl Page puts it, "[A]ll forms of human judgment will always be situated within and determined by an essentially contingent framework," "and no form of human judgment can in principle transcend that contingent situatedness in any final way."[79]

Doubtless, no one in the nineteenth or twentieth centuries can deny the historicity of human being and human thought. The trouble with historicism as described here, however, is that when a human being assents to it, his act of assent does something that the content of historicism claims is impossible to do knowingly and so responsibly. To know that historicism is true one has to do something it rules out.[80] There are ways of stating the historicist position that are not obviously self-refuting in this way. And it seems that historicism could be stated as true, although not as known to be true.[81] Nonetheless, it remains the case that talking about the finitude of human reason seems ineluctably to suppose that, knowing the bounds of that finitude, we are beyond it—which is ruled out by historicism.[82]

77. Carl Page, *Philosophical Historicism and the Betrayal of First Philosophy* (University Park: University of Pennsylvania Press, 1995), 3–4.

78. See Leo Strauss, "The Origins of the Idea of Natural Right," in Strauss, *Natural Right and History* (Chicago: University of Chicago Press, 1953), 81–119.

79. Page, *Philosophical Historicism*, 92.

80. Page, *Philosophical Historicism*, 95.

81. Page, *Philosophical Historicism*, 96–97.

82. Page, *Philosophical Historicism*, 112; see also 113–18 for argument that historicism means that historically conditioned philosophical accounts of human reason and action are arbitrarily constructed and so nihilistic, as Stanley Rosen maintains.

The second answer to historicism is theological. It consists in saying that the same power that makes revelation revelation, that enables us to recognize public revelation as revelation, that invites us and enables us to assent to it in an act that is beyond our natural capacity, the act of faith, is also the power that maintains the accessibility of revelation from the time it was completed until now. Further, this answer consists in pointing out the special instrument the Power in question uses in order to enable us to be sure that we have the same understanding of Christ as he had of himself, as St. Paul had of him, as St. John had of him. That instrument is— surprise!—dogma itself. Of course, dogma serves to assure us that with its help we rightly recover the sense of St. Paul's letters and St. John's gospel only if we embrace it with the same act of faith with which we embrace the creed.

Dogma lets us more easily recover the sense of history, reconstruct it accurately, and recover the original witness recorded in the New Testament. Dogma is counterhistoricist, just as, in the fourth century, Nicaea lets us recover the sense of the pre-Nicene fathers who sound, by a later theological standard, "subordinationist." As Newman says, dogma is conservative of its past antecedents; "it is an addition which illustrates, not obscures, corroborates, not corrects, the body of thought from which it proceeds."[83] It lets us see the past better, just as it is only the mouth of the stream that lets us appreciate the spring of its origin. In this sense, the theological reality of Tradition, whose ultimate agent is the Holy Spirit, is the antihistoricist principle of the course of revelation in time.

What is being said here is that what Yves Congar counted as a *presupposition* of dogma, the continuity of meaning from Christ to the witness to Christ to the New Testament, to dogma is something that we can *recognize* only in virtue of dogma itself. To say this is not to involve us in some invalidating circularity. It is merely to point to the fact that Catholic faith is a package deal. The parts of it—Scripture, Tradition, magisterium, dogma—stand or fall together. Scripture is voiceless or cacophonous without Tradition. Tradition is antihistoricist but cannot maintain itself without those who guard the deposit; guarding the deposit sometimes requires solemn statement of what it contains.

83. Newman, *Essay on Development*, 200.

PHILOSOPHICAL PRESUPPOSITIONS 103

It has been said in the postmodern era that there is "nothing outside the text." Where there is no God, such a saying condemns us (or liberates us) to an illimitable pluralism of contemporarily construed meanings for every text, and not only that of Scripture. But if the world and history are equally texts of God's generosity and saving providence, all the mini-idealisms sponsored by postmodern principle are brought to book—to the Book. In the legacy St. Augustine bequeathed to the Church, as Alasdair MacIntyre points out, the Author of Scripture is at the same time the chief Agent of the salvation history it records. Those who read Scripture understand it as revealing the meaning of another text by the same Author, the text of nature and the text of history. And it falls to the Author, God, betimes to declare the meaning of Scripture and history through the authorities of the Church he has established.[84]

84. MacIntyre, *Three Rival Versions of Moral Enquiry*, 94.

CHAPTER 5

THE LOGICAL VERIFICATION OF DEVELOPMENT

Let us recall the progress of this book so far. In chapter 1, development was described as the unfolding of many doctrines from one revelation, or from the one idea of Christianity, and where the many enable us to see the one more clearly, with greater understanding.

In chapter 2, it was observed that dogma, the idea of dogma as an infallibly defined statement of a truth of the Catholic faith, emerges at Nicaea, together with the recognition of an organ of ecclesial teaching that defines and teaches dogma authoritatively, the ecumenical council.

Chapter 3 laid out the theological framework within which such a notion of dogma as emerged at Nicaea makes sense. This framework includes: 1) the cognitive character of revelation accomplished historically in word and deed; 2) the conjoint role of both Scripture and Tradition in communicating a closed revelation to us, where Tradition is both the framework in which Scripture is rightly read, the space in which the written and then proclaimed word of God can be rightly apprehended, and is as well the very hearing of it in new circumstances; 3) the magisterium as an instrument of Tradition and of the Holy Spirit; and 4) the anticipation of dogma and its development in Scripture.

Chapter 4 undertook to state the philosophical presuppositions of the development of Catholic dogma, which included: 1) understanding knowing as the identity in act of knower and known; 2) whose instruments are propositions whose predicates capture the essential intelligibilities of the known reality to which the subject refers, and which intelligibilities are made present to the mind conceptually; 3) the implication of which view of things is the propositional and conceptual character of revelation, which, when expressed dogmatically, asserts 4) a dogmatic realism implying a metaphysical realism generally, itself indicated already in Scripture; 5) which realism escapes the Kantian strictures on human knowledge, enabling the formulation of analogically expressed truths about God and the human soul, since the formal object of the human intellect is being, and not merely material being; and 6) which realism escapes as well the historicist strictures on the reasonable affirmation of the continuity of propositionally articulated meaning, historical and metaphysical, through time, since, once again, the formal object of the human intellect is being, not temporal being, and since (a theological reason) the propositional and textual character of Scripture and dogma reflect the divinely textual character of creation and salvation history.

Now we turn to (1) the theological justification of developments, (2) the necessary role of logic therein, (3) the apodictic forms of logical justification, and last, (4) the truths embedded in the plan of saving history which only a certain other kind of logic discerns and vindicates.

The justification of developments as genuine

Cardinal Newman's *Essay* provides no theory, certainly no comprehensive theory, of how the development of dogma occurs in every instance. He offers an elaborate argument unto our making a reasonable judgment that developments are to be expected, as noted above (see the *Essay*, chap. 2, section 1). He gives a similarly elaborate argument as to the many kinds of development of the idea of Christianity we may expect: political, logical, historical, ethical, metaphysical (chap. 1, section 2). But none of this amounts to a detailed *explanation* of how each and every development *has* occurred and how each and every future development *will* occur. What Newman does offer us are "tests" "for ascertaining the correctness of developments *in general*."[1] These tests are the seven "notes" of genuine developments which he explains at length (chapter 5) and applies in the second part of the *Essay*—preservation of type, continuity of principles, power of assimilation, logical sequence, anticipation of future developments, conservative action on the past of the newly formulated dogma, chronic vigor. Of these tests he says:

They are insufficient for the guidance of individuals in the case of so large and complicated a problem as Christianity; though they may aid our inquiries and support our conclusions in particular points. They are of a scientific and controversial, not of a practical character, and are instruments rather than warrants of right decisions.[2]

The tests are instruments of the right doctrinal decision, not warrants, for the only warrant of the definition of a dogma is that it is seen to be contained in revelation, the word of God. This point has been indicated before, but it bears repeating: the definition of the Church binds us to making an assertion, but not to the exegetical or theological argument that manifests the assertion.[3] Definition and promulgation of and assent to dogma is in the first place an exercise of faith, not of reason, either antecedent or subsequent to the act of faith.

There are two reasons there can be no comprehensive theory of doctrinal development that will satisfy the mind, either of the theologian or the believer. The first reason is the inability of reason to bring history, the

---

1. Newman, *Essay on Development*, 78. Emphasis added.

2. Newman, *Essay on Development*, 78.

3. See Ambroise Gardeil, OP, for whom the work of the theologians is merely dispositive, in *Le donné révélé et la théologie*, 2nd ed. (Paris: Les Éditions du Cerf, 1932 [1909]), 179–81; Henri de Lubac, SJ, "The Problem of the Development of Dogma," in *Theology in History*, 248–80, trans. Anne Englund Nash (San Francisco: Ignatius, 1996), 262 (first published in 1948); Karl Rahner, SJ, "Considerations on the Development of Dogma," in *Theological Investigations*, vol. 4, 3–35, trans. Kevin Smyth (Baltimore: Helicon, 1966), 27–31 (first published in 1958); Yves Congar, *La Foi et la théologie*, 176.

history of Christianity, the history of the *idea* of Christianity—in itself most intelligible—into logical form. This is part of the power of Newman's *Essay*, of its slow accumulation of historical context and detail. Anticipations of development there may be, but no predictions of this, that, or the other development. History is too variegated, too granular, too subject to chance and freedom, both divine and human, for that.

The second reason there can be no comprehensive theory of doctrinal development that will satisfy the mind in its every desire is that the agent of doctrinal development is the Church as a whole, acting first through the *sensus fidei* of the faithful and then decisively through the organs of her magisterium. Like the confession of faith in the creed, the dogmas of the Church are given to us *"quasi ex persona totius ecclesiae, quae est per fidem unitur/*as it were by the person of the whole Church, which is united by faith."[4] But the Church as a whole is mysterious in her being and agency. She possesses, as it were, a personality, sometimes figured as Christic (the Body of Christ), sometimes as Marian (the Bride of the Lamb), sometimes as Pneumatic (the Temple of the Holy Spirit). But in each characterization, the description of the Church connects her to a divine person, Son or Spirit. Her personality, and therefore her agency, which comes to evidence and publicity in the teaching and ruling of pope and bishops, is therefore mysterious, in the proper sense of "mystery": something holy and transcendent is disclosed and signified as operative in the world.[5] *Predicting* how the agency of the Church will play out, an agency which manifests and is the instrument of divine agency, is beyond the ken either of faith or reason, or reason illumined by faith.

So to speak is to speak from the standpoint, as it were, prior to dogmatic decision. But after dogmatic decision, we must speak another way. *Post factum definitionis*, it is one of the tasks of the theologian to justify the dogmatic decisions of the Church.[6] That is part of the discharge of the task of faith seeking understanding, and hence precisely of defending

---

4. *Summa theologiae* II-II, Q. 1, a. 9, ad 3.

5. For the personality of the Church, see Benoît-Dominique de La Soujeole, OP, *An Introduction to the Mystery of the Church*, trans. Michael J. Miller (Washington, DC: The Catholic University of America Press, 2014), 504–11.

6. See de Lubac, SJ, "The Problem of the Development of Dogma," 261–66, who distinguishes the role of logic before and after the definition of a dogma.

the Church's teaching against the charge of inventing a teaching not in the deposit. And the tests or notes of Newman here come into their own. The notes are ordered to helping us recognize a development as genuine, as something really contained in the deposit of faith that the Church but guards and does not add to.[7]

In discharging this task, the theologian vindicates the claim of the First Vatican Council, repeating Vincent of Lérins, that although there is progress in understanding the deposit of faith, this progress remains "within its exact kind, that is to say, in the same doctrine, in the same sense, and with the same meaning."[8] Now, demonstrating this continuity or identity of meaning is, as already indicated in chapter 2, a matter of logic. So it is also for Newman. He thinks it is evident that the Catholic Church of the nineteenth century is the *historical* successor of the ancient Church. "The only question that can be raised is whether the said Catholic faith, as now held, is *logically*, as well as historically, the representative of the ancient faith."[9] The second part of the *Essay* is ordered to showing that it is. If the statements that articulate revelation in Scripture, in prophecy and apostolic witness, as well as in patristic Scriptural commentary and dogmatic definition are a matter of the conceptual presence of the intelligibilities of the mysteries of faith to the believing mind, and if the art of ordering concepts, seeing relations of identity and nonidentity, is a matter of logic, then the verification of the continuity of meaning from revelation to dogma is a matter of logic, and of logic alone. What else could serve to get that job done? Newman's notes attest the privileged place of logic in the vindication of developments as genuine. It is not just the second and fourth notes, continuity of principles and logical sequence, that indicate this. The power of assimilation (third note) is the

---

7. The notes are Newman's way of explicating how Vincent of Lérins's insistence that developments do not change or deform the deposit is to be manifested; see Reinhard Hütter, "Progress, Not Alteration of the Faith: Beyond Antiquarianism and Presentism. John Henry Newman, Vincent of Lérins, and the Criterion of Identity of the Development of Doctrine," *Nova et Vetera* (English) 19 (2021): 333–91, at 370–71.

8. *Dei Filius*, chap. 4, my translation; DH 3020, ND 136. For Vincent, see the "Comminatory" (*Commonitorium*), trans. C. A. Heurtley, in *Nicene and Post-Nicene Fathers*, 2nd ser., vol. 11, *Sulpitius Severus, Vincent of Lérins, John Cassian*, 123–59, edited by Philip Schaff and Henry Wace (Peabody, MA: Hendrickson, 1994), chap. 23, no. 54, p. 148.

9. Newman, *Essay on Development*, 169, emphasis added. See Thomas G. Guarino, *Vincent of Lérins and the Development of Christian Doctrine* (Grand Rapids, MI: Baker Academic, 2013).

power of assimilation of something *logically* coherent with what is already taught; conservative action on past adumbrations of the dogma (fifth note) is conservation of the same *meaning*—the past teaching is corroborated, not corrected, as he says.[10]

Newman repeats this estimation of the contribution of logic to Christian teaching in *The Idea of a University*.

> What is revealed? all doctrinal knowledge flows from one fountain head. If we are able to enlarge our view and multiply our propositions, it must be merely by the comparison and adjustment of the original truths; if we would solve new questions, it must be by consulting old answers. The notion of doctrinal knowledge absolutely novel, and of simple addition from without, is intolerable to Catholic ears, and never was entertained by any one who was even approaching to an understanding of our creed. Revelation is all in all in doctrine; the Apostles its sole depository, the inferential method its sole instrument, and ecclesiastical authority its sole sanction. The Divine Voice has spoken once for all, and the only question is about its meaning.[11]

"The inferential method its *sole* instrument." Doubtless what theologians call positive theology relies on history to gather the material of systematic or speculative theology. But the instrument of this latter theology is logic. The necessity of this demonstration of continuity follows from the reasonability of faith, which it is one of the tasks of theology to defend.

Inevitable logic

Before describing the forms of the logical justification of developments, another way of recognizing a development as genuine must be considered. It really does enable us to know developments as genuine. But it does not explain how they are justified by reference to their presence in or connection to what has *already* been revealed. This other way is the way of the connatural knowledge of the mysteries of faith. Connatural knowledge is affective knowledge; it delivers intelligible results but feels more like, well, feeling or experience.[12]

10. Newman, *Essay on Development*, 200.

11. John Henry Newman, *The Idea of a University*, ed. with introduction by I. T. Ker (Oxford: Clarendon Press, 1976), 190 (223 in the online edition of 1852).

12. "Connatural knowledge" goes by other names. As Francisco Marín-Sola has it, "We are

St. Thomas explains the connatural knowledge of an object as follows when discussing how the gift of wisdom, one of the gifts of the Holy Spirit, operates to make us wise. He compares it to how the virtue of chastity enables us to make judgments about what is chaste and what is not. Whoever has some knowledge of the commandments and of social norms and some experience can reason out whether some action is chaste or not. But the virtue of chastity lets us know immediately and without argument that some action or dress or language is or is not chaste. It does this simply by conforming us to the object of chastity so that it becomes second nature to us, so to speak, and we immediately recognize what does or does not agree with this nature. So, following Dionysius the Areopagite, St. Thomas teaches us that in a similar way the gift of wisdom makes us "patient" to divine things. "Sensitivity or connaturality of this kind regarding divine things occurs [in us] by way of charity."[13] Conformed to divine things as the chaste man is conformed to ordered sexual love, the gift of wisdom enables us to judge of divine things—to judge which things really are divine—in contemplating them and in acting upon them.[14]

St. Thomas had already spoken of the gift of wisdom in treating the invisible missions of both Spirit and Word into our hearts. There, he teaches that this indwelling of the Word conforms us to him just insofar as the Word breathes forth Love, the Holy Spirit, who moves us to further union with him. This he says on the authority of John 6:45, according to which if we believe in Christ, we will come to him. This conformation is by way of an abiding habit, not just of fleeting act, and so enables a sort of immediate knowledge of divine things: the Son is sent to us so that we may not just know him, but "perceive" him (*cognosicitur et percipitur*). But perception bespeaks a kind of "experimental knowledge" of the known object (*experimentalem quandam notitiam*).[15]

---

here referring to the channel of affection, of the will, of piety, of feeling, the experimental way, the mystical way, in short, that way of which St. Thomas so often speaks, and describes as the way by mode of *connaturalness*, by a certain *affinity*, quasi *experimental*, by *contact*, and other like qualifiers," in his *The Homogeneous Evolution of Catholic Dogma*, trans. Antonio T. Piñon (Manila: Santo Tomas University Press, 1988), no. 216, p. 400. Connatural knowledge is understood in contrast to knowledge by study or systematic inquiry. See the nice compendium of texts in no. 219, pp. 404–7.

13. *Summa theologiae* II-II, Q. 45, a. 3, c. My translation.

14. *Summa theologiae* II-II, Q. 45, a. 4, c. and ad 1.

15. *Summa theologiae* I, Q. 43, a. 5, ad 2.

Francisco Marín-Sola nicely summarizes the knowledge in question, and relates it to the *sensus fidei* that all the baptized possess in one degree or another.

[H]e who possesses divine faith, and to a much greater degree, he who possesses sanctifying grace with its virtues and gifts, possesses and carries within himself, in the manner of a nature, the very same object from which all the statements of faith proceed, and with which they are all concerned; the object from which, and from which alone, all dogmatic progress ensues, and can ensue, since nothing can ever be dogmatic or belong to divine faith if it is not a real expression of the Divinity. Thus, the believer, and, even more so, the saint, possess within themselves a new sense, which St. Paul calls the *sense of Christ*, and which we might very well call the *sense of faith*, or the *eyes of faith*.[16]

It is when St. Thomas speaks of the gift of understanding, however, that he brings this topic of connatural knowledge into the closest proximity with the knowledge of doctrine. He is explaining why faith is called a "virtue" and "understanding" a gift of the Holy Spirit.

Whence if some things are apprehended immediately and without argument, this apprehension is not said to be a matter of *ratio* but of *intellectus*, just like first principles which someone at once approves as soon as they are heard.... Faith makes us hold to spiritual things as it were wrapped up as they are in enigmas and seen in a mirror, and thus perfects the mind in a human way [human as depending on sensible likenesses of spiritual things]. And so faith is called a virtue. But insofar as the mind is raised up by a supernatural light such that it is led to behold spiritual things, this is above the [natural] human way [of knowing]. And this is done by the gift of understanding, which illumines the mind about what is heard, such that they are approved as soon as they are heard in the way first principles are, and thus it is the gift of "understanding."[17]

Once again, we learn that the gift of the Holy Spirit gives us an immediate apprehension of some truth concerning the mysteries of God. When we hear the enunciation of the truth, we know it is good and true. But the gift does not bring with it any discursive knowledge of how the truth is related to other truths of the mysteries of God.

16. Marín-Sola, *Homogeneous Evolution*, no. 218, p. 403.
17. *In III Sent.* d. 35, q. 2, sol. 1. My translation. The background here is both Biblical and Aristotelian: for the gifts of the Holy Spirit, Isaiah 11:2; and for the intellectual virtue of understanding (*intellectus*), *Nicomachean Ethics*, book 6, chap. 6.

So, connatural knowledge can play a role, has played a role, in the discernment of developments as genuine and true developments, and this is as much to say that it can play a role in development itself. But it does not discharge the task of showing how they are contained in and related to the deposit of revelation as communicated to us in Scripture and Tradition. This is easily seen if we remember the initial contrast noted above between how the chaste man knows something is chaste or not and how the man of ordinary practical experience or the moral theologian knows that same thing. For the task of showing how developments are contained in and related to the deposit of revelation, we want something analogous to the reasoning of the moral theologian. We want not just knowledge of the fact, a grasp of some truth that connatural knowledge or the *sensus fidei* can give us of a genuine development, but knowledge of the reasoned fact. We want to know the reasons, the connections to first principles, for why the fact is so.

There is another proposal for explaining how the development of dogma takes place and can be recognized as genuine that is conveniently taken up here. It so explains things, however, as to obviate the need of any demonstration of some development as already implicit in or contained in what has been confessed before as belonging to the deposit of revelation. Because of its appeal to experience, it may look like an invocation of some connatural knowledge of revelation, although in fact it is not.

This proposal was formulated by Maurice Blondel at the beginning of the twentieth century in his *History and Dogma*. This work was occasioned by Alfred Loisy's deployment of a historical-critical reading of New Testament Christology, the results of which were that Christ did not claim to be divine, and that the imputation of divinity to him, if it is to be discerned at all in the New Testament, is very late, and takes place only in the address of the gospel to people more Hellenistic than Jewish.[18] Blondel elucidates the principle that enables the Catholic historian to see more in the facts of Christian history than a purely positivist historian (Loisy) can discern, and so enables us to see how these facts, these early witnesses to the reality of Christ, develop coherently and intelligently into the more fully articulated dogmas of Catholic Christianity.[19]

18. Loisy, *Autour d'un petit livre* (Paris: Picard & Fils, 1903), part 4.
19. Maurice Blondel, *The Letter on Apologetics & History and Dogma*, trans. Alexander Dru

This principle of development is indeed *Tradition*, which becomes in Blondel's hands the spectacles that correct Loisy's myopia. Blondel's account of Tradition, however, makes it more creative of subsequent articulations of faith than can be credited. This is because he makes it deliver the reality of Christ to us independently of the words of witness, of preaching, of Scripture. So, he says, tradition "preserves not so much the intellectual aspect of the past as its living reality." "It relies ... on texts," he says, but "primarily on something else, on an experience always in act."[20] Experience of what, we may ask? "It helps us reach the real Christ whom no literary portrait could exhaust or replace, without being confined to the texts."[21] Through our love of and obedience to Christ, tradition serves "as a vehicle for a doctrine which literature does not relate in its entirety."[22]

Thus, we have an extralinguistic, extraconceptual, more primordial experience of Christ given to us especially in the practical and affective order. Because of this experience, in virtue of this access, we will put into words more than what has already been contained and conveyed in the words of witness, of the New Testament. This looks at first glance like the connatural knowledge of which St. Thomas speaks. But it is not. Connatural knowledge does not give us new things not already contained in the word of God. But Blondel's Tradition does. It seems to be more creative than a fundamental theology that recognizes the closure of revelation with the death of the last apostle can countenance.[23]

---

and Illtyd Trethowan (Grand Rapids, MI: Eerdmans, 1994), 223: "[T]here must be an explanatory principle and a source of movement which accounts for the double coming and going—the movement from the historical data to faith which goes beyond what these provide for an ordinary witness—and the movement from faith to really objective affirmations and to realities which constitute Sacred History."

20. Blondel, *History and Dogma*, 267.

21. Blondel, *History and Dogma*, 268. This is repeated on 269.

22. Blondel, *History and Dogma*, 274.

23. Yves Congar much appreciated Blondel's contribution to a theology of Tradition, but not uncritically. In his *Tradition and Traditions*, there is an apt summary of Blondel's position: "Dogma, though dependent on historical documents, draws upon another source: the experience of an ever present reality to which the documents bear witness at their own level and in their own way" (362). However, Congar says, while "the Church's faith can penetrate the meaning of texts and events" ... "it is not (strictly) creative.... In reacting against apologetic rationalism on the one hand and historicism on the other, did Blondel, perhaps, minimize the part played by the arguments which render the evidence of value to discursive reason?" (367). In other words, Blondel's proposal seems to come very close to acknowledging some sort of "ongoing revelation," condemned by Pius X in *Lamentabili* (DH 3421).

Blondel's proposal is sometimes thought to be strengthened by an appeal to St. Thomas's analysis of the act of faith. In his treatment of faith, St. Thomas asks whether the object of faith is something "complex" or "incomplex."[24] He answers that it is complex, in the sense that it is captured in *enunciabilia*—the enunciable propositions of faith are complex, asserting a predicate of a subject. On the other hand, the object in the sense of the reality that is believed is incomplex, something simple. His answer to the second objection is that "the act of faith does not terminate in the enunciable [the proposition] but in the reality" (*"actus credentis non terminatur in enunciabile, sed ad rem"*). Some take this to mean that the act of faith initiates some contact with the reality—with divine Reality—other and richer and more personal than what the proposition gives us. This would characterize Marie-Dominique Chenu's position, where the "realism" and formulas of faith are played off against one another.[25] Unfortunately, as was noted in chapter 4, such a suggestion seriously distorts St. Thomas's meaning. Just after saying that the act of faith terminates in the reality, he adds: "For we do not form enunciables except in order to have knowledge of things through them, just as in science, so also in faith" (*"non enim formamus enuntiabilia nisi ut per ea de rebus cognitionem habeamus, sicut in scientia ita et in fide"*).[26] The idea, then, is that propositions of faith function no differently than propositions do in some science. The light of faith is greater than the light of the natural intellect, true enough. But it does not make the propositions we assent to in virtue of this light function differently than any other true proposition.

24. *Summa theologiae* II-II, Q. 1, a. 2.

25. See Marie-Dominique Chenu, OP, "Vérité évangelique et métaphysique Wolffienne à Vatican II," *Revue des sciences philosophiques et théologiques* 57 (1973): 632–40, at 637–38, and his earlier "L'unité de la foi: Réalisme et formalisme," *Vie Spirituelle. Supplément* 52 (1937): 1–8, translated as "The Unity of Faith: Realism and Formalism," in M.-D. Chenu, *Faith and Theology*, 1–7, trans. Denis Hickey (New York: Macmillan, 1968). Chenu opposes the realism and formalism (propositionalism) of faith to each other rather than seeing that the proposition is the instrument of faith's realism. For a careful analysis of Chenu's theology of faith, see Henry Donneaud, OP, "La constitution dialectique de la théologie et de son histoire selon M.-D. Chenu," *Revue Thomiste* 96 (1996): 41–66.

26. Jan Walgrave seems to share Chenu's understanding; see his *Unfolding Revelation: The Nature of Doctrinal Development* (Philadelphia: Westminster, 1972), 98–99. He calls on St. Thomas's *De Veritate* Q. 14, a. 8, ad 5 and ad 11, for help, but these texts do not really change the teaching of the *Summa*, although they alert us to the fact that the propositions of faith do not exhaust the Object they inform us of.

In both cases, the reality is given to us just exactly as the proposition delivers it to us: we know of the reality just what the concepts of the subject and predicate hand over to us, no less, but also, no more. There is no help for Blondel's position here.

Because of the influence of Blondel on Henri de Lubac, however, his view of how Tradition operates in the development of dogma has had a great influence.[27] It is hard to judge whether or not de Lubac himself escapes the criticism made above of Blondel. Like Blondel, he also reaches for an access to Christ considered in his reality as the "redemptive Action" of God and in our knowledge of this as the whole of revelation, which he styles "the Whole of Dogma." From this Whole, as from an ingot of gold, the several and discrete coins of individual dogmas are struck off and minted, such that we need not concern ourselves with a logical demonstration of a development's presence in the deposit prior to magisterial definition of it.[28] There need be no such demonstration prior to definition, and such demonstration is not the warrant for magisterial definition of dogma, anyway, which, to repeat, is no theological *argument* but the magisterial perception that the dogma is revealed. This is surely to be granted and is easily accounted for by the connatural knowledge of divine things by the gifts of the Holy Spirit. Still, relative to the *theologian's* task of showing how a development is contained in the deposit, de Lubac's adoption of Blondel seemingly makes it in principle impossible to fulfill, even though de Lubac readily speaks of the theologian's responsibility to fulfill it.[29] If I read Blondel aright, the present experiential knowledge of Christ that warrants the development makes finding it even implicitly in the previous teaching of the Church impossible and unnecessary. If the "Whole of Dogma" is no mere collection of "principles" and "premises," is it similarly nonconceptual?[30] The "Whole," we learn, is an undivided

---

27. For a sympathetic appreciation of de Lubac on development, see Nicholas J. Healy, Jr., "Henri de Lubac on the Development of Dogma," in *Ressourcement After Vatican II: Essays in Honor of Joseph Fessio, S.J.*, 346–365 (San Francisco: Ignatius, 2019).

28. Henri de Lubac, SJ, "The Problem of the Development of Dogma," 274.

29. De Lubac, "The Problem of the Development of Dogma," 266.

30. De Lubac, "The Problem of the Development of Dogma," 275. De Lubac also envisages a more-than-ordinary logic for dealing with the revealed mysteries of faith (265–67). What this would be exactly is difficult to say; the logic we learn as sophomores is either applied or it is not: concepts may be analogical, but it is hard to envisage an analogical application of logic.

reality, possessed in a sort of "higher state of awareness."[31] But if there is such a higher awareness of the "Whole of Dogma" that is the basis for the development of doctrine, then once again, showing the presence of a development in the prior traditional teaching of Scripture and magisterium will be impossible and unnecessary. For it seems to follow that what now the magisterium perceives in the deposit of revelation was not necessarily perceived conceptually and so communicably in any way before by courtesy of any "principle" or "premise."[32]

De Lubac is noted for the "Christological concentration" of revelation he effects in this essay.[33] We can read him as meaning nothing more than the Whole, the Design, of which Yves Congar speaks. And this is important in providing a way to discern the Marian dogmas as already noted in chapter 3. On the other hand, his solution for explaining development by appealing to the possession of this Whole of Dogma and redemptive Action in a state of higher awareness—higher than our awareness of premise and principle?—is hard to make sense of.

Both of these notions, the Whole of Dogma concentrated in Christ and the characterization of its subjective mode of possession owe something to Pierre Rousselot, who speaks of the "concrete" and "personal" knowledge of Christ the apostles possessed both affectively and conceptually, the Christ who in his humanity just is the intelligible truth of Christianity.[34] This concrete and personal knowledge of the apostles, affective and conceptual, is transmissible to the Church by means of catechesis (for the conceptual content) and by way of the *habitus* of faith, which gives a sympathetic, connatural knowledge of Christ.[35] Perhaps we could say de Lubac's "higher state of awareness" (higher than awareness of any principle or premise) is a function of Rousselot's connatural knowledge of Christ by way of the *habitus* of faith.

31. De Lubac, "The Problem of the Development of Dogma," 274, 275. Nichols notes de Lubac's dependence on Pierre Rousselot, SJ, for whom see below.

32. For the same account, see Henri de Lubac, SJ, *La Révélation Divine*, 3rd ed. (Paris: Les Éditions du Cerf, 1983), 157–59.

33. Aidan Nichols, OP, *From Newman to Congar: The Idea of Doctrinal Development from the Victorians to the Second Vatican Council* (Edinburgh: T&T Clark, 1990), 201; Healy, "Henri de Lubac on the Development of Doctrine," 354–356.

34. Pierre Rousselot, SJ, "Petite théorie du développment du dogme," *Recherches de Science Religieuse* 53 (1965): 355–90, at 364–65 and 374–75.

35. Rousselot, "Petite théorie," 365, 385–86

THE LOGICAL VERIFICATION OF DEVELOPMENT   117

Now, it is by way of this connatural knowledge, a knowledge *per modum naturae*, by which Rousselot wants "to explain the knowledge that the Church apprehends of dogmatic truths that are the object of new definitions."[36] The Church as a whole may judge the truth of new doctrines by way of connaturality, which is readily to be granted.[37] But he seems also to think of the connatural and sympathetic possession of Christ by the Church as productive of new definitions not hitherto contained in the conceptual possession of the Church, actual or implicit.

Other theologians make similar moves with appeals to experience and "contact" with the reality revelation speaks of. They seem to be looking for an extraconceptual but still cognitively laden possession of revelation that will then subsequently be cashed out in hitherto unformulated dogmatic propositions. Karl Rahner, for instance, speaks of the experience of a lover, whose knowledge of his beloved does indeed have a propositional component, but which "is infinitely richer, simpler and denser than any body of propositions."[38] If we impute to the apostles and to the Church such an experience of Christ, then we have a mechanism for understanding how the Church can enunciate dogmatic propositions that are not evidently logically related to a previous deposit.[39] The light of faith, moreover, gives a real "contact" with the reality of what is believed, and this, too, explains how new dogmatic formulations are arrived at.[40] An experience of something, of a person, can certainly include more than what we have already expressed in word and statement. But it is hard to see how it could be that the Church today has an experience like that of the apostles.

As to the light of faith, Edward Schillebeeckx makes the same appeal: the "light of faith enables me to grasp more in the mystery of revelation than is said about it in conceptual terms and than history tells us about it."[41]

---

36. Rousselot, "Petite théorie," 378. Objectively considered, one may "pretend" (*feindre*) for the sake of method that "the whole of the deposit reduces to the gospel or to the New Testament" (387).

37. Rousselot, "Petite théorie," 387.

38. Karl Rahner, SJ, "The Development of Dogma," in *Theological Investigations*, vol. 1, 39–77, trans. Cornelius Ernst, OP (Baltimore: Helicon, 1961), 64.

39. Rahner, "The Development of Dogma," 65–66; and 68, for the supposition that the Church has an experience "in principle the same as that of the apostles."

40. Rahner, "The Development of Dogma," 50–54. Propositions assented to by the light of faith, therefore, do not function as do ordinary propositions.

41. E. Schillebeeckx, OP, "The Development of the Apostolic Faith into the Dogma of the

So, the light gives us more than is contained only and exactly in the propositions of faith. He, too, invokes an "experiential knowledge of the church in contact with the saving reality itself."[42] As with Rahner, it is hard to know whether anything real is being referred to.

If a cognitively laden but extraconceptual possession of revelation (apart from a possession in *praxis*, of course, which is not itself altogether bereft of propositional direction, like Rome's refusal to rebaptize in the third century) names nothing real, and if the conceptual mediation of revelation ends "with the death of the last apostle" as explained above, where the relation of Scripture to Tradition was discussed, such that its deposition in concept and proposition—"the pattern of the sound words"—is the only place of its location, then the theological task of showing the relation of the "new" dogma to the "old" expressions of the gospel remains outstanding. It remains necessary, however, if the reasonability of assent to what the Church proposes is to be made evident. What will do this except logic?

Forms of the logical justification of developments

If connatural knowledge cannot show *how* a development is contained in the deposit, and if "experience" or "contact" with saving reality seem to call for an extraconceptual possession of revelation that prevents showing its previous presence in the deposit, then theology's discharge of the task of showing the rational credibility of some development of dogma will be accomplished on the following two understandings. First, as chapter 4 claimed and as the brief review of twentieth century figures calls to mind, there is no extraconceptual, extrapropositional human possession of the

---

Church," in *Revelation and Theology*, vol.1, 57–83, trans. N.D. Smith (New York: Sheed and Ward, 1967), 75. He says also that the light of faith does not bring with it an "infusion of content" (76), so it is hard to see exactly what he means. This article first appeared in 1952.

42. E. Schillebeeckx, OP, "Revelation Scripture, Tradition, and Teaching Authority," in *Revelation and Theology*, vol. 1, 3–24, at 17. This article first appeared in 1963. Schillebeeckx wants to understand the relation between experience and concept as does D. de Petter; see E. Schillebeeckx, "The Concept of Truth," in *Revelation and Theology*, vol. 2, 5–29, trans. N.D. Smith (New York: Sheed and Ward, 1968), 18–20. This article first appeared in 1954. For Schillebeeckx's subsequent unfortunate slide into dogmatic relativism, see his "Toward a Catholic Use of Hermeneutics," in E. Schillebeeckx, *God the Future of Man*, 1–49, trans. N.D. Smith (New York: Sheed and Ward: 1968), at 32–33, 37–40.

intelligibility of things, even revealed things. Second, the path between what was conceptually present and affirmed already in the deposit and what is affirmed in the supposed development will be conceptual, which is to say that this path can be nothing but a logical path.

The most detailed account of this path was provided by Francisco Marín-Sola, OP, in his *The Homogeneous Evolution of Catholic Dogma*, already referred to.[43] Marín-Sola distinguishes three degrees of doctrinal development or progress: passage from the explicitly revealed deposit to what is formally or immediately implicit in it; passage from the deposit to what is virtually or mediately implicit in it; and passage from the deposit to what is purely virtually or mediately contained in it, which he calls the "connexively mediate."[44] The formally implicit distinguishes things only nominally distinct; the virtually implicit distinguishes conceptually distinct things; the connexively implicit distinguishes things really distinct.[45]

There are four ways in which things are merely nominally distinct: as a definition from the defined; as an essential part from its whole; as a particular from a universal; and as one correlative from another.[46] So rational animal and man; soul and person; Peter and man; son and father. The virtually implicit names the distinction between a thing's essence and its properties, or between a cause and its effect.[47] The connexively implicit is really distinct from what is ordinarily but not necessarily connected with

43. Marín-Sola was born in 1873 and entered the Dominican missionary province of the Holy Rosary in 1888. After philosophical and theological studies, he taught in Manila, Spain, the United States, and the University of Fribourg. He died in 1932. For an appreciation of his view of development, see Reinhard Hütter, "Progress, Not Alteration of the Faith: Beyond Antiquarianism and Presentism. John Henry Newman, Vincent of Lérins, and the Criterion of Identity of the Development of Doctrine," 380–383, and his *John Henry Newman on Truth and Its Counterfeits: A Guide for Our Times* (Washington, DC: The Catholic University of America Press, 2020), 155–66. In addition to the development of doctrine, Marín-Sola also devoted a considerable part of his professional life to the understanding of grace and freedom, for which see Michael Torre, *Do Not Resist the Spirit's Call: Francisco Marín-Sola on Sufficient Grace* (Washington, DC: The Catholic University of America Press, 2013).

44. Marín-Sola, *Homogeneous Development*, nos. 30–34, pp. 152–54.

45. Marín-Sola, *Homogeneous Development*, no. 23, p. 150. The terminology here is various. F. Suarez calls Marín-Sola's connexively implicit the virtually implicit; properly speaking, it is for Suarez the "merely virtual," understood as a theological conclusion following from premises only one of which is revealed, and asserting something not only conceptually but really distinct from the revealed premise, and indefinable. See no. 73, pp. 185–86. According to Marín-Sola, "virtually implicit" conclusions as he understands them are definable in that they necessarily follow from revelation.

46. Marín-Sola, *Homogeneous Development*, no. 32, p. 153.

47. Marín-Sola, *Homogeneous Development*, no. 42, p. 159.

it by physical or chemical or biological law.[48] For instance, ordinarily it is the case that no mother is a virgin. But this is not metaphysically necessary, and, in the case of Mary, not true. The bond of the connexively implicit can be broken miraculously. But the bond of the virtually implicit cannot be broken under any circumstances, for that would imply that something be and not be.[49]

Evidently, the terms of Marín-Sola's classification of logical connections depends on the logical doctrine of the predicables contained in the fifth chapter of the first book of Aristotle's *Topics*.[50] The predicables name the five ways a predicate may be related to a subject. They are genus, species, specific difference, property, and accident. Socrates is an animal, a man, rational, ironical, and bald. Genera name essential factors making kinds, but which kinds contain species of a more determinate intelligibility, themselves distinguished by essential differences. Properties strictly speaking are always and necessarily said of what they are properties of, because they are necessarily connected with the essentials of genus or species. Accidents may or may not belong to the subject of which they are truly predicated without making or implying any difference as to what the subject essentially is. Accidents may be important, as are wickedness and uprightness. But as to essentials, Iago and Othello are both men, both animals, both rational, and both capable of speech (a property).

48. Marín-Sola, *Homogeneous Development*, no. 37, pp. 155–56.

49. Marín-Sola, *Homogeneous Development*, nos. 37, 39, pp. 155–56, 156–57. Reginald Schultes, OP, does not distinguish as does Marín-Sola, and note should be taken of this difference, especially since many are acquainted with Schultes's work through Garrigou-Lagrange's reliance on it. In his *Introductio in Historiam Dogmatum Praelectiones* (Paris: Lethielleux, 1922), Schultes counts as formally implicitly revealed nominally distinct formulations of revelation, as for instance a definition of what is named in Scripture, or a particular contained in a revealed universal, or parts in a revealed whole, or the correlative of something revealed (173–74). He calls the virtually revealed what is contained in some revealed principle or cause whence it may be deduced (175–76). This includes theological conclusions, dogmatic facts (e.g., a declaration of the legitimacy of an ecumenical council), canonizations. Theological conclusions are indefinable for Schultes (195–203), but definable for Marín-Sola. See Matthew Minerd's remark on this issue in the introduction to *The Thomistic Response to the Nouvelle Théologie*, ed. and trans. Jon Kirwan and Matthew K. Minerd (Washington, DC: The Catholic University of America Press, 2023), 63. Schultes provides a greater separation between dogma and theological science.

50. For a basic presentation, see John Oesterle, *Logic: The Art of Defining and Reasoning* (New York: Prentice-Hall, 1952), chap. 2, or Francis H. Parker and Henry B. Veatch, *Logic as a Human Instrument* (New York: Harper and Brothers, 1959), 116–25, 228–30. For appeal to the doctrine of the predicables in St. Thomas, see for instance *Quaestiones disputatae de potentia*, Q. 7, a. 3, ad 2; *Contra gentes* I, chap. 17, no. 7; chap. 32, no. 4; *De ente et essentia*, chap. 3–4.

The predicables not only name all the possible relations between a subject and predicate, but also indicate the order of our coming to know things.[51] What is first apparent to us in our sensory exploration of the world are the accidental features of things. Colors, shapes, weights, densities, hardness and softness, smells, plasticities, tastes, clicks and clacks, tones and tunes—these are the things that meet us first. But some immediately encountered features seem more permanent, more connected with what they qualify, than others. So, from many different contingent accidents we come to intuit the properties that are the stable platforms from which various accidents come and go without importantly changing the subject. Men may be black or white or yellow, but they must all have a three-dimensional surface capable of supporting such accidents of color. Once we know enough of the properties of things, we can start to classify things on the supposition that important essential differences distinguish them, even if we cannot yet name them, and the world is no longer a chaotic riot of colors and shapes and noises, but an ordered array of plants and animals, of birds and bears and fishes, of spiders and flies and gnats and "other bugs."

The basic distinction of the predicables is between essentials (genus, species, difference, and properties flowing from the foregoing) and accidentals. Predicable relations are objective, and they suppose the truth of the "realism" spoken of in chapter 4, the fact that human knowing apprehends the intelligibilities of things. They name the results of our cognitive engagement with the things and features of the things of the world, together with their relations, the actions they undertake, and the passions they are subject to. The predicables, if they really do rightly name these cognitive results, are at home only in a logic that is more than purely extensional, where there is no supposition of the possibility of human insight into the natures of the things our common names classify. Understood so, the predicables can be at home in a logic only if nominalism is understood to be false.[52] In this way, the very logic needed to explain how the theologian discharges his task in considering the development of dogma is very

51. See the exposition of this fact in Sokolowski, *Phenomenology of the Human Person*, chap. 7 and 8.

52. For more on this, see Henry Babcock Veatch, *Two Logics: The Conflict Between Classical and Neo-Analytic Philosophy* (Evanston, IL: Northwestern University Press, 1969).

uncontemporary, and it alerts us to the difficulties of understanding development of dogma today. Marín-Sola's consideration of development is at home only in this uncontemporary context.

Marín-Sola is careful to point out the various relations of properties to essences (= genera and differences). Sometimes properties are fully manifest and sometimes not.[53] Every man has the capacity to become ironic, like Socrates. But not every man is actually ironical. Only someone of cultivated manners and practiced wit is actually ironical. There is also a distinction of causes to be made. Metaphysical causes are identical with their effects, and physical causes are not. So, Marín-Sola illustrates, the absolute immutability of God is the ground of his eternity, and they are not in fact really distinct. But fire, which has the capacity to burn, does not always burn. The effect is really distinct from the cause, as the third chapter of Daniel shows us.[54]

If logic is the instrument of showing that a development is genuine, as Newman argues *en bloc* (see the first section of this chapter, above), then Marín-Sola is merely distinguishing the various more determinate logical relations that perform this theological task, and he emphasizes that whatever is metaphysically included or virtually implicit in the realities made known by revelation is itself also revealed. The evident and unbreakable necessity of the relation guarantees this. Marín-Sola's first illustration of the speculative, strictly logical justification of dogma is the teaching of Nicaea that the Son is consubstantial with the Father. How was this truth revealed? "It was revealed in other truths in which it is implicit out of which it is educed through reasoning or inference." These other truths, he says, are two: "[F]irst, 'Jesus Christ is the true Son of God,' or 'Jesus Christ is true God'; second, 'in God there can be no division, but only mere unicity, of substance.'"[55] Indeed, Christ is true Son, as is manifest from the fact that he is not made but is "the only begotten Son" (Jn 1:18) through whom all things are made, the Son in a proper sense as distinct from the prophets who are servants (Mt 21:33–41). But "to be a true *son* requires to be *of the substance* of the father, since that is the definition of

---

53. Marín-Sola, *Homogeneous Development*, nos. 43–45, pp. 160–63.

54. Marín-Sola, *Homogeneous Development*, no. 50, p. 165.

55. Marín-Sola, *Homogeneous Development*, no. 202, pp. 359–60.

sonship."[56] This is a matter of the formally or immediately implicit. The absence of division in God, on the other hand, is a restatement of his simplicity, which is asserted in asserting his transcendence to the world of composite beings, as well as from the impossibility that he can be rightly imaged (Ex 20:4) and that there can be an idol appropriate to him, as also from the nondistinction of nature and individual in God (only God is God—Is 43:10–14; 44:6–8), as from the fact that, as creator, he does not receive existence, and also as from his eternal perfection to which nothing can be added nor nothing removed.[57] If there can be no division in God, then Father and Son are the same numerically one divine substance, consubstantial.

If we revisit the argument for the consubstantiality of Father and Son that Bernard Lonergan offered and which we reviewed in chapter 2, we find the same strict logic. There is an argument from the mutual exclusivity of their knowledge of one another asserted in Matthew 11:27. No one knows the Father but the Son or the Son but the Father. The exclusive knowledge of one of the other is conceived of here as a property. The exact same property is asserted of Father and Son; they each possess the same property; and therefore Father and Son are the same nature or substance, inasmuch as properties flow from essences. And here, while there is a conceptual distinction between substance and essence, there is no real distinction. The real distinction of Son from Father, on the other hand, does not imply any real distinction of substance. Lonergan argues also from the fact that "I AM," the name God gives himself in Exodus 3:14 and which is a privileged expression of Old Testament monotheism, is predicated also of the Son in John 8:24, 8:28, 13:19, and so on. The name that bespeaks uniqueness of being is predicated of both; practically speaking, the same essence that must be numerically one is predicated of both. Lonergan points to the fact that the same power of creation is attributed to both in 1 Corinthians 8:6, among other places, and from this, too, there results the affirmation of their consubstantiality: the same power, the same property, is predicated of each.[58]

---

56. Marín-Sola, *Homogeneous Development*, no. 202, p. 360.

57. See Thomas Joseph White, *The Trinity: On the Nature and Mystery of the One God* (Washington, DC: The Catholic University of America Press, 2022), chap. 13.

58. Bernard Lonergan, *The Triune God: Doctrines*, 289.

It can be noted that the same kind of logical argument is deployed by St. Thomas in showing that the Son of God is God. So for instance in the fourth book of the *Contra gentiles*, arguing against Arius, he appeals to John 5:19—"for whatever the Father does, that the Son does likewise." The same power (property) is attributed to each, and the numerical identity of the power implies numerical identity of the nature.[59] Against the opinion of Photinus that Christ is but the adopted Son of God, St. Thomas marshals the facts that, like God, Christ sanctifies (Heb 2:11; 13:12) and forgives sins (Mt 1:21). From the operation to the power to the nature, the argument is bound together by strict necessity: if Christ can do what only God can do, he is God by nature and not by merit.[60]

Perhaps the most celebrated instance of the logical justification of a development simply because it is so short, sweet, clear, and therefore easy to remember is the teaching of the Third Council of Constantinople on the human will of Christ. In Marín-Sola's exposition, it follows from these two truths:

[F]irst, "Jesus is not only a true man but also a perfect man, or in a connatural state, or like us in everything except sin or anything opposed to the end of redemption"; second, "no one can be a *perfect* man, or man in a *connatural* state, or man *like us in everything* [Heb 4:15], without a human will and the other physico-natural powers or properties (although one can be truly and essentially a man without them)."[61]

This example is important for Marín-Sola because it illustrates the necessity of distinguishing human nature taken abstractly from the nature or essence in that state in which no integral part is lacking to it (so, its "connatural" state) and from the nature perfected by the virtues, intellectual and moral.[62] From the nature taken abstractly, it by no means follows that Christ exercised human freedom. But from his nature taken integrally and as perfected by the virtues, it follows not only that there is radically

---

59. *Contra gentiles*, book 4, chap. 7, no. 20.

60. *Contra gentiles*, book 4, chap. 4, no. 15.

61. Marín-Sola, *Homogeneous Development*, no. 204, pp. 364–65. A "physico-natural" power is a power immediately ready to be manifested in act, as, say, the freedom of a person in a vegetative state is not.

62. Marín-Sola, *Homogeneous Development*, no. 443, p. 160.

THE LOGICAL VERIFICATION OF DEVELOPMENT 125

present the power of intellectual appetite, but also its manifestation and operation in the life of Christ in free acts of will.[63]

The emphasis in the foregoing on metaphysical necessity should not mislead one in thinking that even where such necessity is in play, one therefore has an apodictic demonstration of the presence of the dogma in question in the deposit. There are too many questions of exegesis and interpretation, of how to reach a proper reading of some scriptural witness in the context of the whole of Scripture, of the analogy of faith uniting one's grasp of the entire design of revelation, for that easily to be attained.[64] This does not mean the metaphysical connections where they are evident do not really contribute to our ability to see the new formulation in the old deposit. It means that we attain to a credible judgment that the new formulation is contained in the old deposit on par with the judgment of credibility in believing that God has spoken in the first place. The logic of development will be of same kind as the logic that, in principle, can lead to the act of faith itself.

Confirmation by the logic of antecedent and converging probabilities

Much of the Church's extraordinary definition of dogma has concerned the divine person and two natures of Christ (Nicaea, Ephesus, Chalcedon, Second Constantinople). There was also concern for the two wills and two operations of Christ, as well as the question of the iconic representability of his human nature (the Lateran Synod of 649, Third Constantinople, Second Nicaea). Overlapping with questions of the divinity of Christ's person, there have been important Trinitarian clarifications (First Constantinople, several Synods of Toledo in the seventh century,

---

63. The corrective of Marín-Sola's position that Reginald Garrigou-Lagrange makes at this point should be noted. It is to the effect that while what is metaphysically connected to a revealed reality can be known necessarily, it is known as part of what is revealed only if it is attested to. See R. Garrigou-Lagrange, OP, *The One God: A Commentary on the First Part of St. Thomas' Theological Summa*, trans. Dom. Bede Rose, OSB (Jackson, MI: Ex Fontibus Company, 2012). 54. And for the revealed as what is attested to, see Ed. Dhanis, SJ, "Révélation explicite et implicite," *Gregorianum* 34 (1953): 187–237. On this showing, not every theological conclusion, as certain as it may be, is definable. See Schultes, *In Historiam Dogmatum*, 206–7.

64. See *Dei Verbum*, no. 12, and Marín-Sola, *Homogeneous Development*, no. 218, p. 404.

Fourth Lateran). Questions about the relation of nature and grace have also been answered (Synod of Carthage of 418, the *Indiculus gratiae* of the fifth century, the Second Council of Orange, the Council of Trent on Original Sin and Justification in the sixteenth century). Then there were questions on the nature of man (Vienne, Fifth Lateran). There have also been numerous questions about the efficacy and nature of the sacraments (from early on, but notably Trent, again, on the Eucharist, especially). Because of the nature of all these issues, the fitting instrument for theologians and popes and bishops to think them out and sometimes to express them has been a metaphysical grasp, increasingly explicit, of created reality and, so far as is possible, of uncreated reality. Just note how many times the word "nature" was used in the foregoing brief description of dogmatic concerns! It is Marín-Sola's signal contribution to an understanding of dogmatic development and its justification to map out the ways in which metaphysical thinking, concerned as it is to put its hand on necessities, plays a role.

At certain points, however, metaphysical insight will not be an entirely adequate instrument to vindicate a development of doctrine as genuine, albeit a dogma contained in the received deposit of revelation. This is so with the dogmas of our Lady's Immaculate Conception and Bodily Assumption into Heaven.

Here is how Marín-Sola justifies the definition of the Immaculate Conception by Pope Pius IX in 1854. When St. Gabriel the Archangel and the Church address Mary as "full of grace" (Lk 1:28), this means that "to Mary, in her capacity as Mother of God, must be attributed all that degree of grace or holiness, all that degree of immunity from sin, that is compatible with the honor of her Son, that is, with her redemption by Christ." This, he says, is simply the explication of Scripture. There is to be added to it a premise of reason, that "it is possible at once to be conceived without original sin and to be redeemed by Christ."[65] This possibility can be realized, moreover, by "a true and proper preservative redemption by Jesus Christ."[66] The distinction between redemption after the fact of sin and contracting guilt and a redemption prior to sin that keeps one from guilt,

---

65. Marín-Sola, *Homogeneous Development*, no. 209, p. 377.
66. Marín-Sola, *Homogeneous Development*, no. 209, p. 379.

the distinction of John Duns Scotus, thus makes it possible that her Son will effect the fullness of realization of grace in Mary, so that she can be the worthiest mother of God as it is possible to be. Marín-Sola concludes that the dogma of the Immaculate Conception of Mary "follows from the dogma [of the divine motherhood of Mary] with certainty through exactly the same process employed by Tradition and theology to demonstrate that the Mother of God had to be immune from all actual sin."[67]

Many readers sympathetic to Marín-Sola's overall project are nonetheless not convinced that by such reasoning he gives us certainty, that he gives us a demonstration that truly locates the dogma in the deposit of faith. It is not that the distinction between the application of the grace of Christ prevenient to and consequent to the exercise of human agency is not satisfactory. But it seems rather that *gratia plena* is taken as a sort of blank check on which the theologian can write out any sum desirable according to later calculations of the kinds and degrees of grace worked out by theological science long after the closure of revelation. Yves Congar observes that it is not the philologist but rather the Tradition of the Church that will give us the meaning of *kecharitomene* in Luke 1:28. It gives us this meaning by "the analogy of faith,"[68] by an examination of the pattern or design of the economy of salvation as a whole expressed in many texts throughout both Testaments that call to one another, reflect one another, and link up to one another.[69] All are concerned with what befits Mary as a worthy mother of God. Seeing and verifying what this consists in insofar as it includes exemption from original sin, however, commits the theologian to another form of reasoning than Marín-Sola employs. It is a logic—not the logic of the *Topics* but rather of the *Rhetoric*, as we shall soon see.

It is noteworthy that Reginald Garrigou-Lagrange offers what he takes to be a demonstration of the Bodily Assumption of Mary whose point of departure is likewise the truth that she is full of grace. Together with the

67. Marín-Sola, *Homogeneous Development*, no. 209, p. 380.

68. Cf. Rom 12:6 and *Dei Verbum* no. 12.

69. Yves Congar, "Theological Notes on the Assumption," in *Faith and Spiritual Life*, 3–10, trans. A Manson and L. C. Sheppard (New York: Herder and Herder, 1968 [French, 1962]), 4, 6. See also Congar, *Foi et théologie*, 113–14, where, following R. Garrigou-Lagrange, he observes that in treating the Immaculate Conception, Marín-Sola fails to distinguish the revealed in its material reality from the revealed as something attested to.

truth that she was also "blessed by God among women in an exceptional way," for which Luke 1:42 is the authority, it follows that she was exempt from the divine maledictions of Eve pronounced in Genesis 3:16–19. Thus, she did not bring forth children in pain, and she did not return to the dust from which Adam was made.[70] He offers also a second demonstration, one based on Mary's association with Christ in his victory over sin and death. In both cases, Garrigou-Lagrange says, the argument is "explicative": it does not move from one concept to another, but merely unpacks what is in "fullness of grace" and "victory over sin and death."[71] He too recognizes arguments of fittingness for the Bodily Assumption of Mary, arguing from the love of Christ for his mother, for instance.[72] But it seems clear that he counts most on what he deems to be demonstrations that unfold the formalities of concepts. If we are dissatisfied with Garrigou-Lagrange and Marín-Sola at these points, where shall we turn?

In addition to the logical paths that lead the mind from a thing to its definition, from one thing to its correlative, from essences to properties, and so on, we need in addition a more supple logic, one that can lead us to facts not yet affirmed. Once we have the facts of the Word made flesh, of Christ's true divinity, of his true sonship, of the Spirit's sanctifying role and of his being sent by both Father and Son, we can put together the Christological and Trinitarian dogmas of the Church in such a logically compelling way that more satisfactorily makes a coherent whole out of Sacred Scripture than any other way. But we are in a different logical territory when we assert Mary's Immaculate Conception and her Bodily Assumption into heaven. These facts are not asserted in the New Testament the way the Incarnation is asserted (Jn 1:14) or the fullness of the divinity of Christ is (Col 2:9) or the relation of begottenness (Jn 1:14) or the distinction of Son and Spirit (Jn 14:16), and so on. How then can we assert them at all?

We are in similar territory, moreover, when it comes to recognizing in the papacy and the college of bishops the fulfillment in ecclesial history of the Lord's promise to keep the Church in the truth.[73] And we are in

---

70. Reginald Garrigou-Lagrange, OP, *The Mother of the Saviour and Our Interior Life*, trans. Bernard J. Kelly, CSSp (St. Louis: Herder, 1943), 144.

71. Garrigou-Lagrange, *The Mother of the Saviour*, 145.

72. Garrigou-Lagrange, *The Mother of the Saviour*, 148.

73. Congar, *La Foi et la théologie*, 102–3.

like territory once again when we definitively affirm as an infallible truth pertaining to faith that the Church has no authority to ordain women to the priesthood, as John Paul II taught.[74] What kind of logic encompasses a demonstration not of metaphysical necessities so much as of revealed facts? We bring such facts to logical form by what Cardinal Newman called informal inference.[75] We bring them to form by way of establishing the antecedent probability of the fact and bringing to bear converging evidences of the actual confirmation of this fact.[76] This has very much to do with the role Congar sees the design of revelation or the analogy of faith playing in the discernment of dogma, his attention to which we adverted to in chapter 3 in discussing revelation.

The logical moves in question are easily illustrated because they are so commonly used. In a good crime novel, one key is the determination of the motive of the murderer; the fun of Agatha Christie's *Murder on the Orient Express* is Inspector Poirot's discovery that all the passengers in the coach but one have an excellent motive to murder Ratchett. Discovery of a motive is discovery of a likely cause of the murder; it is the discovery of an antecedent probability. The other key in a crime novel is the amassing of circumstantial evidence: bloodstain on the shirt, inability to furnish an alibi, suspect's prior knowledge of the victim's itinerary, and so on and so forth. None of them by themselves prove, since all of them, when reduced to logical form, are arguments that affirm the consequent: if p, then q; but q, therefore ... therefore, *nothing*. The suspect may have blood on his shirt from a bad shave. But many such evidences in harmony with the antecedent probability make for certainty. If all converge on him, the conclusion is that he is guilty as charged. So Newman's comparison of convergent probabilities to a cable: one may not trust oneself to just one of the wires of which a cable is made; but a traveler would be mad not to trust himself to the Brooklyn Bridge.[77]

---

74. Apostolic Letter, *Ordinatio sacerdotalis* (1994) (DH 4983; ND 1760). *Ordinatio sacerdotalis* engages the teaching that the Church can definitively and so infallibly teach what is necessarily connected to the deposit of faith.

75. John Henry Newman, *An Essay in Aid of a Grammar of Assent*, ed. I. T. Ker (Oxford: Clarendon Press, 1985), 187–213, esp. 208–9 (online, 289–329, esp. 321–22).

76. Meszaros, *The Prophetic Church*, 74–79, for confirming evidences; 121–25, for antecedent probabilities. See Aristotle, *Rhetoric*, book 1, chap. 2; 1356b1–1358a1.

77. For the cable wire illustration, see Meszaros, *The Prophetic Church*, 76–77 (Newman: *Letters*

Such a pattern of argument can be applied to the Bodily Assumption of Mary as follows.[78] The first set of considerations establishes the antecedent probability of Mary's bodily assumption into heaven. They all have this form: "If X is true, then we should expect Mary to be assumed bodily to heaven." The second set of considerations follows, as it were, the reverse form: "If Mary was assumed bodily to heaven, we should expect Y. But we find Y." Therefore? Therefore nothing—unless there are a sufficient number of such considerations to make the denial of Mary's assumption improbable.

There are four arguments demonstrating antecedent probability.[79] The first is from Mary's motherhood of Jesus. If she was physically the mother of Jesus, then it is the same flesh that belongs to both the Christ and his mother. But if this flesh is risen in Christ, it is not fitting that it see corruption in Mary's grave. Also, she conceives first in her mind, personally, what she conceives in her womb. This is to say that Mary is morally the mother of Jesus, and most worthily, with full and perfect human and graced freedom, untouched by sin in any way (which follows from the doctrine of the Immaculate Conception). Therefore, it seems inconsequent that she would share that penalty of sin which is the corruption of the body. The Mother of Life should still live, and as Mother—with her body sharing the same glory as her Son. The second argument is from the virginity of Mary, which itself befits her as mother of one whose Father is God. The sexual reproduction of animal species including that of man is in this present order a stratagem to overcome death. Were there no death, there would be no sexual concourse. And where there is no sexual concourse, it is fitting that there would be no death. The third argument unfolds the moral union of

---

and Diaries, XXI, 146). Newman illustrates both lines of argument in the preface to the French edition of his *University Sermons*.

78. For the Marian dogmas, see Andrew Meszaros, "John Henry Newman and the Thomistic Tradition: Convergences in Contribution to Development Theory," *Nova et Vetera* (English) 19 (2021): 423–68.

79. Joseph Duhr, SJ, reports the prominence of the arguments from Mary's motherhood and virginity in the Byzantine fathers; see his *The Glorious Assumption of the Mother of God*, trans. John Manning Fraunces, SJ (New York: P. J. Kennedy & Sons, 1950), 28. For considerations of the fittingness of the assumption, see John Henry Newman, "On the Fitness of the Glories of Mary," in Newman, *Mary: The Virgin Mary in the Life and Writings of John Henry Newman*, 149–166, ed. Philip Boyce (Grand Rapids, MI: Eerdmans, 2001), and Matthew Levering, *Mary's Bodily Assumption* (Notre Dame, IN: University of Notre Dame Press, 2015), chap. 6.

Mary with her Son, already touched on in the first argument. Mary shares with Christ the suffering of the cross (Jn 19; Lk 2:35), and does so with the perfection enabled by her sinlessness, and it is therefore fitting that she share his victory over death and in its perfection, realized now before the end of the age. Fourth, Mary is the image of Zion and Israel and so of the Church and represents in herself the perfection promised the Church in the final age, which includes resurrection into glory. It is therefore fitting that she share in this perfection even now, before the coming of that age.[80]

We pass to the kind of arguments that Newman calls "informal inferences," arguments that give probable evidences of Mary's assumption. First, if Mary was assumed into heaven, we should expect to find scriptural invitations so to think. We should find scriptures suggestive of, if not compelling, the admission of her assumption, and of course, we do. There is the "full of grace" of Luke 1:28. There is the equivalent "blessedness" of Mary and the fruit of her womb in Luke 1:42.

There are more scriptural indications. There is a complex but beautiful illation from the identification of Mary as the new Ark of the new covenant in Christ in Luke 1:39–45, explained by Benedict XVI in a homily for the Feast of the Assumption. The Ark of the Covenant, containing the tables of the covenant, was a particular seat of God's presence both before and after the erection of the temple. Mary, in retracing the steps by which the Ark traversed the hill country of Judea, is a sort of final Ark, since on her visit to Elizabeth, she already contains the one in whose blood is consecrated a last and eternal covenant (Lk 22:20). She is so identified because John leaps in Elizabeth's womb just as David danced before the Ark of the Covenant. Now, the Ark that appears in the temple of heaven in Revelation 11 is the Woman clothed with the sun and bearing the Son in Revelation 12. They are two visions of the same reality. The heavenly temple contains the Ark of the final covenant consecrated in the blood of Christ, and the Ark is once again Mary. The visions together indicate that the eschatological and eternal embodiment of the Messiah is shared by his Mother.[81]

---

80. This argument is touched on by Yves Congar in short essay entitled "Theological Notes on the Assumption," 9. It is also touched on by Joseph Ratzinger, *Daughter of Zion: Meditations on the Church's Marian Belief*, trans. John M. McDermott, SJ (San Francisco: Ignatius Press, 1983), 76–77.

81. See Ratzinger, *Daughter of Zion*, 81–82, and as Benedict XVI, his homily for the Solemnity of the Assumption, August 15, 2011, available at the Vatican website.

Thinking of the Assumption, Ratzinger thinks also of Colossians 3:3, according to which our life is now hidden with God, as it were, sharing his ascension, of which Ephesians 2:6 says more strongly that God has "raised us up with him, and made us sit with him in the heavenly places in Christ Jesus." "We"—not Christ, but those belonging to Christ—now sit with him in heaven. In hope, to be sure, we want to follow where our Head has led the way. But the present tense of the verse can be read to insist on a more literal reading: "We" now sit with Christ in heaven, bodily, in the person of Mary.[82]

Joseph Ratzinger understands Mary within the ancient perception of her as the Second Eve and so uniting the Testaments. The Marian dogmas simply articulate perspectives that embrace this unity.[83] For instance, a fundamental pattern of revelation is God's identification of himself by his relation to human beings. He is the God of Abraham, Isaac, and Jacob. This tells us who God is; it also tells us the destiny of those he takes to himself in this way. Thus, to the Sadducees, who deny the Resurrection generally, he says that God, the God of Abraham, Isaac, and Jacob, is the God "not of the dead but of the living" (Mk 12:27). They will certainly be raised up. But Mary is "most blessed" (Lk 1:48), most venerated. And this veneration fittingly corresponds to her sharing now in the resurrection of her Son.[84]

Louis Bouyer completes this thought in terms of the bridal imagery of the Testaments. If Mary figures the Bride of the Lamb in Revelation 12 and 22, if she thus personifies a fulfillment of the nuptial imagery of the Old Testament for Israel and Zion displayed in Hosea 1–3, Isaiah 54–55, and other places, is it to be thought that the Lamb is now widowed? Can he be the Spouse of the Church he is according to Ephesians 5:32 if there is no eschatological fulfillment even now of the Church's destiny?[85]

Let us pass to other corroborations more briefly. In the second place, if Mary was assumed into heaven, we should expect to find some patristic witness to it. Although it is relatively late, beginning with St. Epiphanius

---

82. Ratzinger, *Daughter of Zion*, 79–81.

83. Ratzinger, *Daughter of Zion*, 32.

84. Ratzinger, *Daughter of Zion*, 75–76.

85. See Louis Bouyer, *The Seat of Wisdom: An Essay on the Place of the Virgin Mary in Christian Theology*, trans. A. V. Littledale (New York: Pantheon, 1960), 10–19.

of Salamis in the fourth century and St. Gregory of Tours in the sixth, it is there. Third, if Mary was assumed into heaven, we would expect some liturgical witness to this on the part of the worshipping Church, and there exists such witness from the sixth century on.[86] The ecclesial witness to the Bodily Assumption in liturgical festival and popular devotion from the sixth century onwards does not indicate some oral tradition handed on from the apostles, but rather the recognition of the fact of the assumption by the *sensus fidei* of the faithful and a confirmation of its truth by those conformed to Christ by charity, and, indeed, by those conformed to the one most perfectly conformed to him, Mary. Fourth, if Mary was assumed bodily into heaven, we should expect the great masters at the first flowering of scientific theology to affirm it, and St. Albert, St. Thomas, St. Bonaventure, and Duns Scotus all do. Fifth, if Mary was assumed bodily into heaven, we should expect no veneration of her relics, and there is none.[87]

Congar observes that the recognition of the papacy and the college of bishops as the historical fulfillments of the Lord's promise to keep the Church in the truth follows a pattern similar to that of locating the justification of the Marian doctrines in the design of the events and persons of the Old Testament, in the prophecies and figures of New Testament realities in the Old. The shape of the papal office in its mature form in, say, the fifth century with Leo the Great cannot be deduced from the New Testament. But the antecedent probability of the continuation of the Petrine ministry of strengthening his brothers, of a ministry by which the successors of the apostles are strengthened, is high. It is admirably articulated by Newman himself in the *Essay on Development* as we saw in chapter 3, but we return to the argument in order to note its structure. The essence of all religion is authority, Newman notes, and points to the authority of conscience as the authority that rules natural religion.[88] But the Christian revelation comes to us as revelation, and does so publicly, openly, with warrants to its quality as revelation easy enough to find for those who seek them.[89] So if it is to remain in the world as revelation, and

---

86. See Manfred Hauke, *Introduction to Mariology*, trans. Richard Chonak (Washington, DC: The Catholic University of America Press, 2021), 274–75, 277–78.

87. Cf. Duhr, *The Glorious Assumption*, 32.

88. Newman, *Essay on Development*, 86

89. Newman, *Essay on Development*, 79–80.

if there are to be developments, there must be some organ that can determine which developments are genuine and which not, and must be able to do so publicly, openly, with warrants easy enough to find for those who seek them. As for the informal arguments that converge on the location of this organ in the pope of Rome, Newman lists the converging witness to this from the history of the ancient Church, beginning with Clement of Rome, Ignatius of Antioch, and Irenaeus of Lyon, and ending with the fifth century.[90] To his list may be added the things that Ludwig Hertling piles up in in his monograph, things ranging from letters of communion between the churches, boiled down in the end for convenience's sake to the claim to be in communion with Rome, and the observation that the concern so to be in communion with Peter is older than the canon of the New Testament.[91]

The recognition of the bishops themselves as collectively capable of determining matters of faith was touched on in chapter 2. Let us rather turn to a recent teaching, the teaching that women cannot be ordained priests, to close this chapter. The structure of the teaching is complex. In *Ordinatio sacerdotalis*, John Paul II exercises his ordinary and noninfallible teaching authority to "confirm" (Lk 22:32) the universal and ordinary teaching authority of the bishops which *is* infallible and "declare that the church has no authority whatsoever to confer priestly ordination on women and that this judgment is to be definitively held by all the faithful." In declaring that this teaching is to be "definitively held," he is teaching that it is infallible but may belong only to the secondary object of magisterial teaching authority, which truths are to be "held" and assented to but not assented to and "believed" by Catholic and supernatural faith.

The idea that the teaching authority of the Church extends beyond what is contained in the deposit of faith to include things that are necessarily connected with it is itself enunciated by the Congregation for the Doctrine of the Faith in *Donum veritatis*, on the Ecclesial Vocation of the Theologian (1990)[92] and in the CDF's explanation of the Profes-

---

90. Newman, *Essay on Development*, 157–65.

91. Ludwig Hertling, SJ, *Communio: Church and Papacy in Early Christianity*, trans. Jared Wicks, SJ (Chicago: Loyola University Press, 1972), 29–35, 47–55, 65–69.

92. DH 4877.

sion of Faith (1998).[93] That the scope of magisterial authority extends to what is necessarily logically or historically connected to what is entirely within the deposit of faith is itself revealed, as Marín-Sola argues. For it is revealed that the Church has the duty of safeguarding the revealed deposit. But she would not be able to do this "if she were not infallible with respect to what is mediately revealed" (a proposition of reason).[94] Declaring the truth of truths beyond the deposit but logically connected thereto is a necessary means to the safekeeping of the deposit. Moreover, Marín-Sola points out, such declaration of truths is the practice of the Church.

Such detour into the complexity of the teaching of *Ordinatio sacerdotalis*, however, does not address the main issue, which is how to see its teaching contained in or related to the deposit of faith. It is not enough to observe that the proposition that women can be ordained to the presbyterate has no support in either Scripture, where all apostles and apostolic authorities succeeding them are male, or Tradition, which knows of absolutely no ordination of women to the priesthood of either the first or second rank (priest or bishop), or in prior theological tradition, which produces arguments for the restriction of orders to men of various value. Unless the fact of the nonordination of women is not a brute fact or the result of culture or custom alien to the gospel, there must be some positive intelligibility to this fact. What is it?

It is the same kind of intelligibility discerned for the Marian doctrines of the Church, an intelligibility which takes seriously the grammar of sexual difference for the expression of revelation. Mary's virginal conception of the Son of God is a theological word that cannot be spoken independently of her feminine reality. It bespeaks in an exemplary because embodied fashion the fact that every human hearing of the word of God is purely receptive. The word of God comes from beyond us even as the Word that Mary conceives is announced to her and comes to her. The grammar of revelation is a sexually inflected grammar. This sexually inflected manner of expressing divine truths is continued in the sacramental

---

93. DH 5071, 5072. On the secondary object of ecclesial infallible teaching, see Avery Dulles, SJ, *Magisterium: Teacher and Guardian of the Faith* (Naples, Fla.: Sapientia Press, 2007), 73–74, 76–81.

94. Marín-Sola, *Homogeneous Development*, no. 212, p. 391.

economy of the Church. God made human is God made man because only so does the Incarnation fittingly introduce in history the spouse of the corporate person who has always been figured in the Old Testament as Daughter Zion, a feminine reality vis-à-vis the transcendent God. The supreme sacramental celebration of the new covenant found in the Eucharist recapitulates this history, the actual history of Christ who is the Bridegroom (Mk 2:19; Jn 2:1–12; 2 Cor 11:2; Eph 5:32), in that the one who makes the bread the Body and the wine the Blood acts not only in the power of Christ but in his person. Apart from the male character of the priesthood the sacramental display of the work of Christ and his covenant relation with the Church is obscured and rendered difficult of discernment. In this way, the Eucharist would become wholly a matter of words, and even the unsubstitutable reality of the Bread and the Wine questionable in setting aside the historical reality of the man Christ.[95]

The grammar of sexual difference as deployed in revelation provides the antecedent probability of the impossibility of ordaining women to the priesthood; the constant practice of the Church, noted by both *Inter insigniores* and *Ordinatio sacerdotalis*, provide converging evidence of this truth.

95. See the so-called "iconic" argument in the Congregation of the Doctrine of the Faith's *Inter insigniores* (1976); DH 4598–4606.

CHAPTER 6

VATICAN I AND THE DOGMA ABOUT DOGMA

Dogma was invented by the Council of Nicaea. The invention, dogma, is a reflexive grasp of what is contained in revelation as true. As chapter 2 had it, that is just what it is to assert that the Son is *homoousios tô patri*. The assertion sums up what Scripture teaches about the Son, the Logos of whom John speaks in the first chapter of his gospel, takes that teaching as true and as telling us objectively what is the case about Jesus of Nazareth, and formulates it in such a way that the orthodox can, and the Arians cannot, assent to it.

Nicaea, however, did not itself formulate what a dogma is. It did not reflect on what it had invented in teaching that the Son is consubstantial with the Father. That was the part of the First Vatican Council. Nicaea formulated what the Son is—in a dogma. The First Vatican Council formulated what dogma is in a reflexive grasp of what Nicaea discovered and many other councils employed. That reflexive grasp consists in apprehending dogma as a true and infallibly proposed statement of what is contained in revelation. The Vatican Council reflexively grasps dogma as a reflexive grasp of what is truly and infallibly proposed to faith by divine revelation and therefore proposed as a true and immutable teaching.

We can put the contrast another way. Nicaea gives us a dogma about the Word. It gives us a word about the Word. The Vatican Council gives us a dogma about dogma, a word about dogmatic words. It produces a meta-dogma.

The work of this chapter falls into six parts. What did the First Vatican Council dogmatically teach about dogma? Second, why did it teach that? Third, how can we recognize this teaching of the First Vatican Council as itself a legitimate development of dogma? That is, how can we recognize it as contained in the deposit of faith? Fourth, did the Second Vatican Council contradict this teaching, not in words, but in practice? Fifth, what must be true of dogmatic language if the dogma about dogma is true? This fifth question leads to a sixth and final issue, how to account for the universal accessibility of dogma.

Dei Filius and the dogma about dogma

In four successive chapters the First Vatican Council's dogmatic constitution on the Catholic faith addressed God, revelation, faith, and the relation between faith and reason.[1] Chapter 1 teaches that God is one and living, "Creator and Lord of heaven and earth, almighty, eternal, immense, incomprehensible, infinite in intellect and will and every perfection."[2] The chapter and its canons reprove the errors of atheism, materialism, and pantheism. They condemn the teaching that the world emanates from the divine substance and teach rather that the world is created from nothing. The second chapter teaches that though God can be known by the light of reason as the origin and end of the world, revelation is absolutely nec-

---

1. See the papers from the symposium on *Dei Filius* by Simon Gaine, OP, Rudi te Velde, and others published in *Nova et Vetera* (English), 20 (2022), and especially that of Andrew Meszaros, "*Dei Filius* IV: On the Development of Dogma," 909–38.

2. *Dei Filius*, chap. 1. My translation. DH 3001; ND 327.

essary for man to know the supernatural end to which he has been called and the things of divinity that surpass reason's scope. This revelation is to be found in the books of Scripture and the apostolic tradition entrusted to the Church. Moreover, "that meaning of Sacred Scripture is to be held as the true one which holy mother Church has held and holds," for it belongs to her to judge this true sense of Scripture.[3] Chapter 3 teaches that faith is a supernatural virtue by which we believe to be true what God has revealed, "not because we perceive the intrinsic truth of things by the light of natural reason but on account of the authority of the revealing God."[4] The Catholic Church is the guardian and teacher of what is revealed. Therefore, "all those things are to be believed by divine and Catholic faith that are contained in the word of God, written or handed on, and are proposed by the Church as divinely revealed, whether by a solemn judgment or by her universal and ordinary teaching authority."[5]

The things the Church proposes to be believed by divine faith in a solemn judgment are called dogmas. Chapter 4 first explains that what we know by faith on the one hand and by reason on the other form two distinct orders of knowledge, and that in the order of what we know by faith there are mysteries properly so called that we could not know unless they were revealed. It declares, second, that reason enlightened by faith can nonetheless come to some understanding of these mysteries. Third, it declares that since the two orders have their origin in God, they cannot contradict one another, and therefore, every assertion contrary to revealed truth is false. The knowledge of faith, moreover, is an aid and guide to the knowledge attainable by reason. Last, the chapter reinforces the distinction between the orders, the distinction between philosophy and the doctrine of faith, in the following terms.

The doctrine of faith which God has revealed has not been proposed to us as some philosophical invention to be perfected by human genius, but as a divine deposit handed over to the spouse of Christ [the Church] to be faithfully guarded and infallibly declared.[6]

---

3. *Dei Filius*, chap. 2. My translation. DH 3007; ND 217.
4. *Dei Filius*, chap. 3. My translation. DH 3008; ND 118.
5. *Dei Filius*, chap. 3. My translation. DH 3011; ND 121.
6. *Dei Filius*, chap. 4. My translation. DH 3020; ND 136.

Then the council adds a dogma about dogma in the following words.

From this it follows also that that the meaning of dogmas which holy mother Church has once declared is to be perpetually retained, nor can one ever depart from that sense under the guise and in the name of a more profound understanding.[7]

This the council confirms with a citation from the *Commonitorium* of Vincent of Lérins. After first declaring his hope for dogmatic development in the course of the time of the Church, he says: "May understanding, knowledge, and wisdom therefore increase and make great and powerful progress, both for the individual and for the whole Church." But he adds that this progress is a progress only in understanding what has been revealed: what dogmatic progress attains to must remain "precisely in its own kind, which is to say in the same teaching, in the same sense, and in the same judgment."[8] Last, the council expresses the same teaching in the third canon attached to the chapter.

If anyone says that it is possible that at some time and according to the progress of science a meaning is to be attributed to the dogmas once proposed by the Church that is different from that which the Church has understood and still understands, *anathema sit.*[9]

The dogma about dogma is to the effect that the meaning of dogma does not change, that once declared, its perfection is not found in altering its sense according to the progress of human knowledge, scientific or philosophical. Rather, the Church's duty is to guard and declare it just as she does the deposit that has been entrusted to her, and it is evidently not guarded or declared if the dogmas that express it are relative from age to age to the surrounding scientific and philosophical culture. The meaning and truth of dogma is as immutable as the meaning and truth of revelation, as the meaning and truth of the word of God, of which the expressions of revelation in the words of Scripture and Tradition and Dogma participate.

---

7. *Dei Filius*, chap. 4. My translation. DH 3020; ND 136.
8. Vincent of Lérins, *Commonitorium*, chap. 23. My translation.
9. *Dei Filius*, chap. 4, canon 3. My translation. DH 3043; ND 139.

VATICAN I AND THE DOGMA ABOUT DOGMA 141

The reason for the dogma about dogma

Dogmas do not come from nowhere. Of course, they come from the revealed word of God. In another sense, they do not come except from a historically conditioned moment of the Church's mindful possession of the deposit of faith. Defending the deposit evidently means defending it against actual, historically instantiated threats. Arianism threatened the deposit in the fourth century. Rationalism and "semi-rationalism" threatened it in the nineteenth century.

Rationalism is evidently the background to chapters 1 and 2 of *Dei Filius*. The necessity of the world as a moment of divine self-constitution, pantheism, and the denial that creation is *ex nihilo*, all of which are common positions within German idealism, are reproved in chapter 1 and its canons, as well as materialism.[10] The idea that God is known only by a tradition passed down from an original revelation to Adam and Eve ("traditionalism"), and Kantian agnosticism with regard to the existence of God are targeted in chapter 2.[11]

It is "semi-rationalism" that is the background to chapter 4, however. This position holds that once revelation has disclosed to us such mysteries as the Trinity and the Incarnation, then human reason can come to know them by its own power—human reason can come to know them with the same understanding it brings to the knowledge of purely natural and created things. Those who held positions to this effect were Georg Hermes (1775–1831), Anton Günther (1783–1863), and Jakob Frohschammer (1821–1893).[12] That human reason extends to proving such things as the Triunity of God and the Incarnation of the Son of God is reproved in chapter 4, where the council teaches that such mysteries cannot be known

---

10. Jean Michel Alfred Vacant, *Études Théologiques sur les Constitutions du Concile du Vatican d'après les Actes du Concile. La Constitution Dei Filius*. 2 vols. (Paris: Delhomme et Briguet, 1895), 1:207–15. For the history of the redaction of *Dei Filius*, see Roger Aubert, *Vatican I* (Paris: Éditions de l'Orante, 1964), 56–60, 126–31, 182–94.

11. Vacant, *Concile du Vatican*, 1:301–2.

12. For the condemnation of the writings of Georg Hermes, see Gregory XVI, *Dum acerbissimas* (1835), DH 2738–2740, repeated by Pius IX, *Qui pluribus* (1846), DH 2775–2777, ND 106–108; and of the writings of Anton Günther, Pius IX, *Eximiam tuam* (1857), DH 2828–2831; and of the writings of Jacob Frohschammer, Pius IX, *Gravissimas inter* (1862), DH 2850–2861. These condemnations were repeated in the *Syllabus* of Pius IX (1864), DH 2908–2914, ND 112/8–112/11.

unless revealed, and that, even if we come to some understanding of them, they remain hidden to us in their ultimate intelligibility.[13]

The semi-rationalism of Anton Günther, however, not only obscured the boundary between faith and reason, but also proposed a novel interpretation of the force of the Church's dogmatic statements.[14] Such statements, Günther held, are made with the philosophical and scientific conceptualities available at the time of the definition. With further scientific and philosophic progress, however, they can be given a better but different sense than that which was originally understood. The condemnation of this view is what we have quoted above from chapter 4 and its third canon.

Now, we are interested not so much in Günther's own view of things, but how his view was understood by the council, and so, what exactly was condemned. The council's understanding, however, was the understanding of Johannes Franzelin (1816–1886).[15] Here is Franzelin in his great work, the *Tractatus de divina traditione et scriptura*, from Thesis XXV on Tradition, "On the joint task of the guardians and teachers of the faith, and on the manner of explaining the deposit."

Günther distinguished historical facts recorded in the Scriptures and the understanding of these facts. He called this understanding the "doctrinal tradition" and the "conscience of the Church." He further came to the considered opinion that this understanding received constant additions by force of philosophical science, to the point that what was imperfect in the Apostles compared to the holy Fathers was still by no means perfect in them and even completely lacking on account of a defect of true philosophy, until at length it could now, once the true (Güntherian) philosophy was discovered, lay down a path by which it might attain to the highest understanding of the whole of revealed doctrine and so could proceed to the conclusion of the "doctrinal tradition," or, as he himself said, to that beyond which there is nothing further. Within this progress of science and

---

13. For a detailed history of the redaction of chapter 4 of *Dei Filius*, see Georges Paradis, SJ, "Foi et raison au premier Concile du Vatican," in *De Doctrina Concilii Vaticani Primi: Studia Selecta*, 221–81 (Vatican City: Libreria Editrice Vaticana, 1969). This study first appeared in the *Bulletin de littérature ecclésiastique*, 63 (1962): 200–26, 268–292; 64 (1963): 9–25.

14. See the chapter on Günther in Aidan Nichols, OP, *Conversation of Faith and Reason: Modern Catholic Thought from Hermes to Benedict XVI* (Chicago: HillenbrandBooks, 2011).

15. Nor should it be thought that Franzelin misunderstood Günther—quite the contrary. Still, we are interested in what the council understands by its teaching, not in the first place in Güntherism.

by the explication of the truth through the course of the ages, it belongs to the magisterium of the Church to define that way of understanding dogmas among the various ways of doing so available at whatever time that is *most apt* for that time. In this definition, the Church is infallible because of the assistance of the Holy Spirit, but not because the defined way of understanding the dogmas is simply speaking perfect and true. Rather, given the progress of the human intellect in the other sciences and generally in philosophy, in psychology, in the philosophy of nature, even that definition already given by the Church will appear imperfect, and another, more perfect, will be necessary. Therefore, the definitions that have been published by the Church in various ages are, Günther says, to be recognized as containing *some truth*, but not the truth and the true understanding of the dogmas simply speaking. So the definition of Ephesus about the unity of the person of Christ contains *some truth* in it, that Christ the man was conjoined to God the Word from the beginning of his existence, but did not contain nor could not contain the supreme understanding of the dogma, because the philosophy of the 19th century was lacking to the fifth century.[16]

The supreme understanding of the Incarnation, according to Günther, is that two persons, divine and human, are united in one composed person.[17]

Now, it is just this understanding of dogmatic relativity to philosophy that we find in Franzelin's schema for the First Vatican Council, parts of which became, at length, *Dei Filius*.[18] Hence the denial of the council that the doctrine of faith is not some philosophy to be improved by human ingenuity in the course of time. And hence the council's insistence that dogma defined in the fifth or the sixteenth century be understood today as it was understood when defined. Here is how Franzelin puts the issue in his note to chapter 11 of his proposed schema.

[P]rogress in the understanding of revealed truth is perversely understood by some. For they think that this most of all depends on philosophical science, and that theological disciplines are to be treated like philosophical ones (Syllabus of Errors, Prop 8). Hence they say that the understanding of dogmas varies in different ages on account of the diverse state of the philosophical sciences; in the Apos-

---

16. Johannes Baptist Franzelin, SJ, *Tractatus de Divina Traditione et Scriptura*, 3rd ed. (Rome: Typographia polyglotta, 1882), 304–5.

17. Franzelin, *De Divina Traditione*, 305, note 1.

18. See chap. 11 of Franzelin's draft schema "Contra errores ex rationalismo derivatos," redacted by the Theological Commission and distributed December 10, 1869, in Johannes Dominicus Mansi, *Sacrorum Conciliorum Nova et Amplissima Collectio*, vol. 50 (Graz: Akademische Druck – und Verlagsanstalt, 1961), 67–68. See also Vacant, *Concile du Vatican*, 2:282–87.

tles it was not indeed false but imperfect; in the holy Fathers it was more perfect than in the Apostles but still very far from its ultimate perfection; but now in virtue of the true philosophy and in the light of the sciences of more recent times the full understanding of revealed truths is to be attained to.... Thus, they say, in the fifth century there was excluded the *separation* of the two persons, one of the man Jesus and the other of the Son of God; but the condemnation of this separation included the unity of the person of Christ "according to the psychology of that time," and so there was defined one hypostasis or person in two natures. But according to the true philosophy of our age, they say, two persons ought now to be understood, divine and human, continuing in that union; and therefore there is not to be understood the real unity of the person of Christ, as was understood at that time, but one person composed from two persons.[19]

So, just as today for some, the unity of divinity and humanity in Christ is held to be a psychological unity, something achieved in consciousness, according as the man Jesus is perfectly given over to the divine Word, or according as he enjoys the beatific vision even in his earthly life.

It is supremely noteworthy that the Church's dogma about dogma is here seen to be Christologically motivated, just as was the teaching defined at Nicaea. There is indeed a "Christological concentration" of dogma on the level of the content of dogma, a notion dear to Henri de Lubac but also recognized by Cardinal Newman.[20] Here, the immutability of dogma connects us to the fact that the Incarnation does not subject eternity to time, as if the divine and human natures were changed by their union in Christ, but rather guarantees the capacity of human language to express divine truth once and for all within time, just as Jesus Christ is the same yesterday, today, and forever.

The truth of the third canon of chapter 4 of *Dei Filius*

If now we have some understanding of why the First Vatican Council undertook to distinguish philosophical progress from dogmatic stability

---

19. Mansi, 50:99–100. Franzelin does not name Günther in this note to chapter 11. He is mentioned in the *relatio* of Archbishop Simor of March 18, 1870, presenting a reformed draft of the *Constitutio De Fide Catholica* (Mansi, 51:48). Franzelin's schema and his notes are also reproduced in Vacant, *Concile du Vatican*, 1:570–608 for the schema and notes as a whole, and 605 for the note on chapter 11.

20. Newman, *Essay on Development*, 93–94, 324–26.

and to insist that dogmas maintain their meaning across the ages, how shall the dogma enunciated in the third canon of chapter 4 be vindicated? It is easy to see that given the claims of philosophers to express the truth of the Trinity and the Incarnation better than and very differently than that of the ancient councils, there was a high antecedent probability that such a definition take place.

The definition is easily discerned in Scripture and Tradition. I give Franzelin's justification of it from his *De traditione*.[21] He first notes that because things implicit in the deposit of faith become explicit, and because things once clearly proposed by the Church can be subsequently distorted and turned to a *"sensum alienum,"* those who are infallible guardians of faith must also be infallible teachers of faith.[22] This he establishes by noting the conjunction of guarding the deposit and teaching it in the Pastoral Letters of St. Paul.[23] Second, infallible explanation of the faith includes more clearly proposing it, more distinctly defining it, and sincerely defending it. The successors of the apostles as teachers in Matthew 28 and as those who have the Spirit of truth in John 14 cannot be guardians of the deposit without being able to carry through these very things of explaining, proposing, defining, and defending the faith.[24] And Franzelin invokes patristic witness for the role of the Lord and his Spirit in the discharge of this task by the successors of the apostles.[25] He notes expressly, however, that the discharge of this task by no means involves some new revelation, the closure of which has been previously defended (Thesis XXII). Rather the *explicatio* of the faith occurs by way of explicitly proposing what is implicit in the deposit, and doing so against error, and defining what has been obscurely expressed or what informs some practice.[26] This section closes by invoking the citation of Vincent of Lérins quoted by *Dei Filius*.

Then, third, Franzelin comes to Günther. Now, the denial of Günther's position and the truth of the third canon of chapter 4 of *Dei Filius*

---

21. See also Vacant, *Concile du Vatican*, 2:286–87, who first appeals to the immutability of truth in general.

22. Franzelin, *De Divina Traditione*, 295.

23. Franzelin, *De Divina Traditione*, 296–97.

24. Franzelin, *De Divina Traditione*, 298.

25. Franzelin, *De Divina Traditione*, 298.

26. Franzelin, *De Divina Traditione*, 303.

are formally contained in Scripture. Franzelin's task is difficult therefore only because it is so simple. It is a matter of noticing how words and concepts work, what they are.

Definitions of faith must be believed with the force of the form of words and with the force of the concepts with which they are proposed. For this comes about by the assistance of the Holy Spirit, such that nothing is contained in these definitions of the Church that is not objectively revealed and immutably true.[27]

Definitions of faith, after all, merely recapitulate what is contained in the immutably true word of God. Thus, "it can never be the case that a concept once used does not remain infallibly true for all time and as something revealed by God as dogma."[28]

When the council adopts and defines this understanding of defined dogma, it fixes for us something in the order of our knowledge of revelation correlative to what the Council of Trent did in the sacramental order.[29] The sacraments confer the grace of which God alone is the creator. Dogmas manifest the truth of which God alone is the speaker. The sacraments do things that only God can do unto our being saved. Dogmas speak a word that only God can speak unto our knowledge of the economy of salvation. Insofar as Pius IX rightly discerns a sort of working out of Protestant principles of the sixteenth century in the atheism, materialism, and pantheism of the nineteenth century, as he observes in the prologue to *Dei Filius*,[30] it is altogether just that he sees the Vatican Council as continuing in the steps of the Council of Trent.

The Second Vatican Council and dogmatic continuity

The First Vatican Council thus gives us to understand that dogmatic truth maintains its sense and truth through time, and what was affirmed, say, at Ephesus in 432 is to be affirmed today, and that therefore divine and human properties are to be affirmed of one and the same Son, person, hypostasis. The Second Vatican Council also speaks of dogma and its development in the Constitution on Divine Revelation, *Dei Verbum*, but without

27. Franzelin, *De Divina Traditione*, 305–06.
28. Franzelin, *De Divina Traditione*, 306.
29. Meszaros, *The Prophetic Church*, 225–28.
30. Tanner, *Decrees of the Ecumenical Councils*, 2:804.

VATICAN I AND THE DOGMA ABOUT DOGMA   147

using the word (*evolutio*). It does so in speaking of the Church's tradition (*traditio*) of revelation. We are told that this tradition "progresses" in that there is a growth of understanding of what is handed on (no. 8), even as, relative to the deposit of revelation, the First Vatican Council spoke of a progress in understanding and knowledge and wisdom (*Dei Filius*, chap. 4).[31]

Dei Verbum adds to the teaching of *Dei Filius* a carefully considered list of the ways by which development occurs: by contemplation and study; by the experience of an intimate understanding of divine things; by episcopal preaching (no. 8). There is, then, the logical putting of two and two together in study, the connatural knowledge of the mysteries by our conformation to them, and the discernment of those truths that are espied by surveying the great canvass of the divine plan recorded across both testaments of the Scriptures and articulated in the preaching of the liturgy. All three of these ways were addressed in the previous chapter.

Nothing the Second Vatican Council says denies the canon of the First Vatican Council on the abiding character of the sense and truth of dogma, and it repeats the teaching that papal definitions of dogma are irreformable in the Dogmatic Constitution on the Church, *Lumen gentium* (no. 25). However, it has been thought that the council denies this abiding character in practice. It is thought, moreover, that it does so in the one document where it *does* claim to "develop" (*evolvere*) prior teaching, the Declaration on Religious Freedom, *Dignitatis humanae* (no. 1c). Here, the council claims to examine "the sacred tradition and doctrine of the Church, from which it proffers new things, always in harmony with the old" (no. 1a), evoking Mt 13:52, a traditional warrant for development.[32]

31. The language of "progress" (*proficere*) is from Vincent of Lérins. The First Council references Vincent; the Second does not. He had fallen from the favor he enjoyed in the nineteenth century because of suspected semi-Pelagianism. For discussion and exoneration of Vincent, see Thomas G. Guarino, *Vincent of Lérins and the Development of Christian Doctrine* (Grand Rapids, MI: Baker Academic, 2013), xx–xxix.

32. The literature on *Dignitatis humanae*—historical, hermeneutical, controversial—is extensive, to say the least. I list four introductory studies by distinguished Catholic theologians. F. Russell Hittinger reads the declaration in continuity with previous magisterial teaching in "The Declaration on Religious Liberty, *Dignitatis Humanae*," 359–382, in *Vatican II: Renewal Within Tradition*, ed. Matthew L. Lamb and Matthew Levering (Oxford: Oxford University Press, 2008); Nicholas J. Healy Jr. notes interpretative issues and the most important ways of receiving it in

Dignitatis humanae is divided into two parts, the first of which asserts the religious freedom of the individual and the religious liberty of the Church by appeal to reason, the second of which asserts these same things by appeal to revelation.

Part 1 asserts first that all persons possess the natural right of freedom from coercion in matters religious (no. 2), and second that religious groups or communities are also by right free from coercion (no. 4), understanding that these rights extend to both private and public acts (no. 3). These are the two main assertions of part 1. *Dignitatis humanae* presents reasons for these assertions. That persons have such a right to freedom in matters religious is grounded in their obligation to seek the truth about God and their duty to conform their lives to the religious duties they discover (nos. 2 and 3). The right is in the first place a right not be interfered with in the discharge of religious duty, and it should be recognized as a civil right (no. 2). However, since the pursuit of religious truth and the performance of religious duty serve the good of the citizens of the state, the state has an obligation to promote the religious life of its citizens (no. 3)—as the United States arguably does, for instance, by providing chaplains in the armed services. But since the proper end of the state is to care for the temporal common good of man, it is not within its competence to direct or prevent religious activity that is ordered to an end beyond the power of the state to realize (no. 3). That religious freedom extends to communities as well as individuals is founded on the social nature of man (no. 3). Furthermore, it can be that according to circumstance of the prevalence of one religion within a state, it is proper for the state to recognize this religion in its law and constitution (no. 6), as long as the rights of all citizens to religious freedom are respected. This is the sole mention of any possible "establishment" of Catholicism.

"*Dignitatis Humanae*," 367–92, in *The Reception of Vatican II*, ed. Matthew L. Lamb and Matthew Levering (Oxford: Oxford University Press, 2017); Avery Cardinal Dulles, SJ, defends the declaration as a homogenous development of Catholic doctrine in "*Dignitatis Humanae* and the Development of Catholic Doctrine," 43–67, in *Catholicism and Religious Freedom: Contemporary Reflections on Vatican II's Declaration on Religious Liberty*, ed. Kenneth Grasso and Robert P. Hunt (Lanham, MD: Sheed and Ward, 2006); finally, Thomas G. Guarino notes the discontinuities of the declaration while maintaining that it offers no substantial reversal of defined doctrine in *The Disputed Teachings of Vatican II: Continuity and Reversal in Catholic Doctrine* (Grand Rapids, MI: Eerdmans, 2018), 177–97.

Part 2 turns to a consideration of religious freedom in the light of revelation. The individual person's right to religious freedom is grounded in the freedom of the act of faith (no. 9). The voluntary nature of Christian faith is witnessed to in the example of Christ and the apostles (nos. 10–11). The freedom of the Church to evangelize, worship, and conduct her own affairs is grounded in the authority given her by Christ, the Son of God, and so is a divine authority (no. 13).

Where is it to be thought that *Dignitatis humanae* revokes prior magisterial teaching? There is no teaching or even mention of the Church's right to rule and so to punish (coerce) her own members. Prior teaching touching on that is therefore presumably left "intact" (no. 1). The declaration rather addresses the *state's* intrinsic lack of any authority for religious coercion, and it refuses by its silence on the matter to countenance the ecclesial request that the state exercise its power on her behalf.[33] Pope Leo XIII already taught the state's incompetence in and of itself in matters religious.[34] It is the silence on establishment that provokes the charge of a reversal of teaching. Just so, Avery Dulles picks out two themes in previous papal teaching of the nineteenth century. First, "did these popes teach as a matter of divine law that Roman Catholicism should be established as the religion of the state?" For *Dignitatis humanae* never says so, and, in its silence on establishment, seems to deny that there is such a universal norm. Second, "Did they reject the religious freedom of non-Catholics, individually and corporately, to practice their religion publicly and to propagate their beliefs?"[35]

In *Mirari vos* (1832), Pope Gregory XVI opposes religious indifferentism, the opinion that one profession of faith is as good as another for obtaining salvation, as long as a morality that conforms to objective norms is followed (no. 13), and that on this basis, "freedom of conscience" relative to religion is to be recognized for all (no. 14).[36] In the same vein, in *Quanta cura* of 1864 Pope Pius IX opposes the same error of indif-

33. Thomas Pink, "Conscience and Coercion: Vatican II's Teaching on Religious Freedom Changed Policy, Not Doctrine," *First Things* Aug/Sept 2012: https://www.firstthings.com/article/2012/08/conscience-and-coercion, at p. 9. Nor is there any judgment on the Church's past invocation of the secular arm.

34. Leo XIII, *Immortale Dei* (1885); DH 3168.

35. Dulles, "*Dignitatis Humanae* and Development," 51.

36. Gregory XVI, *Mirari vos*; DH 2730.

150   CHAPTER 6

ferentism, according to which "the best constitution of society and civil progress ... require that human society be conducted and governed without regard being had to religion any more than if it did not exist," "and without any distinction being made between true religion and false religion."[37] *Dignitatis humanae* by no means endorses such indifferentism as the basis of civil organization. Rather, the state is to promote the religious life of its citizens, without, however, presuming to direct it. As to distinguishing true and false religions, Leo XIII subsequently says in *Immortale Dei* (1885) that the Church does not condemn "those rulers who, for the sake of securing some great good or hindering some great evil, allow patiently custom or usage to be a kind of sanction for each kind of religion having its place in the State."[38] A principle of toleration is enunciated not on any modern liberal theory of government, but on the natural law obligation of states and rulers to maintain civil peace. In other words, Leo takes account just as *Dignitatis humanae* does of the religious pluralism of many societies. And for that matter, as has been said, neither is *Dignitatis humanae* silent about the possibility, circumstances dictating, of the state recognition of Catholicism (no. 6).

There are also, however, Proposition 55 of Pius IX's Syllabus of Errors (1869), which reproves the assertion that the Church is to be separated from the state, and Proposition 77, which reproves the following: "In our age it is no longer advisable that the Catholic religion be the only State religion, excluding all other forms of worship."[39] The first is from an allocution on the persecution of the Church in Columbia. The second is from an allocution on the situation of the Church in Spain. Is the implication of Proposition 77 that Catholicism ought to be the state religion in *every* age, and so also in "this age"? Or does "in our age" place, as it were, a sort of expiration date on it, in that we must distinguish what is appropriate to diverse ages? Dulles follows Roger Aubert for the second interpretation.[40] How one is to generate a universal affirmative statement as to what every state is obliged to do in every age and in every circumstance from these

---

37. Pius IX, *Quanta cura*, in *The Papal Encyclicals 1740–1878*, ed. Claudia Carlen (Beloit, Kans.: McGrath Publishing Co., 1981), 382.

38. Leo XIII, *Immortale Dei*; DH 3176.

39. Pius IX, Syllabus of Errors; DH 2955, 2977.

40. Dulles, "*Dignitatis Humanae* and Development," 53.

quite determinate and prudential judgments of Pius IX and Leo XIII, and to recognize it as a universally applicable divine law, is a puzzle.

As to the second theme Dulles articulates, the denial of freedom to non-Catholics, we have already adverted to the principle of toleration of Leo XIII in *Immortale Dei*. This second theme, rephrased, concerns the recognition of religious freedom as a human right, suitably enacted by law as a civil right. What the popes reprove, however, is religious liberty asserted on the basis of "indifferentism," which by no means is the foundation of the argument *Dignitatis humanae* gives for this right, quite the contrary.

Dignitatis humanae says in one and the same breath that it leaves intact Catholic teaching as to the duties of individuals and societies or states to the true religion, the Catholic religion, and that it wants to develop the teaching of recent popes on the rights of persons vis-à-vis the state (no. 1). What, then, is really new in this declaration? For Dulles, it is the Church's recognition of a natural right of every man to immunity from state religious coercion and a positive right to be supported (if not directed) in discharging the obligation to seek religious truth, even if the individual does not in fact discharge this obligation, while at the same time rightly not giving recognition to any right to disseminate error.[41]

The necessity of this recognition is appreciated today when we consider the Church's claim that she herself enjoys an irrefragable freedom, one grounded in the natural law and in revelation, to evangelize all men and all societies (no. 13). The council fathers here think globally, and not just within the parameters of putting Humpty Dumpty together again in Europe after the Enlightenment, after the smashup of the French Revolution, after the passing of the Holy Roman Empire. The Church cannot claim before religiously differentiated and religiously indifferent societies that she has a right to exercise this freedom if there remains the suspicion that once it is politically possible, she will invoke the secular arm to disenfranchise the adherents of other religions and even of nonreligious ideologies. Therefore she renounces any right to do so by recognizing the equally irrefragable right of individuals and societies to pursue the truth and live by what they think they have found of it. In this light, we see how

41. Dulles, "*Dignitatis Humanae* and Development," 58–59.

152   CHAPTER 6

necessary the Declaration on Religious Freedom was and remains when we think of Christians and the Church today in places like Saudi Arabia, China, Russia, Pakistan, and elsewhere.

The assertion of the rights of the individual and of the rights of the Church and so of Catholic Christian citizens does not relieve believing citizens of their own obligation to Christianize the societies they live in, and to bring them to that state where the objective moral order and un-prejudiced openness to revealed truth that the ideal of a secular Christendom, the outline of which was elaborated by Charles Journet long before the council, can be realized.[42] The idea of secular Christendom is the idea of a regime where Church membership makes one an ideal citizen, but is not required for legal citizenship (as in "consecrational Christendom").[43] In other words, according to Journet, *Dignitatis humanae* makes for a new application of the principle of the subordination of the temporal to the spiritual order. As Roger Nutt and Michael De Salvo put it, "*Dignitatis Humanae* helps make possible the existence of states not just Christian but *freely* Christian."[44] They will be Christian in a new, higher way.

These few pages on *Dignitatis humanae*, wholly inadequate as they are for certainly adjudicating the charge that the declaration denies prior infallible magisterial teaching, are nonetheless useful for indicating the issues raised in addressing the question, and are therefore in turn useful for thinking about development. The issues are both historical and theological. Historically, what did the prior papal magisterium teach as to the establishment of the Church by the state, and why did it teach this? What did the declaration teach, and on what grounds? Theologically, did what the popes of the nineteenth century teach amount to an infallible teaching that every state is bound, or ideally bound, to establish the Church? If they did not propose their teaching as infallible—"defining and declaring" as with, say, the Marian dogmas—did the acceptance of their teaching by the bishops amount to an exercise of the universal ordinary magis-

---

42. The council recognizes this obligation in the Decree on the Apostolate of Laity, *Apostolicam actuositatem*, nos. 7 and 14.

43. Charles Journet, *The Church of the Word Incarnate: An Essay in Speculative Theology*, vol. 1, *The Apostolic Hierarchy*, trans. A. H. C. Downes (London: Sheed and Ward, 1955), 214–15.

44. Roger W. Nutt and Michael R. De Salvo, "The Debate on *Dignitatis Humanae* at Vatican II: The Contribution of Charles Cardinal Journet," *The Thomist* 85 (2021): 175–226, at 180 (emphasis added), and see 225–26.

VATICAN I AND THE DOGMA ABOUT DOGMA   153

terium? The principal difficulty to asserting this, to my mind, lies simply in determining whether there really was a determinate teaching that proposed a determinate relation of Church and state that could evidently be applied to all the modern nations of Europe and the Americas. If we cannot do that, the charge against *Dignitatis humanae* must be dropped for lack of evidence.

The universal accessibility of dogma

The implication of accessibility

When the third canon to chapter 4 of *Dei Filius* refers to the sense or meaning of dogma, it speaks of it as what the Church "has understood and still understands." The use of the present and the present perfect tenses is of course deliberate. It implies that the temporal difference between the past time of the dogma's definition and the present time in which it is reasserted makes no difference in meaning. What the Christian people of Constantinople understood by Chalcedon in the fifth century is what the Catholic people of Chicago understand by it today. Moreover, the singular subject of this understanding, "Church," is also significant. Since the Church is apostolic, there is unanimity across time, a sort of diachronic unity of faith. But this one, single Church is the Catholic Church, catholic or universal not just in time but in space. The implication is that the cultural differences between Germans and Americans now, or between Italians and Vietnamese now, as also the cultural differences between, say, the Ugandans and the Europeans of the nineteenth century, an age of great missionary enterprise and the very age in which the Church enunciated the dogma about dogma, make for no difference in meaning. And there is the associated implication that the French and the Ugandans had and still have equal access to this same meaning. In addition to diachronic, there is also synchronic unity. The meaning of dogma, it seems, is transtemporal and transcultural. This is the abiding meaning of Vincent of Lérins's dictum that the teaching of the Church is believed *ubique, semper, et ab omnibus.*[45]

---

45. Vincent of Lérins, *Commonitorium*, chap. 2.

That the meaning of dogma, like the meaning of the gospel itself, should be accessible to all cannot come as a surprise to any Catholic Christian. Just because the gospel is first of all proposed to us in a story where people live in a highly structured society of law and custom, and just because it is proposed to us in a story embedded in a mixed economy of agriculture and manufacture, and just because it has to do with love and hate, sin and forgiveness, birth and death, God and man, it is accessible to the ordinary sensibility and ordinary language of every time and place. It may be that there is an ancient political background to the characterization of a ruler as "shepherd" of his people. It may be that there is an important Old Testament background, in Ezekiel especially, to Jesus's calling himself the Good Shepherd. Still, when he says that the Good Shepherd leaves the ninety-nine to seek out the lost sheep, there is a sort of fundamental meaning to the parable that cannot be lost on anyone. Or again, one does not have to be a farmer or scavenger to understand what finding buried treasure in a field means.

Now, dogma declares the nature and moral character of the God revealed in the story of Jesus of Nazareth, as well as the identity of the one who reveals it, Jesus the Son of God. Whenever we meet a "dogma," we can always let it sink back into the original matrix of revelation it is defining or clarifying. We can always let the doctrine of the Trinity sink back into the accounts of Jesus's prayer to his Father and his promise of an Advocate. When we see "transubstantiation" at Trent, we can always think back to the words of institution, "This is my body," and note that the assertion is unqualified. And when we run into another rather extraordinary word, at least in English, "consubstantial," we can think back to the one who said "the Father and I are one," or who said that only the Father knows the Son and only the Son know the Father.

There is also another thing to remark about the language of dogma, and that is its fundamentality. For instance, the Council of Trent teaches that the institution of sacramental confession is from divine law.[46] It says also that only priests have the power of binding and loosing sin, the power, that is, to absolve a penitent from sin in the sacrament of penance.[47]

46. 14th session, November 25, 1551, canon 6; DH 1706, ND 1646.
47. 14th session, canon 10; DH 1710, ND 1650.

VATICAN I AND THE DOGMA ABOUT DOGMA   155

Is there anything difficult here? "Law" is a sort of basic notion of the moral and political life, as an ordinance or rule governing action. We speak of the Ten Commandments as divine law, and sometimes as expressing the natural law. The Tridentine context presumes a distinction between ecclesiastical law and divine law, and wants us to confess that the sacrament of penance is divinely established and is no merely ecclesiastical arrangement. When Trent speaks of sin as something immoral in God's eyes, and of "power" as a capacity to effect some change, these are not difficult notions. They are not difficult except of course insofar as they are linked up with God, such that, to be sure, divine forgiveness is a supernatural mystery compared with the natural mystery of human forgiveness.

To deny that these notions are difficult or recondite, however, is not to say that there is no lengthy Scriptural and patristic track to follow for the complete understanding of them, not to mention a philosophical consideration of power and law, for after all, the more perfect understanding of a notion includes how it is used and the circumstances of its use and how it has been received from age to age. One wants to be aware also of voluntarist and seventeenth- and eighteenth-century distortions of the understanding of law. Nonetheless, the Tridentine canons just mentioned are surely within the competence of the mind to comprehend, no matter what our cultural distance from the Baroque.

An objection

Sometimes, however, it is alleged that the differences between the ancient conciliar use of some terms is so far removed from our own that we cannot be sure of what we are assenting to when we assent to the Church's dogma. The ground of this allegation is the ineluctable historical conditioning of the terms used, such that what the term wants to speak always comes with some cultural resonances, some time-bound noise. It follows, it is said, that we cannot hear the conciliar word clearly, and have not the skill to discern where the intended word of faith ends and the occluding noise begins. For instance, the Christological dogmas of the Church, collectively, teach that there is one person and two natures in Christ—one divine person and two natures, human and divine, in Christ. Karl Rahner was uncertain of what this teaching commits a Catholic to, because of the alleged amalgamation of grain and chaff in the culturally conditioned formulas that propose it to us. So, like Anton Günther before him, he thought he would still be thinking with the Church if he conceived the union of the human and divine in Christ as an event accomplished in the human consciousness of Christ.[48]

As to the general argument to the effect that we do not really understand what we are asserting today when we repeat the formulas of Nicaea and Chalcedon and so on, it ends up in a denial that revelation has ever occurred. If we cannot tell what was really spoken by the Church as an authoritative interpretation of Scripture and Tradition, then Scripture and Tradition are no longer capable of putting us in possession of the revealed word of God. And if we are not in possession of the revealed word, then it is not revealed. Just as a word that is not heard has not been spoken, or a lesson that has not been received by the student has not been taught by the teacher, so also for revelation, an equally relational reality: if the reality is not and cannot be received by faith, it is because it has not been disclosed.[49] It seems as well to follow from Rahner's argument that neither did the original framers of the dogmas really know that what they were saying was the word of revelation and nothing but that. And how can this line of thought not also affect what we think prophet and apostle, and even the Lord himself—historically conditioned as they all were—accomplished? The only revelation Rahner's argument leaves us with is the wordless revelation of the "supernatural existential," or as expressed more accessibly, the only thing we are left with is the wordless revelation of the God who has come close to every man in the offer of grace.

It is not surprising, of course, that such objections to the accessibility of dogma as Karl Rahner makes are made in the very age, our own, in which historicism is pervasive and to some seems obvious. His objection

48. For the theory of such historical conditioning of dogma as to produce amalgams of binding gospel truth and time-bound error, see Karl Rahner, "Yesterday's History of Dogma and Theology for Tomorrow," in *Theological Investigations*, vol. 18, 3–34, trans. Edward Quinn (New York: Crossroad, 1983); and for the Christology he thought he had license to assert within the "limits" of "classical Christology," see his *Foundations of Christian Faith: An Introduction to the Idea of Christianity*, trans. William Dych (New York: Seabury, 1978), 279–304. For analysis, see Thomas Joseph White, OP, *The Incarnate Lord: A Thomistic Study in Christology* (Washington, DC: The Catholic University of America Press, 2015), 91–100.

49. See John Lamont, "The Historical Conditioning of Church Dogma," *The Thomist* 60 (1996): 511–35.

is itself historically conditioned, very much a product of the peculiar prejudices of the post-Kantian age. So much we gather from Rahner's own view of the historical conditioning of dogma. Should not this retorsion of the argument back on itself, in which the head is seen to circle round and start swallowing the tail, induce us to reject it root and branch?

Person and nature

We must look more closely at the particular argument of radical reframers of dogma in the contemporary age, reframers of the Christological dogma of the Church. And it may be that the self-evidence of the truth of the Incarnation itself may let us recapture the evidentiary force of dogma, and let us regain a confidence in the realism and objectivity not only of our religious language but of language itself. The "covenant" between word and world of which George Steiner speaks is sealed by Christ.[50] That is, the original covenant between word and world, the covenant divinely spoken that founds the world in Genesis 1, that names it with human names in Genesis 2, is now fulfilled by the everlasting covenant Christ establishes in his blood.

"Person" and "nature" are, like the ideas of power and forgiveness, fundamental notions. How do they function in the declaration that Christ is one person subsisting (existing) in two natures? Fr. Rahner thinks this is not at all clear since, he alleges, if we say as the councils seem to give us leave to, that Jesus of Nazareth is God, we shall be led into error unless a very fundamental adjustment is made to this statement. Just as such, he says, asserting this statement in the way we assert ordinary statements about things in the world, we would be led to confuse divinity and humanity, one of the very things Chalcedon forbids us to do.[51] "Jesus is God," then,

---

50. George Steiner, *Real Presences* (London: Faber and Faber, 1989), 89–90: "The covenant between word and object, the presumption that being is, to a workable degree, 'sayable,' and that the raw materiality of existentiality has its analogue in the structure of narrative—we recount life, we recount life to ourselves—have been variously expressed. There are different stories of the history. In Adamic speech, the fit is perfect: all things are as Adam names them. Predication and essence coincide seamlessly. In Platonic idealism, to which the main Western metaphysics and epistemology have been satellite, the dialectical discourse, if critically and stringently pursued, will elevate the human intellect towards those archetypes of pure form of which words are, as it were, the transparency."

51. Rahner, *Foundations*, 290–91: "For when we say that Peter is a man, the statement expresses a real identification in the content of the subject and predicate nouns. But the meaning of 'is' in

---

158   CHAPTER 6

is not an ordinary identity statement, Rahner says. And in thinking about the basic constitution in being of Jesus Christ, we are perfectly at leave to suppose that the union of divinity and humanity in Christ is adequately accounted for by conceiving it as an event in the human consciousness of Christ, commending himself to the Father in an unsurpassable way, and experiencing God immediately in the vision of the Logos.[52] Could it be that Fr. Rahner simply forgets the communication of idioms that governs Chalcedon and Ephesus and Nicaea before it, according to which divine things are predicated, not of the human nature, but of the one *suppositum*, the one hypostasis, the Logos, born eternally of God, born temporally of Mary? He states it accurately just a few pages before his essay into Nestorianism.[53]

It is indeed an essay into Nestorianism, however, and is by no means permitted by Chalcedon. The recognition of two persons in Christ is explicitly forbidden when Chalcedon asserts one hypostasis, one person: "each nature is preserved and comes together in one person, one hypostasis, not parted or divided into two persons." A "person" is an individual, and who is this one person in Christ? Evidently, the one Son of God eternally born of the Father, now born in time of Mary the Virgin, "the only-begotten divine Word, the Lord Jesus Christ." "Word," "Son," "Lord," "Jesus," "Christ" all name the same one, the same one person or hypostasis. But as to natures, there are two of them in Christ, divine and human. Evidently, if Chalcedon is not a purely verbal solution to Christological controversy, there must be some real distinction between person and nature in Christ, between what there is one of and what there are two of in him. What is it? Since the person here is the Word, who comes down from heaven, since the person here is the Lord Christ who takes flesh "because of our salvation," which is to say, in order to work our salvation, it is con-

---

statements involving an interchange of predicates in Christology is not based on such a real identification.... For in and according to the humanity which we see when we say 'Jesus,' Jesus 'is' not God, and in and according to his divinity God 'is' not man in the sense of a real identification." This forgets that predication is of the supposit: "the rose is red" means that the thing that is rosy is also ruddy, not that rosiness is ruddiness. So also, to say that Jesus the man is God is not to say that humanity is divinity, but to say that the one who is human is one who is also divine.

52. Rahner *Foundations*, 253–54, 279–80, 302–4; "Dogmatic Reflections on the Knowledge and Self-Consciousness of Christ," in *Theological Investigations*, vol. 5, 193–215, trans. Karl H. Kruger (New York: Seabury Press, 1966), 206–7.

53. Rahner, *Foundations*, 287–88.

venient to say that the one person or hypostasis in Christ is one *agent*, and agent does nicely as a synonym for person. There is one agent, one doer, one actor in Christ, the Word of God, begotten of God, who as man is called Jesus and who as fulfilling his mission among us is called Christ.

And of the natures, which remain two, we can say of them compatibly with identifying the one person as one agent, that they name two agencies—they name two ways of being an agent, two ways of exercising agency. A man who is both smith and carpenter exercises his agency as a carpenter in making a stool from the lumber in his shop. He exercises quite another agency, the agency of a smith, in making a wrought iron stool. To say that Chalcedon commits us to confessing one agent possessing two agencies, one Word of God possessing not only the divine agency he holds in common with Father and Spirit, but also our human way of being an agent, adequately states what the dogma asserts. Of course, to find out who the Agent is, and what his agencies accomplish, we must read Scripture.

An important question at just this juncture is whether this restatement entails that we have changed the conceptual meaning of the dogma, whether in fact concepts have been exchanged: the concept of person for the concept of agent, the concept of nature for the concept of agency. The answer is that in fact nothing has been changed by the words, and no concept has been exchanged for a different one. In context, it should be fairly clear that agent and person cover much if not exactly the same ground and have the same meaning. "Treat me like a person" is pretty much the same as "treat me like an agent—someone *compos sui.*" Again, if natures are ways of operating, species-defining ways in which a substance makes its way in the world, then "agency," in the above sense stipulated by the context, does the same work, brings the same reality to mind.[54]

Now, the way in which the concepts are worked out in the process of stating the truth of the Incarnation, the way we see they must work themselves out in making sense of the Chalcedonian settlement, according to which "person" names an individual-with-a-nature, an actor with a way of acting, and nature names a basic way of acting according to which, within

---

54. "Agency" here designates the principle of acting, of doing, of operating as an agent. Recall the standard definitions of nature: a principle of motion and rest in that to which it belongs essentially and not accidentally (Aristotle), or the first principle of the operations of a substance (Thomas).

the world, we distinguish species from one another (canine, bovine, human), this way is also a sort of self-evidencing of their rightness, appropriateness, and truth. Person and nature remain basic words without which it is difficult to imagine us making our way in the real world full as it is of human agents and their typical, natural way of moving about in the world of things and other persons. But just so, they show in their own order the truth of the Incarnation. The revealed word can get itself into human words just as the subsistent Word of God can get himself into—express himself in—a human nature assumed in the womb of Mary. The possibility of this putting human words to use in order to express revealed truth is guaranteed by the fact that we really are addressed by God, and is itself a testimony to the supernatural character of both the event of the Incarnation and the conciliar teaching. To repeat, the covenant of the Incarnation reestablishes for us the original covenant between word and world of which Steiner speaks.

The statement "Jesus of Nazareth is God" is thus very much an "ordinary" identity statement. It is an ordinary identity statement according to the analysis of classical logic, where the predicate brings to light something true but previously unexpressed of the subject.[55] Just as the Word gets himself into the words of Scripture without compromising his transcendence, so he gets himself into the humanity of Jesus, and so, subsequently, does he get himself into the dogmatic language of the Church. For just as all words are knockoffs of the Word by whom the heavens and earth were made, and scriptural words knockoffs of the revealed Word, so the humanity of Jesus—which is a nature that is a created participation of the divinity of which the Word is the perfect expression and so another knockoff—inserts the Word into the world and history in a more intense way. But in all these ways in which the Word becomes one of its possible created expressions, he adds nothing to himself, and becomes what is other to him by assuming to himself some created thing. He does this, however, without change or deformation either to what is assumed or to himself. He does this without change or deformation of what is assumed because in taking to himself scriptural words or the humanity of Jesus,

---

55. Not according to modern logic, of course, which merely relates things but does not say what they are. See Henry Veatch, *Two Logics*, chap. 1.

the assumption presupposes the very creation and so the integrity of the things assumed—whether the words of Scripture or the nature assumed from Mary. He does this without change or deformation to himself because he is not defined by what is not him, and so can become it without ceasing to be himself.[56]

Common sense and the magisterium on dogmatic language

In the aftermath of Catholic Modernism, Réginald Garrigou-Lagrange (1877–1964) undertook a sustained vindication of the general accessibility, transcultural and transtemporal, of Catholic dogmatic pronouncements in a book entitled *Le Sens commun: La philosophie de l'être et les formules dogmatiques*.[57] The occasion for this long argument was the theory of dogma offered by Édouard Le Roy (1870–1954). According to Le Roy, dogmatic statements have a purely practical meaning. They do not inform us positively about the subjects of their affirmations, but merely direct our practical action.[58] We confess as Catholics, for instance, that God is personal, that Jesus returned to life after his death, that the consecrated elements at Mass are the Body and Blood of Christ. But these statements tell us nothing about God in himself, or about the nature of the life of Christ today, or about the ontology of the Eucharist. That God is personal directs us to treat God like a person—to deal with him so.[59] The resurrection of Christ tells us to pray to him and to obey him as if he were alive. And as for the Eucharist, we are to worship the consecrated Bread and Wine as if they were the bodily and personal presence of Christ.

---

56. The same point is sometimes made by saying that divine revelation and the Incarnation establish a real relation of created things—words, the humanity of Jesus—to divinity, but no real relation of divinity to created things.

57. The first edition was in 1909, but the standard edition is the third, reviewed and corrected (Paris: Nouvelle Librairie Nationale, 1922). I will cite the translation, *Thomistic Common Sense: The Philosophy of Being and the Development of Doctrine*, trans. Matthew K. Minerd (Steubenville, Ohio: Emmaus Academic, 2021).

58. Édouard Le Roy, "Qu'est-ce qu'un dogme?" *Le Quinzaine* 63 (1905): 495–526, which was reprinted in his *Dogme et critique* (Paris: Librairie Bloud et Cie, 1907).

59. See the analysis of Le Roy's proposal of 1905 by Léonce de Grandmaison, SJ, "What Is a Dogma?" in *Defending the Faith: An Anti-Modernist Anthology*, 213–41, edited and translated by William Marshner (Washington, DC: The Catholic University of America Press, 2017).

Le Roy defended this proposal on the grounds that if we take an "intellectualist" view of dogma and suppose dogmas inform us about their subjects, they must do so either in commonsense terms or in technical scientific or philosophical terms. If the latter, they are inaccessible to the ordinary Catholic. If the former, they bring down holy and transcendent realities to a language that is incapable of naming the real, a language expressing fictions of our convenience but not facts. Whence his mistrust of commonsense language?

Underlying Le Roy's proposal as to the practical meaning of dogma is indeed a theory about the meaning of ordinary language. Here he follows Henri Bergson (1859–1941), whose star was still ascendant in the first part of the twentieth century. For Le Roy and Bergson, the real that surrounds us is properly known only in philosophical intuition, and it is something flowing and oceanic, and not composed of discrete and separate things. It is *la durée*, where everything is immanent to everything else, rather like the Heraclitean flux known to first-year students of the standard history of philosophy. By our common language, to be sure, with our names common and proper, we pick things out and treat them as separate and stable things. But this is so only for our practical purposes. Common language, the common sense of common life, therefore, is radically nominalist. The names are our conventions for our convenience's sake; they do not render the real to us in its own reality.

Garrigou-Lagrange, on the other hand, has a much greater confidence in the realism of the Bible and Tradition taken at their word, even, a commonsense word. But of course, it was incumbent on him to defend his confidence. The key to his defense is that commonsense terms, even as technical, metaphysical terms, all do their work within the single horizon of being, the subject of the Aristotelian metaphysics. And just as the ordinary man knows that the holy is above him and beyond his imagination, so the Catholic metaphysician understands how the technical terms of metaphysics can be analogically applied to the one who, as *Esse subsistens*, is the creator of *ens commune*.

Against the philosophical and theological proposal of Le Roy, therefore, Garrigou-Lagrange musters what he calls "the conceptual realist theory of common sense." He first establishes that the formal object of the human intellect is being on the ground that definitions expressed in concepts aim at the intelligibility of the things of our experience, that is to say, some possibility of being, and on the ground that human affirmations aim at the actuality of being grasped in judgment.[60] This position on the realism of what it is that the human intellect aims to possess is of course the more general truth that the dogmatic realism discovered in chapter 2 on Nicaea points to and which was recalled in chapter 4. The position is, as he says, a refutation of nominalism.

It then falls to his project to inventory, as it were, the contents of conceptual realist common sense, the contents recognized in what he calls its "classical" expression, to be found according to Garrigou in Aristotle, the scholastics, Thomas Reid, Leibnitz, and indeed in what Leibniz called the *philosophia perennis*.[61] These contents divide into two great groups. There is first a group of what were referred to above as basic, fundamental notions, among which are person, substance, nature, cause, man, life. Garrigou's claim is that by common sense, men possess the nominal definitions of these things, from which definitions a mature philosophy will pass over to real definitions.[62] The second great group of the contents of common sense is a collection of first principles: the principles of noncontradiction, of identity, of sufficient reason, of finality.[63] This defense of common sense, Garrigou insists, does not wed the Church or Church doctrine to any determinate philosophic system, Thomist or Aristotelian.[64] It rather simply points to the success of Aristotle and Thomas in locating some of the fundamentals and constants of the human cognitive enterprise.

No one who knows the texts of Aristotle and St. Thomas will be surprised at the way in which Garrigou-Lagrange prizes certain notions like substance and nature for making coherent philosophical sense of the world. And no one who knows these texts will be surprised at Garrigou's express attention to such principles as noncontradiction and finality that are always presupposed and betimes come to determinate expression in their works—noncontradiction in the fourth book of Aristotle's *Metaphysics*; the principle of finality in book 3 of the *Contra gentiles*. What is

60. Garrigou-Lagrange, *Common Sense*, 48–58.
61. Garrigou-Lagrange, *Common Sense*, 84–85.
62. Garrigou-Lagrange, *Common Sense*, 93–98.
63. Garrigou-Lagrange, *Common Sense*, 99–107, 126–31.
64. Garrigou-Lagrange, *Common Sense*, 278–85.

surprising is the attribution to them of a theory of common sense that as one thing, embraces all these things. *Sensus communis*, after all, refers to an internal sense power for St. Thomas, and nothing like what Garrigou is talking about. We likely do not reach any solid ground in naming what he names "common sense" until we get to Thomas Reid (1710–1796).[65]

Still and all, we must cut Garrigou some slack here. The nineteenth and twentieth centuries are heir to many kinds of skepticism, to nominalisms of various sorts, to the acid of Humean empiricism, to the positivist restriction of the human intellect to the empirical sciences engineered by Immanuel Kant, to various German historicisms, and so on. Against the background of any of these movements of intellectual obfuscation and despair, the straightforward assertion of Catholic dogma turns out to be nonsensical. *Le Sens commun* therefore attempts two absolutely necessary tasks of Catholic fundamental theology. There must be a convincing defense of the real unity in faith of a Church some of whose dogmatic pronouncements are 1,500 years old. If this cannot be done, then any claim for the apostolicity of the Church turns out to be vacuous. Further, there must be a convincing defense of the real unity in faith of a Church composed of philosophers and farmers, mechanics and scientists.[66] If this cannot be done, then any claim for the catholicity of the Church turns out to be equally vacuous. All in all, Catholic unity is *doctrinal*.

Whatever must be true for this doctrinal unity to be possible is thus true. The above paragraph is an *a priori* theological argument for conceptual realism, for conceptual realism as the true description of human cognitive functioning just as such—just as *human*—for nothing else will enable a transcultural and transtemporal unity of faith. No theory that ends in epoch-specific idealisms, incommensurable epochal and geographically specific constructions of meaning, will do so. It is also an *a priori* theological argument for the stability—rather, the immutability—of concepts accessible to all men, whatever their station in life, and once again across

---

65. One can consult here the helpful but rather overwrought criticism of Etienne Gilson, "Réalisme et sens commun," in *Réalisme thomiste et critique de la connaissance* (Paris: Vrin, 1939).

66. Garrigou of course recognizes that some dogmatic pronouncements lean more heavenly on a technical or incipiently technical sense of terms than others. The Council of Vienne's definition of the soul as the form of the body does so. There are, then, he says, some degrees of accessibility to be recognized, but even here, the "ordinary man" is not left with no glimpse of the council's concern, the substantial unity of man. See *Common Sense*, 268–70.

culturally divergent spaces and times. *Le sens commun* meets both of these requirements. Is there any other argument that does so?[67]

According to various magisterial statements that bear on this problem, the answer is no. Three significant teachings about the language and conceptuality of dogmatic teaching can be inventoried here.

The first is Pius XII's encyclical letter of 1950, *Humani generis*. He addresses those who hold that the mysteries of faith have never been stated "by truly adequate concepts but only by approximate and changeable notions" that partially express and necessarily distort them. In this light, dogma must find new expression with new concepts that will yield "opposed but still equivalent expression" to divine truth (no. 15).[68] To this resurgence of the view of Anton Günther, he says (no. 16):

> Everyone is aware that the terminology employed in the schools and even that used by the Teaching Authority of the Church itself is capable of being perfected and polished; and we know also that the Church itself has not always used the same terms in the same way. It is also manifest that the Church cannot be bound to every system of philosophy that has existed for a short space of time. Nevertheless, the things that have been composed through common effort by Catholic teachers over the course of the centuries to bring about some understanding of dogma are certainly not based on any such weak foundation. These things are based on principles and notions deduced from a true knowledge of created things. In the process of deducing, this knowledge, like a star, gave enlightenment to the human mind through the Church. Hence it is not astonishing that some of these notions have not only been used by the Oecumenical Councils, but even sanctioned by them, so that it is wrong to depart from them.[69]

The meaning of dogma therefore abides from age to age according to the "principles and notions deduced from a true knowledge of created things."

---

67. The question of the necessary stability of concepts for expressing the same doctrine, the same judgment, was raised again by Henri Bouillard, SJ, at the end of his *Conversion et grâce chez S. Thomas d'Aquin. Étude historique* (Paris: Aubier, 1944), 211–24, where he maintains that the same affirmation can be made with different concepts. See the translation in *Ressourcement Theology: A Sourcebook*, ed. and trans. Patricia Kelly (London: T&T Clark, 2021), 33–40. The incoherence of this proposal is indicated by Garrigou-Lagrange in several responses and exchanges with Bouillard, which can be found in Kirwan's and Minerd's *The Thomistic Response to the Nouvelle Théologie*. Thomas Guarino undertakes a defense of Bouillard in "Henri Bouillard and the Truth-Status of Dogmatic Statements," *Science et Esprit* 39 (1987): 331–43.

68. DH 3882, ND 147.

69. DH 3883, ND 148.

These "notions" are evidently worked out within the realm of faith and with the guidance of the Church, something that Garrigou-Lagrange also notes.[70] It is difficult not to see here some recollection of his work.

The same is true of the teaching of Paul VI in his encyclical *Mysterium fidei* (1965), where he is addressing contemporary and heterodox Eucharistic theologies that wish to abandon the terminology of Trent.

> And so the rule of language which the Church has established through the long labor of centuries, with the help of the Holy Spirit, and which she has confirmed with the authority of the Councils, and which has more than once been the watchword and banner of orthodox faith, is to be religiously preserved, and no one may presume to change it at his own pleasure or under the pretext of new knowledge. Who would ever tolerate that the dogmatic formulas used by the ecumenical councils for the mysteries of the Holy Trinity and the Incarnation be judged as no longer appropriate for men of our times, and let others be rashly substituted for them? In the same way, it cannot be tolerated that any individual should on his own authority take something away from the formulas which were used by the Council of Trent to propose the Eucharistic Mystery for our belief. These formulas—like the others that the Church used to propose the dogmas of faith—express concepts that are not tied to a certain specific form of human culture, or to a certain level of scientific progress, or to one or another theological school. Instead they set forth what the human mind grasps of reality through necessary and universal experience and what it expresses in apt and exact words, whether it be in ordinary or more refined language. For this reason, these formulas are adapted to all men of all times and all places.[71]

This teaching differs from that of Pius XII only in its express characterization of the transcultural value of such conciliar language of substance, person, nature. He takes up the abiding suitability of "transubstantiation" for the expression of the Eucharistic mystery later.[72] Moreover, while he seems evidently under the influence of Garrigou-Lagrange's construction of the worth of dogmatic language, he brings forward patristic insistence on the communicative force and import of stable language in the Church. "The philosophers," St. Augustine says, "use words freely, and they have no fear of offending religious listeners in dealing with subjects that are

---

70. Garrigou-Lagrange, *Common Sense*, 285–86.

71. *Mysterium fidei*, no. 24. This text is available at the Vatican website.

72. *Mysterium fidei*, no. 46.

difficult to understand." But such philosophical freedom is not appropriate within the Church. "We have to speak in accordance with a fixed rule, so that a lack of restraint in speech on our part may not give rise to some irreverent opinion about the things represented by the words."[73]

Finally, let us look to John Paul II's *Fides et ratio* (1998). He is perhaps even more acutely aware of the philosophical challenges to the dogmatic intelligibility and continuity of the Church's teaching and addresses historicism, scientism, and pragmatism explicitly.[74] He states the problem as follows: "The Word of God is destined neither for one people nor for one age. In the same way, dogmatic pronouncements, despite the fact that they reflect the culture of the age from where they come, even so produce truth which is at once constant and decisive." How then to reconcile "the absolute and universal nature of truth" with "the unavoidable historical and cultural conditioning" of its formulation?[75] After a nod to Pius XII and *Humani generis*, he answers as follows:

It is no easy matter dealing with this argument since we must reckon seriously with the varied meanings the words have been accorded in differing ranges of cultures and periods of time. Even so the history of human reflection clearly demonstrates that in and through the progress and variety of cultures basic concepts have preserved both their universal validity for knowledge and the truth of the propositions they express.[76]

Were this not so, human communities would be consigned to islands of intelligibility unable to communicate with one another, which is manifestly not the case. And it is easy to recognize in the reference to "basic concepts" (*principales notiones*) the fundamental notions of Garrigou-Lagrange's *Le Sens commun*.

The First Vatican Council teaches that the Roman Pontiff's definitions concerning faith and morals are "irreformable of themselves and not

---

73. At *Mysterium fidei*, no. 23. The citation is from the *City of God*, book 10, chap. 23.

74. John Paul II, *Restoring Faith in Reason*, a new translation of *Fides et ratio* by Anthony Meredith, SJ, and Laurence Paul Hemming, with commentary and discussion by James McEvoy, ed. Laurence Paul Hemming and Susan Frank Parsons (Notre Dame, Ind.: University of Notre Dame Press, 2002), nos. 87–89, pp. 143–45.

75. John Paul II, *Fides et ratio*, no. 95, pp. 153–55.

76. John Paul II, *Fides et ratio*, no. 96, p. 155. He sends us at this point to the extended discussion of the Congregation for the Doctrine of the Faith's *Mysterium ecclesiae* (June 24, 1973), which is available at the Vatican website.

from the consent of the Church."[77] This teaching is repeated by the Second Vatican Council,[78] and indeed, the same predicate may be affirmed of the definitions of ecumenical councils as well. That they *cannot* be "reformed" in the sense of amending or changing their meaning follows from the fact that they are renderings of the revealed word of God. But that they *need* not be reformed follows from the fact of the constancy of certain human words and concepts, adequate to give this word of God true and by no means approximate, if not exhaustive, expression. It is this second thing that Garrigou-Lagrange vindicates and the papal teaching authority affirms.

77. *Pastor aeternus*, chap. 4, DH 3074, ND 839.
78. *Lumen gentium*, no. 25, DH 4149, ND 877.

EPILOGUE

The above account of development is governed by three principles.

(1) Revelation is closed. It is closed in the sense that there is no further chapter of Scripture to be written, and no further divine deed in history to be enacted, in order to complete the revelation of the Trinity and of the Redemption of the human race by the Incarnation and the mission of the Holy Spirit, before the return of Christ in glory. Such closure, however, does not mean that Christian tradition amounts only to the rereading and repetition of the Scriptures and the monuments of previous tradition such that no new insight into them is possible, that no hitherto unarticulated word interpreting them is to be spoken.

(2) The development of doctrine is "linear." This means that, once defined, a doctrine amounts henceforth to a permanently available, certain, and therefore permanently reliable statement of faith, contained explicitly or implicitly in the deposit of faith, and as long as it is understood in the sense in which it was defined. Linearity does not mean there are no zigs and zags according to the contingencies of history unfolding under the providence of God. But the lines of development do not double back and cross out what once was written. The progress of development does not retract what once was defined and does not contradict it. Like Pilate, the Church can say, "Quod scripsi scripsi," although the Church says this

not from pride of office but from the humility of a hearer of a word that cannot pass away.

(3) Human words and the concepts they evoke can express the truth of divine teaching about divine things. This is so because human words are ordered by God to name the created intelligibilities that, as created, are coherent imitations of the divine wisdom. Therefore, these words can state the truth of things as spoken by God and can furthermore be assumed by God to speak transcendent truths about the transcendent cause of these things.

With each of these principles, this book's account of development looks resolutely backward. It looks to the past deposit of revelation. It looks to the past monuments of previous tradition. It insists on the coherence of any new doctrine with both Scripture and Tradition. It relies on the capacity of language to communicate God's words, because this capacity is ultimately founded on the original creative words of the Hexaemeron.

It used to be that every Catholic account of development shared this backward reference, this backward orientation of the phenomenon of development. But that is no longer so. In the 1960s already Walter Kasper wanted to understand development and the possibilities of future development by thinking of dogma in terms of the future—in terms not of the beginning of Christian history but of its end, the eschaton yet to be fully revealed.[79] Dogma is instrumentally valuable, serving to get us to the end of history with our faith and charity intact.[80] But because the future is only promised, and imperfectly indicated by previous, past revelation, and because of the sinfulness of the Church, dogmas cannot render their service to the unity of the Church if it is thought that they cannot be revised or corrected.[81] Accounts of development that look to a future that

79. Walter Kasper, *Dogma unter dem Wort Gottes* (Mainz: Matthias-Grünewald, 1965).

80. Kasper, *Dogma*, 108: "Dogma is a dynamic and functional concept: it is the result of the previous experience of the Church intimately acquainted with the gospel and an anticipation of future experience, for which the Church must hold herself open. Since Easter, this future of Christian faith is no longer an empty openness, but a decided future.... This does not mean that the Church can now so to speak figure out the concrete ways of the formulation of her solemn declarations of faith. Her statements of faith also stand under the anticipations of the always greater mystery of the future of God."

81. Kasper, *Dogma*, 137: "Dogma, which in itself must serve ecclesial love, can, because of the sinfulness of the actual Church, also sometimes transgress love, in that it is formulated rigidly, coldly,

will control what we formulate as the faith do not, then, necessarily guarantee the linearity of development, and in this respect, revelation seems hardly closed. Accounts that preserve linearity, by contrast, generally look to a revelation that, as closed, is therefore something complete, coherent, final. In that light, whatever interpretation we make of it has to fit with it.

Michael Seewald has recently revisited Kasper's view to recommend it to us as a serviceable way to understand the range of possible developments. "A Church without dogma," he writes, "would be an intellectually underexposed or dishonest assembly that does not know itself and therefore cannot tell others what it believes."[82] That is finely said. But with Kasper, Seewald emphasizes the instrumental character of dogma and its provisionality. "What holds the Church together as the Body of Christ," he says, "is more than the identity and continuity established by dogma."[83] Which is true enough. But sufficient for this identity and continuity is an identity and continuity of consciousness, not a constantly maintained *object* of that consciousness in propositionally expressed truth. To maintain the contrary would be "mechanical"[84] and diminish the scope of freedom God leaves Christians in the formulation of dogma.[85]

Even more recently, David Bentley Hart has taken up this future-oriented account of "development."[86] Hart does not turn to the future, however, until he has dismissed Newman's account of development (and Blondel's theology of tradition). Orientation to a deposit, to an apostolic teaching, must be shown to be unable to produce a convincing story about the unity of Christian tradition. According to Hart, Newman proposes to offer a historical demonstration that Catholic dogmas are genuine, are developments and not corruptions. However, Newman's argument is circular.[87] His argument rather assumes what it seeks to prove,

---

repellently, injudiciously relative to the actual concerns of the other, framed rashly and obstinately. In order to guard the true function of dogma, the Church can and must newly formulate her actual confession of faith when she sees this deformation."

82. Seewald, *Dogma im Wandel*, 287–88.

83. Seewald, *Dogma im Wandel*, 289.

84. Seewald, *Dogma im Wandel*, 289. He is quoting Karl-Heinz Menke, *Macht die Wahrheit frei oder die Freiheit wahr? Eine Streitschrift* (Regensburg, 2017), 108.

85. Seewald, *Dogma*, 291.

86. David Bentley Hart, *Tradition and Apocalypse: An Essay on the Future of Christian Belief* (Grand Rapids, Mich.: Baker Academic, 2022).

87. Hart, *Tradition*, a historical showing, 18, 44, 88; circular, 6.

that there is a coherent theological tradition.[88] So, Hart maintains, when Newman finds a logical connection between an earlier and a later expression of the same dogma, this is "indistinguishable from the retrospective fabrication of some abstract principle that is merely reconcilable with ... the two distinct moments" of the unfolding.[89] Again, Newman's narrative is a reconstruction of the past, not a fair report of it.[90]

This remarkable criticism fails, I think, to understand Newman on his own terms. Newman tells us very clearly what he is up to and what he assumes. He assumes that the mouth of the river tells us more evidently what the spring will amount to. That is to say, he assumes that contemporary Catholic doctrine as a whole is coherent both in itself and with the original idea of Christianity.[91] He takes it that this assumption will enable us more easily to recognize the logical paths that historically led to its contemporary expression. In addition to assuming that there is indeed a logically coherent tradition of Catholic doctrine, Newman assumes also that the evidence is such as to enable us to reconstruct a plausible path from seed to flower—say, from the promise to Peter in Matthew 16 and such cryptic recognitions of Rome as "presiding in charity" to the exercise of the papacy under Leo the Great in the fifth century. Newman does not think history offers any "demonstrations"—except perhaps of the fact that Protestantism looks nothing like the first 1500 years of Christianity.[92] Rather, historical studies show, reasonably but not demonstratively, merely that history can be told in such a way that nineteenth-century Catholic Christianity appears to be not only the historical but also the logical heir of the Christianity of the fourth, fifth, and twelfth centuries. Newman shares with Aquinas the view that sacred theology judges the other sciences and disciplines. So, a theological view of history guides our historical reconstructions, our judgments about what reconstructions are plausible, and what evidences are or are not compelling.[93] To some thinkers, such a procedure will always look circular. Chapter 5 of the *Essay*, on tests for or notes of developments, therefore constitutes the whole

88. Hart, *Tradition*, 52.
89. Hart, *Tradition*, 55.
90. Hart, *Tradition*, 61.
91. Newman, *Essay on Development*, 5, 29–30.
92. Newman's "safe truth"; *Essay on Development*, 7.
93. Newman, *Essay on Development*, 106–7, 114–15, and as bearing on Nicaea, 124.

EPILOGUE   173

of Newman's argument for Hart.[94] Taken strictly, this reduces Newman's argument from a historical to a wholly syllogistic exercise.[95] Hart pays no attention to the dependence of Newman's theologically assessed historical observations on the antecedent probability of development itself,[96] nor to the crucial theological argument on the antecedent probability of our being able to recognize developments as developments of a revelation that comes to us as revelation.[97] For Catholics, the realization of this latter probability, of course, is realized in an office exterior to the course of development, an office that can render judgment on its products.

In other words, Hart does not really warrant the fact of revelation itself—there is no word of God tradition is to maintain.

Be that as it may, Hart supposes that knocking out Newman (and Blondel) gives him leave to turn 180 degrees and look no longer to the past for the justification of development, but to the future. Eschatology replaces archeology. In the expectation and power of the eschatological revelation of God and his Kingdom—the mechanism for the increasing manifestation of which remains, I think, vague in Hart—dogma turns out to be radically revisable, certainly correctible, so that we are no longer held to the wearisome task of defending past dogmatic pronouncements now outmoded in the form and fashion of their expression. On this showing, Christian faith no longer offers the believer the "propositional certitude of dogma."[98] Dogma is provisional and neither true nor false as measured by what precedes it.[99] This lets us see that the real immorality of past Christian theological discourse is to be located not in heresy but in the pretension to police it, to anathematize this, that, or the other teaching.[100] We should rather look to a future where, close to eschatological enlightenment, we are close to a synthesis of Christianity, Vedantic Hinduism, and neo-Platonism.[101] Rather than approaching the enlightenment of final apocalypse, we are, in fact, rather closer here to the histor-

94. Hart, *Tradition*, 45.
95. I owe this point to James Edward Kelly of Ave Maria University.
96. Newman, *Essay on Development*, chap. 2, section 1.
97. Newman, *Essay on Development*, chap. 2, section 2.
98. Hart, *Tradition*, 159.
99. Hart, *Tradition*, 160, also 180.
100. Hart, *Tradition*, 169.
101. Hart, *Tradition*, 183, 186.

ical Enlightenment of the eighteenth century, as Hart, wishing to have it all, acknowledges.[102]

On this view of dogma and its course in history, the unity of the Church is a unity beyond discourse, a unity that is patient of a radical incoherence across time. The idea that Kasper, Seewald, and Hart seem to share is this: the eschatological goal of history has already been definitively anticipated in Christ within history, *and this relativizes every attempt to give it conceptual expression*. Why we should believe this, something clean contrary to what has been supposed from the first formulation of dogma in the fourth century, is never quite explained. In any event, for Hart, this frees Catholics from the deadening authority of Rome, Protestants from the straight jacket of *sola scriptura*, and the Orthodox from an imaginary *consensus patrum*.[103] The freedom from dogma promised by von Harnack and Liberal Protestantism in general is restored to all Christians. Except, it is to be wondered whether these Christians are Christians in anything other than sharing a name emptied of any content—a notion as vacuous as that of Newman's "development" is for Hart.

This emptying out of any abiding content of faith, this jettisoning of Newman's dogmatic principle, is sufficient reason for any Catholic to consign Hart's account of development to the dustbin. If there is some content to the gospel beyond the Fatherhood of God (a pure metaphor for Harnack), and the brotherhood of man (policed by obedience to contemporary moral norms), and the immortality of the soul (unto what destiny, exactly?), then we face the task of vindicating not just a common imagination or even a common charity, but also a common mind, and indeed, a mind common with the apostolic Church. For this, we need not freedom from Rome, from Scripture, or from the Fathers, but rather some way intelligibly to orchestrate their contribution to the maintenance of this common mind.

We may be certain of the future that the Spirit will tell us many things we could not previously bear. Developments there will be. Will these things contradict any of the things the Lord himself said and that the Spirit will *also* bring to mind? They cannot do so if our mind is sharing

102. Hart, *Tradition*, 179–80.
103. Hart, *Tradition*, 173–75.

in the mind of Christ (1 Cor 2:16), who is the same yesterday, today, and forever (Heb 13:8). When we look to the future, as Kasper, Hart, and Seewald want us to do, therefore, all we know for sure in fact is that we shall see him return in the same way as he departed (Acts 1:11), identified by the same wounds that identified him after the Resurrection (Jn 20:27). What the Spirit says will therefore be recognized as the same revelation because brought back to the same wounds of which John is the witness (Jn 19:34–35) and that first established it as the faith "once for all delivered to the saints" (Jude 3).

BIBLIOGRAPHY

Anatolios, Khaled. *Retrieving Nicaea. The Development and Meaning of Trinitarian Doctrine*. Grand Rapids, MI: Baker Academic, 2011.

Athanasius. "Against the Arians." Translated by J. H. Newman. Revised by A. Robinson. In *Nicene and Post-Nicene Fathers*. Vol. 4, *Athanasius: Select Works and Letters*, 2nd ser., 303–447. Edited by Philip Schaff and Henry Wace. Peabody, MA: Hendrickson Publishers, 1994.

——. "Defense of the Nicene Creed" (*De Decretis*). Translated by J. H. Newman. In *Nicene and Post-Nicene Fathers*. Vol. 4, *Athanasius: Select Works and Letters*, 2nd ser., 149–72. Edited by Philip Schaff and Henry Wace. Peabody, MA: Hendrickson Publishers, 1994.

——. "On the Councils of Ariminum and Seleucia" (*De Synodis*). Translated by J. H. Newman. Revised by A. Robertson. In *Nicene and Post-Nicene Fathers*. Vol. 4, *Athanasius: Select Works and Letters*, 2nd ser., 448–80. Edited by Philip Schaff and Henry Wace. Peabody, MA: Hendrickson Publishers, 1994.

Aubert, Roger. *Vatican I*. Paris: Éditions de l'Orante, 1964.

Behr, John. *Formation of Christian Theology*. Vol. 1, *The Way to Nicaea*. Crestwood, NY: St. Vladimir's Seminary Press, 2001.

——. *The Formation of Christian Theology*. Vol. 2, *The Nicene Faith, Part One: True God of True God*. Crestwood, NY: St. Vladimir's Seminary Press, 2004.

Block, Benjamin M. "Thomas Aquinas on Knowing the Essences of Material Substances," *The Thomist* 87 (2023): 87–130.

Blondel, Maurice. *The Letter on Apologetics & History and Dogma*. Translated by Alexander Dru and Illtyd Trethowan. Grand Rapids, MI: Eerdmans, 1994.

Boeve, Lieven. *Interrupting Tradition: An Essay on Christian Faith in a Postmodern Context*. Leuven: Peeters, 2003.

Bouyer, Louis. *The Seat of Wisdom. An Essay on the Place of the Virgin Mary in Christian Theology*. Translated by A. V. Littledale. New York: Pantheon, 1960.

Brotherton, Joshua R. "Revisiting the Sola Scriptura Debate: Yves Congar and Joseph Ratzinger on Tradition," *Pro Ecclesia* 25 (2015): 85–114.

———. "Development(s) in the Theology of Revelation: From Francisco Marín-Sola to Joseph Ratzinger," *New Blackfriars* 97 (2016): 661–76.

Catechism of the Catholic Church. 2nd ed., rev. Vatican City: Libreria Editrice Vaticana, 1997.

Chadwick, Owen. *From Bossuet to Newman.* 2nd ed. Cambridge: Cambridge University Press, 1987.

Chenu, Marie-Dominique, OP. "Vérité évangelique et métaphysique Wolffienne à Vatican II," *Revue des sciences philosophiques et théologiques* 57 (1973): 632–40.

Congar, Yves, OP. *La Foi et la Théologie.* Tournai: Desclée, 1962.

———. *Tradition and Traditions: An Historical Essay and a Theological Essay.* Translated by Michael Naseby and Thomas Rainborough. New York: Macmillan, 1967.

———. *The Meaning of Tradition.* Translated by A. N. Woodrow. San Francisco: Ignatius Press, 2004.

———. "Theological Notes on the Assumption." In *Faith and Spiritual Life*, 3–10. Translated by A. Manson and L. C. Sheppard. New York: Herder and Herder, 1968.

Congregation for the Doctrine of the Faith. *Inter insigniores, On the Question of the Admission of Women to Priestly Ministry.* October 15, 1976. http://vatican.va.

———. *Dominus Iesus, Declaration on the Unicity and Salvific Universality of Christ and the Church.* August 6, 2000. http://vatican.va.

Daley, Brian E., SJ. *God Visible: Patristic Christology Reconsidered.* Oxford: Oxford University Press, 2018.

Decrees of the Ecumenical Councils. Vols. 1 and 2. Edited by Norman P. Tanner, SJ. London: Sheed & Ward and Georgetown University Press, 1990.

De Grandmaison, Léonce, SJ. "What Is a Dogma?" In *Defending the Faith: An Anti-Modernist Anthology*, 213–41. Edited and translated by William Marshner. Washington, DC: The Catholic University of America Press, 2017.

De La Soujeole, Benoît-Dominique, OP. *An Introduction to the Mystery of the Church.* Translated by Michael J. Miller. Washington, DC: The Catholic University of America Press, 2014.

De Lubac, Henri, SJ. *La Révélation Divine*, 3rd ed. Paris: Les Éditions du Cerf, 1983.

———. "The Problem of the Development of Dogma." In *Theology in History*, 248–80. Translated by Anne Englund Nash. San Francisco: Ignatius, 1996. First published in 1948.

Denzinger, Heinrich. *Enchiridion symbolorum definitionum et declarationum de rebus fidei et morum/Compendium of Creeds, Definitions, and Declarations on Matters of Faith and Morals.* Edited by Peter Hünermann, and by Robert Fastiggi and Anne Englund Nash for the English edition. 43rd ed. San Francisco: Ignatius Press, 2012.

Dhanis, Ed., SJ. "Révélation explicite et implicite," *Gregorianum* 34 (1953): 187–237.

Duhr, Joseph, SJ. *The Glorious Assumption of the Mother of God.* Translated by John Manning Fraunces, SJ. New York: P. J. Kennedy & Sons, 1950.

Dulles, Avery, SJ. *Models of Revelation.* Garden City, NY: Doubleday, 1983.

———. *Magisterium: Teacher and Guardian of the Faith*. Naples, Fla.: Sapientia Press, 2007.

———. "From Images to Truth: Newman on Revelation and Faith," *Theological Studies* 51 (1990): 252–67.

———. "*Dignitatis Humanae* and the Development of Catholic Doctrine." In *Catholicism and Religious Freedom: Reflections on Vatican II's Declaration on Religious Liberty*, 43–67. Edited by Kenneth Grasso and Robert P. Hunt. Lanham, MD: Sheed and Ward, 2006.

Farkasfalvy, Denis, O. Cist. *A Theology of the Christian Bible: Revelation – Inspiration – Canon*. Washington, DC: The Catholic University of America Press, 2018.

Franzelin, Johannes Baptist, SJ. *Tractatus de Divina Traditione et Scriptura*. 3rd ed. Rome: Typographia polyglotta, 1882.

Franzelin, Johannes Baptist, SJ. Draft schema "Contra errores ex rationalismo derivatos," redacted by the Theological Commission and distributed December 10, 1869. In Johannes Dominicus Mansi, *Sacrorum Conciliorum Nova et Amplissima Collectio*. Vol. 50, pp. 59–119. Graz: Akademische Druck – und Verlagsanstalt, 1961.

Gardeil, Ambroise, OP. *Le donné révélé et la théologie*. 2nd ed. Paris: Les Éditions du Cerf, 1932.

Guarino, Thomas G. *Vincent of Lérins and the Development of Christian Doctrine*. Grand Rapids, MI: Baker Academic, 2013.

Garrigou-Lagrange, Reginald, OP. *Le Sens commun*. 3rd ed, reviewed and corrected. Paris: Nouvelle Librairie Nationale, 1922.

———. *Thomistic Common Sense: The Philosophy of Being and the Development of Doctrine*. Translated by Matthew K. Minerd. Steubenville, OH: Emmaus Academic, 2021.

———. *The Mother of the Saviour and Our Interior Life*. Translated by Bernard J. Kelly, CSSp. St. Louis: Herder, 1943.

———. *The One God: A Commentary on the First Part of St. Thomas' Theological Summa*. Translated by Dom. Bede Rose, OSB. Ex Fontibus Company, 2012.

Gilson, Étienne. "Réalisme et sens commun," in *Réalisme thomiste et critique de la connaissance*. Paris: Vrin, 1939.

Greer, Rowan. "The Christian Bible and Its Interpretation." In Roman Greer and James Kugel, *Early Biblical Interpretation*, 107–208. Edited by Wayne Meeks. Philadelphia: Westminster, 1986.

Gregory XVI, Pope. *Dum acerbissimas*. Brief (on the errors of Georg Hermes). September 26, 1835. http://vatican.va.

Gregory Nazianzen. Oration 31, the Fifth Theological Oration.

Hamanns, Herbert. *Die Neueren Katholischen Erklärungen der Dogmenentwicklung*. Essen: Ludgerus – Verlag Hubert Wingen KG, 1965.

Hart, David Bentley. *Tradition and Apocalypse: An Essay on the Future of Christian Belief*. Grand Rapids, MI: Baker Academic, 2022.

Hart, Trevor. "Revelation." In *The Cambridge Companion to Karl Barth*, 37–56. Edited by John Webster. Cambridge: Cambridge University Press, 2000.

Hauke, Manfred. *Introduction to Mariology*. Translated by Richard Chonak. Washington, DC: The Catholic University of America Press, 2021.

Healy, Nicholas J., Jr. "Dignitatis Humanae." In *The Reception of Vatican II*, 367–92. Edited by Matthew L. Lamb and Matthew Levering. Oxford: Oxford University Press, 2017.

———. "Henri de Lubac on the Development of Dogma." In *Resssourcement After Vatican II: Essays in Honor of Joseph Fessio, S.J.*, 346–65. Edited by Nicholas J. Healy Jr. and Matthew Levering. San Francisco: Ignatius, 2019.

Hertling, Ludwig, SJ. *Communio: Church and Papacy in Early Christianity*. Translated by Jared Wicks, SJ. Chicago: Loyola University Press, 1972.

Hittinger, F. Russell. "The Declaration on Religious Freedom, *Dignitatis Humanae*." In *Vatican II: Renewal Within Tradition*, 359–82. Edited by Matthew L. Lamb and Matthew Levering. Oxford: Oxford University Press, 2008.

Hütter, Reinhard. *John Henry Newman on Truth and Its Counterfeits: A Guide for Our Times*. Washington, DC: The Catholic University of America Press, 2020.

———. "Progress, Not Alteration of the Faith: Beyond Antiquarianism and Presentism. John Henry Newman, Vincent of Lérins, and the Criterion of Identity of the Development of Doctrine." *Nova et Vetera* (English) 19 (2021): 333–91.

Irenaeus of Lyons. *Against Heresies*. In *The Ante-Nicene Fathers*. Vol. 1. Edited by Alexander Roberts, James Donaldson, and Arthur Cleveland Coxe. New York: Cosimo Classics, 2007.

John of the Cross. *The Ascent of Mount Carmel*.

John Paul II, Pope. *Ordinatio sacerdotalis, On the Reservation of Priestly Ordination to Men Alone*. Apostolic Letter, May 22, 1994.

———. *Fides et Ratio, on the Relationship between Faith and Reason*. Encyclical letter. September 4, 1998. http://vatican.va.

———. *Restoring Faith in Reason: A New Translation of the Encyclical Letter* Faith and Reason *of Pope John Paul II*. Translated by Anthony Meredith, SJ, and Laurence Paul Hemming, with commentary. Notre Dame, IN: University of Notre Dame Press, 2002.

Journet, Charles. *The Church of the Word Incarnate*. Vol. 1, *The Apostolic Hierarchy*. Translated by A. H. C. Downes. London: Sheed and Ward, 1955.

Kasper, Walter. *Dogma unter dem Wort Gottes*. Mainz: Matthias-Grünewald, 1965.

Kelly, J. N. D. *Early Christian Doctrines*. New York: Harper and Row, 1960.

———. *Early Christian Creeds*, 3rd ed. New York: Longmans, 1972.

Lamont, John. "The Historical Conditioning of Church Dogma," *The Thomist* 60 (1996): 511–35.

Lash, Nicholas Lash. *Newman on Development: The Search for an Explanation in History*. Shepherdstown, WV: Patmos Press, 1975.

Leo XIII, Pope. *Pastor Aeternis, on the Restoration of Christian Philosophy*. Encyclical Letter. August 4, 1879. http://vatican.va.

———. *Immortale Dei*. http://vatican.va.

Le Roy, Édouard. "Qu'est-ce qu'un dogme?" *Le Quinzaine* 63 (1905): 495–526. Reprinted in his *Dogme et critique*. Paris: Librairie Bloud et Cie, 1907.

Levering, Matthew. *Mary's Bodily Assumption*. Notre Dame, IN: University of Notre Dame Press, 2015.

Levering, Matthew. *Engaging the Doctrine of Revelation*. Grand Rapids, MI: Baker Academic, 2014.

———. *An Introduction to Vatican II as Ongoing Theological Event*. Washington DC: The Catholic University of America Press, 2017.

Lienhard, Joseph, SJ. *The Bible, the Church, and Authority: The Canon of the Christian Bible in History and Theology*. Collegeville, MN: Liturgical Press, 1995.

Loisy, Alfred. *Autour d'un petit livre*. Paris: Picard et Fils, 1903.

Lonergan, Bernard J. F., SJ. *Collected Works of Bernard Lonergan*. Vol. 11, *The Triune God: Doctrines*. Translated by Michael G. Shields. Edited by Robert M. Doran and H. Daniel Monsour. Toronto: University of Toronto Press, 2009.

———. "The Dehellenization of Dogma." In *A Second Collection*. Philadelphia: Westminster, 1974.

MacIntyre, Alasdair. *Three Rival Versions of Moral Enquiry: Encyclopaedia, Genealogy, and Tradition*. Notre Dame, IN: University of Notre Dame Press, 1990.

Mansini, Guy, OSB. *Fundamental Theology*. Washington, DC: The Catholic University of America Press, 2018.

Marín-Sola, Francisco, OP. *The Homogeneous Evolution of Catholic Dogma*. Translated by Antonio T. Piñon. Manila: Santo Tomas University Press, 1988.

May, Gerhard. *Creatio Ex Nihilo. The Doctrine of 'Creation out of Nothing' in Early Christian Thought*. Translated by A. S. Worrall. London: T&T Clark, 1994.

Merrigan, Terrence. *Clear Heads and Holy Hearts: The Religious and Theological Ideal of John Henry Newman*. Foreword by Ian Ker. Louvain: Peeters Press, 1991.

Meszaros, Andrew. *The Prophetic Church: History and Doctrinal Development in John Henry Newman and Yves Congar*. Oxford: Oxford University Press, 2016.

———. "John Henry Newman and the Thomistic Tradition: Convergences in Contribution to Development Theory," *Nova et Vetera* (English) 19 (2021): 423–68.

———. "*Dei Filius* IV: On the Development of Dogma," *Nova et Vetera* (English) 20 (2022): 909–38.

Montagnes, Benoît, OP. "La parole de Dieu dans la creation," *Revue Thomiste* 54 (1954): 213–41.

Neuner, J., and J. Dupuis. *The Christian Faith in the Doctrinal Documents of the Catholic Church*. 7th ed. New York: Alba House, 2001.

Newman, John Henry Cardinal. *An Essay on the Development of Christian Doctrine*. 6th ed. Foreword by Ian Ker. Notre Dame, IN: University of Notre Dame Press, 1989. This is a reprint of the edition of 1878.

———. *An Essay in Aid of a Grammar of Assent*. Edited by I. T. Ker. Oxford: Clarendon Press, 1985.

———. *The Idea of a University*. Edited with introduction by I. T. Ker. Oxford: Clarendon Press, 1976.

———. "1852 Discourse V. General Knowledge Viewed as One Philosophy." In *The Idea of a University*, 421–34. Edited with introduction by I. T. Ker. Oxford: Clarendon Press, 1976.

———. "Sermon 15: The Theory of Developments in Religious Doctrine." In *Fifteen Sermons Preached Before the University of Oxford Between A.D. 1826 and 1843*, 312–51. London: Longmans, Green, 1896.

———. Appendix 5, "Orthodoxy of the Faithful during Arianism." In *Arians of the Fourth Century*, 445–68. London: Longmans, Green, 1901.

———. "On the Fitness of the Glories of Mary." In *Mary: The Virgin Mary in the Life and Writings of John Henry Newman*, 149–66. Edited by Philip Boyce. Grand Rapids, MI: Eerdmans, 2001.

Nichols, Aidan, OP, *From Newman to Congar: The Idea of Doctrinal Development from the Victorians to the Second Vatican Council*. Edinburgh: T&T Clark, 1990.

Oesterle, John. *Logic: The Art of Defining and Reasoning*. New York: Prentice-Hall, 1952.

Origen. *Commentary on the Gospel According to John, Books 1–10*. Vol. 80 of *Fathers of the Church*. Translated by Ronald E. Heine. Washington, DC: The Catholic University of America Press, 1989.

Page, Carl. *Philosophical Historicism and the Betrayal of First Philosophy*. University Park: University of Pennsylvania Press, 1995.

Paradis, Georges, SJ. "Foi et raison au premier Concile du Vatican." In *De Doctrina Concilii Vaticani Primi: Studia Selecta*, 221–281. Vatican City: Libreria Editrice Vaticana, 1969. This study first appeared in the *Bulletin de littérature ecclésiastique*, 63 (1962): 200–226, 268–92; 64 (1963): 9–25.

Parker, Francis H., and Henry B. Veatch. *Logic as a Human Instrument*. New York: Harper and Brothers, 1959.

Paul VI, Pope. *Mysterium Fidei, on the Holy Eucharist*. Encyclical letter. September 3, 1965. http://vatican.va.

Pius IX, Pope. *Qui pluribus*. Encyclical. November 9, 1846. http://vatican.va.

———. *Eximiam tuam* (errors of Anton Günther). Brief to the Archbishop of Cologne. June 15, 1857. http://vatican.va.

———. *Gravissimas inter* (errors of Jacob Froshschammer). Letter to the Archbishop of Munich-Freising. December 11, 1862. http://vatican.va.

———. *Syllabus of Errors*. December 8, 1864. http://vatican.va.

Pius X, Pope. *Lamentabili* (errors of Modernism). Decree of the Holy Office. July 3, 1907. http://vatican.va.

Pius XII, Pope. *Humani generis, Concerning Some False Opinions Threatening to*

Undermine the Foundations of Catholic Doctrine. Encyclical letter. August 12, 1950. http://vatican.va.

Pink, Thomas. "Conscience and Coercion," *First Things*, August 2012. http://firsthings .com/article/2012/08/conscience-and-coercion

Prestige, G. L. *God in Patristic Thought.* London: SPCK, 1952.

Rahner, Karl, SJ. *Foundations of Christian Faith. An Introduction to the Idea of Christianity.* Translated by William Dych. New York: Seabury, 1978.

———. "The Development of Dogma." In *Theological Investigations.* Vol. 1, 39–77. Translated by Cornelius Ernst, OP. Baltimore: Helicon, 1961.

———. "Considerations on the Development of Dogma." In *Theological Investigations.* Vol. 4, 3–35. Translated by Kevin Smyth. Baltimore: Helicon, 1966. First published in 1958.

———. "Dogmatic Reflections on the Knowledge and Self-Consciousness of Christ." In *Theological Investigations.* Vol. 5, 193–215. Translated by Karl H. Kruger. New York: Seabury Press, 1966.

———. "Yesterday's History of Dogma and Theology for Tomorrow." In *Theological Investigations.* Vol. 18, 3–34. Translated by Edward Quinn. New York: Crossroad, 1983.

Ratzinger, Joseph. *The Theology of History in St. Bonaventure.* Translated by Zachary Hayes. Chicago: Franciscan Herald Press, 1971.

———. *Daughter of Zion: Meditations on the Church's Marian Belief.* Translated by John M. McDermott, SJ. San Francisco: Ignatius Press, 1983.

———. *Milestones: Memoirs 1927–1977.* Translated by Erasmo Leiva-Merikakis. San Francisco: Ignatius Press, 1998.

———. *God's Word. Scripture – Tradition – Office.* Translated by Henry Taylor. San Francisco: Ignatius Press, 2008.

——— (Pope Benedict XVI). Homily for the Solemnity of the Assumption, August 15, 2011. http://vatican.va.

———. *Das Offenbarungsverständnis und die Geschichtstheologie Bonaventuras: Habilitationsschrift und Bonaventura-Studien.* In *Joseph Ratzinger: Gesammelte Schriften.* Vol. 2. Edited by Gerhard Ludwig Müller. Freiburg: Herder, 2009.

Rousselot, Pierre, SJ. "Petite théorie du développment du dogme," *Recherches de Science Religieuse* 53 (1965): 355–90.

Sadler, Gregory B., trans. and ed. *Reason Fulfilled by Revelation: The 1930's Christian Philosophy Debates in France.* Washington, DC: The Catholic University of America Press, 2011.

Schillebeeckx, E., OP. "The Development of the Apostolic Faith into the Dogma of the Church." In *Revelation and Theology.* Vol. 1, 57–83. Translated by N. D. Smith. New York: Sheed and Ward, 1967. This article first appeared in 1952.

Schillebeeckx, E., OP. "Revelation Scripture, Tradition, and Teaching Authority." In *Revelation and Theology.* Vol. 1, 3–24. Translated by N. D. Smith. This article first appeared in 1963.

————. "The Concept of Truth." In *Revelation and Theology*. Vol. 2, 5–29. Translated by N. D. Smith. New York: Sheed and Ward, 1968. This article first appeared in 1954.

————. "Toward a Catholic Use of Hermeneutics." In E. Schillebeeckx, *God the Future of Man*, 1–49. Translated by N. D. Smith. New York: Sheed and Ward: 1968.

Schlier, Heinrich. "Kerygma und Sophia. Zur neutestamentlichen Grundlegung des Dogmas." In *Der Zeit der Kirche*, 206–32. Freiburg: Herder, 1966.

Schrodt, Paul. *The Problem of the Beginning of Dogma in Recent Theology*. Frankfurt am Main: Peter Lang, 1978.

Schultes, Reginald, OP. *Introductio in Historiam Dogmatum Praelectiones*. Paris: Lethielleux, 1922.

Seewald, Michael. *Dogma im Wandel: Wie Glaubenslehren sich entwickeln*. Freiburg: Herder, 2018.

Sokolowski, Robert. *Phenomenology of the Human Person*. Cambridge: Cambridge University Press, 2008.

Sokolowski, Robert. *Presence and Absence. A Philosophical Investigation of Language and Being*. Washington, DC: The Catholic University of America Press, 2017.

————. "The Identity of the Bishop: A Study in the Theology of Disclosure." In Robert Sokolowski, *Christian Faith & Understanding: Studies on the Eucharist, Trinity, and the Human Person*, 113–130. Washington, DC: The Catholic University of America Press, 2006.

Spicq, Ceslas, OP. *Saint Paul Les Épîtres Pastorals*. 2 vols. Paris: Gabalda, 1947.

Steiner, George. *Real Presences*. London: Faber and Faber, 1989.

Strauss, Leo. "The Origin of the Idea of Natural Right." In Strauss, *Natural Right and History*, 81–119. Chicago: University of Chicago Press, 1953.

Thomas Aquinas. *Summa theologiae*. Torino: Marietti, 1952.

————. *Summa Theologica*. 5 volumes. Translated by the English Dominican Province. New York: Benziger Bros., 1948.

————. *Summa contra gentiles*. Book 4. Translated by Charles J. O'Neil. Notre Dame, IN: University of Notre Dame Press, 1975.

————. *Scriptum Super Libros Sententiarum*. Edited by P. Mandonnet. 4 vols. Paris: Lethielleux, 1929, 1933, 1947.

————. *Quaestiones Disputatae de Veritate*. In *Quaestiones Disputatae*. Vol. 1. Edited by Raymond Spiazzi, OP. Rome: Marietti, 1949.

————. *Quaestiones Disputatae de Potentia Dei*. In *Quaestiones Disputatae*. Vol. 2. Edited by P. Bazzi, M. Calcaterra, et al. Rome: Marietti, 1949.

Thomas Aquinas. *Commentary on the Epicstle to the Hebrews*. Translated and edited by Chrysostom Baer, O. Praem. South Bend, IN: St. Augustine's Press, 2006.

Torre, Michael. *Do Not Resist the Spirit's Call: Francisco Marín-Sola on Sufficient Grace*. Washington, DC: The Catholic University of America Press, 2013.

Torrell, Jean Pierre, OP. *Saint Thomas Aquinas*. Vol. 2, *Spiritual Master*. Translated by Robert Royal. Washington, DC: The Catholic University of America Press, 2003.

Tyrrell, George. "Revelation." In *Through Scylla and Charybdis: or, the Old Theology and the New*, 264–307. London: Longmans, Green, 1907.

Vacant, Jean Michel Alfred. *Études Théologiques sur les Constitutions du Concile du Vatican d'après les Actes du Concile. La Constitution Dei Filius*. 2 vols. Paris: Delhomme et Briguet, 1895.

Vall, Gregory. *Ecclesial Exegesis: A Synthesis of Ancient and Modern Approaches to Scripture*. Washington, DC: The Catholic University of America Press, 2011.

Vatican Council I. *Dogmatic Constitution on the Catholic Faith (Dei Filius)*. In *Decrees of the Ecumenical Councils*. Vol. 2, *Trent to Vatican II*, XYZ–XYZ. Edited by Norman P. Tanner, SJ. London: Sheed and Ward, 1990. Also: http://vatican.va.

———. *First Dogmatic Constitution on the Church of Christ (Pastor Aeternus)*. In *Decrees of the Ecumenical Councils*. Vol. 2, *Trent to Vatican II*, XYZ–XYZ. Edited by Norman P. Tanner, SJ. London: Sheed and Ward, 1990. Also: http://vatican.va.

Vatican Council II. *Dogmatic Constitution on Divine Revelation (Dei Verbum)*. In *Decrees of the Ecumenical Councils*. Vol. 2, *Trent to Vatican II*, 971–79. Edited by Norman Tanner, SJ. London: Sheed and Ward, 1990. Also: http://vatican.va.

———. *Dogmatic Constitution on the Church (Lumen Gentium)*. In *Decrees of the Ecumenical Councils*. Vol. 2, *Trent to Vatican II*, 849–900. Edited by Norman P. Tanner, SJ. London: Sheed and Ward, 1990.

Veatch, Henry Babcock. *Intentional Logic*. New Haven, CT: Yale University Press, 1952.

———. *Two Logics: The Conflict Between Classical and Neo-Analytic Philosophy*. Evanston, IL: Northwestern University Press, 1969.

Vincent of Lérins. "Comminatory" (*Commonitorium*). Translated by C. A. Heurtley. In *Nicene and Post-Nicene Fathers*. 2nd ser. Vol. 11, *Sulpitius Severus, Vincent of Lérins, John Cassian*, 123–159. Edited by Philip Schaff and Henry Wace. Peabody, MA: Hendrickson, 1994.

Wahlberg, Mats. *Revelation as Testimony: A Philosophical-Theological Study*. Grand Rapids, MI: Eerdmans, 2014.

Walgrave, Jan Hendrik. *Unfolding Revelation: The Nature of Doctrinal Development* Philadelphia: Westminster, 1972.

White, Thomas Joseph, OP. *The Incarnate Lord: A Thomistic Study in Christology*. Washington, DC: The Catholic University of America Press, 2015.

———. *The Light of Christ: An Introduction to Catholicism*. Washington, DC: The Catholic University of America Press, 2017.

———. *The Trinity: On the Nature and Mystery of the One God*. Washington, DC: The Catholic University of America Press, 2022.

Wicks, Jared, SJ. "Six Texts by Prof. Joseph Ratzinger as *Peritus* before and during Vatican Council II," *Gregorianum* 89 (2008): 233–411.

Wilkins, Jeremy D. *Before Truth: Lonergan, Aquinas, and the Problem of Wisdom*. Washington, DC: The Catholic University of America Press, 2018.

INDEX

Abraham, 28, 30, 44, 51, 133
accessibility: of dogma, 4, 139, 154–62, 165n66; of revelation, 103
Acts of the Apostles, 31, 36, 66, 176
Adam, 44–46, 75n10, 92, 92n49, 129, 142, 158n50
agency, 30, 47, 61, 108, 128, 160, 160n54
Alexander of Alexandria, 22
analogy, 94–95
analogy of faith, 126, 128, 130
Anatolios, Khaled, 18
Apostles' Creed, 8–10, 14
Aquinas, Thomas, 48, 73–74, 76–77, 78n17, 78n19, 80, 83, 88, 93–94, 111, 111n12, 112, 114–15, 115n26, 125, 160n54, 164–65, 173
Arian controversy, 16
Arianism, 11
Aristotle, 2, 38, 73, 75–76, 101, 121, 128, 160n54, 163–65
Arius of Alexandria, 17–26, 38–39
Ark of the Covenant, 132
assimilation, 20, 107, 109–10
Athanasius, 18–21, 24–25, 35–36, 39, 52, 89, 96
atheism, 139, 147
Augustine, 39, 77, 96, 101, 167–68
authenticity, 49, 66, 91, 91n46, 99

Babel, 92
Baius, Michael, 15
baptism, 21, 58
Barth, Karl, 93
Basil of Caesarea, 21n26
Behr, John, 19, 21n26
being, 2–3, 101

Benedict XVI, 132
Bergson, Henri, 74, 74n7, 163
Blondel, Maurice, 4, 113–15, 114n23, 116, 174
Boeve, Lieven, 60n43
Bonaventure, 54–55, 134
Bouyer, Louis, 133

Catechism of the Catholic Church, 8–10, 14
Catherine of Siena, 96
causality, 75
Chadwick, Owen, 1
charity, 45, 49–50, 58, 61–62, 91, 111, 134, 171, 173, 175
Chenu, Marie-Dominique, 115, 115n25
Chrismann, Philipp Nerin, 15
Christ. *See also* Son: in Arius, 18, 20; faith and, 6; Father and, 159; freedom and, 125–26; freedom of, 52; in John, 19; in Loisy, 113; Mary and, 129, 131–32; revelation and, 42; Scripture and, 59; witness of, 71; Word and, 161
Chrysostom, John, 39
Church: accessibility of teaching of, 4; doctrinal development and, 108; dogmatic decisions of, 108–9; faith and, 68; in First Vatican Council, 140; Gnosticism and, 66; historicity and, 96–104; Holy Spirit and, 68; Mary and, 132; in Paul VI, 167; revelation and, 148; Scripture and, 56; state and, 151–52; truth and, 129; in Vincent of Lérins, 141, 154
Clement of Rome, 135
cognition: realism and, 73; revelation and, 47–51
Colossians, Epistle to, 18, 28, 129

187

Commonitorium (Vincent of Lérins), 141
communalism, of revelation, 51–52, 61
conceptual affirmations, 72–73
confession, 155
Congar, Yves, 4, 15, 15n4, 46, 57, 65, 70–73,
   93, 99, 103, 114n23, 117, 128, 134
Congregation for the Doctrine of the Faith,
   135–36
continuity of doctrine, 11–12, 147–54
Corinthians, First, 23, 28–29, 31, 53, 90,
   124, 176
Corinthians, Second, 7, 53, 137
Council of Chalcedon, 11, 72–73, 126, 154,
   157, 159–60
Council of Constantinople, 34
Council of Ephesus, 35, 72–73, 126, 147, 159
Council of Nicaea, 4, 15–16, 16n5, 17–34,
   37–38, 72–73, 88, 90, 105, 126, 138–39,
   157, 159
Council of Trent, 15, 46, 127, 147, 155–56,
   167
Council of Vienne, 165n66
Cyril of Alexandria, 35

Daughter Zion, 137
De Decretis (Athanasius), 35–36
Deely, John, 80n23
Dei Filius (First Vatican Council), 15n4, 48,
   65, 142, 144–48, 154
Dei Verbum (Second Vatican Council),
   43n4, 46, 48, 58, 147–48
de Lubac, Henri, 4, 116, 116n30, 117
De Salvo, Michael, 153
Descartes, René, 75n10
Deuteronomy, Book of, 56n26
development of doctrine: defining, 5–13;
   development concept in, 7–8; as genuine,
   106–7; as "linear," 169–70; logical verification of, 105–37
Dignitatis humanae (Second Vatican Council), 148–49, 148n32, 150–51, 153–54
Dionysius the Areopagite, 111
dogma: about dogma, 138–69; accessibility
   of, 139, 154–62, 165n66; defined, 15, 15n5,
   105; development of, theological framing
   of, 41–69; First Vatican Council and,
   138–69; invention of, 14–40; magisterium and, 61–64; meta-, 139; novelty of,
   35–36; philosophical presuppositions of,
   70–104; realism and, 88–89; revelation

and, 139, 141; in Scripture, 65–69; whole
   of, 116–17
Dogma of the Assumption of Our Lady, 15
Donum veritatis (Congregation for the
   Doctrine of the Faith), 135–36
Duhr, Joseph, 131n79
Dulles, Avery, 150
Duns Scotus, John, 52, 128, 134

Enlightenment, 152, 175
Ephesians, Epistle to, 56, 133
Epiphanius of Salamis, 133–34
Essay on the Development of Doctrine
   (Newman), 33, 57n34, 63–64, 87, 106,
   134, 173–74
Eucharist, 7, 50, 57–58, 127, 137, 162, 167
Euthyphro (Plato), 38
Eve, 44–46, 129, 133, 142
exclusivity, epistemological, 81–82
Exodus, Book of, 7, 31, 86, 124

facts, historical, 60, 70–72, 143
faith, 4; analogy of, 126, 128, 130; Christ
   and, 6; Church and, 68; definitions of,
   147; development of doctrine and, 5–6;
   earlier expressions of, *vs.* later, 11–12; in
   First Vatican Council, 168–69; Holy
   Spirit and, 12, 112; infallibility and, 146;
   in Marín-Sola, 112; philosophy and,
   140; in Pius XII, 166; reason and, 139;
   revelation and, 45, 71, 74, 87–88, 118–19;
   Tradition and, 12
Father: baptism and, 21; Christ and, 159;
   in Council of Nicaea, 22–24, 27, 29–30,
   138; *homoousios* and, 25; revelation and,
   42; Rule of Athanasius and, 89; Son and,
   31–32, 123–24; Word and, 160
Fides et ratio (John Paul II), 168
Fifth Lateran Council, 127
First Vatican Council, 4, 15, 43–44, 65, 109,
   138–69
form, 76–77
Fourth Lateran Council, 14, 127
Franzelin, Johannes, 143–45, 145n19, 146
freedom: of Christ, 52; from coercion in
   religious matters, 149; magisterium and,
   61; Mary and, 131; revelation and, 150; in
   Second Vatican Council, 148–49
French Revolution, 152
From Bossuet to Newman (Chadwick), 1

From Newman to Congar: The Idea of Doctrinal Development from the Victorians to the Second Vatican Council (Nichols), 1–2

Galatians, Epistle to, 7, 52
Garrigou-Lagrange, Réginald, 3, 126n63, 128–29, 162–65, 165n66, 167, 169
Genesis, Book of, 16, 29, 42, 75n10, 92–93
Gideon, 44
Gilson, Etienne, 86
Gnosticism, 66
God: analogy and, 95; in Arius, 17; in First Vatican Council, 139–40; knowledge and, 85–86; language and, 93, 95–96; magisterium and, 61; Mary and, 136; mysteries of, 112; name of, 86; realism and, 90; reason and, 139–40; resurrection and, 6; revelation and, 3, 49, 133; Scriptures and, 58; Son and, 125; truth and, 89
grace, 23, 30, 32, 83, 91, 94n57, 112, 120n43, 128–29, 147, 157
Gregory XVI, 150–51
Guarino, Thomas G., 149n32
Günther, Anton, 142–43, 145n19, 146–47, 157, 166

Habilitation (Ratzinger), 54
Hamilton, Paul, 100n76
Hammans, Herbert, 1
Hart, David Bentley, 172–76
Healy, Nicholas J., Jr., 148n32
Hebrews, Book of, 31, 53, 125, 176
Heidegger, Martin, 99, 101
Hengel, Martin, 98
Hermes, Georg, 142
Hertling, Ludwig, 135
Hilary of Poitiers, 39
Hinduism, 174
historical facts, 60, 70–72, 143
historical learning, 10
historicism, 2–4, 11, 100, 100n76, 101–3, 102n82, 114n23, 157, 165, 168
historicity, 96–104
History and Dogma (Blondel), 113
Hittinger, F. Russell, 148n32
Holy Spirit: baptism and, 21; Church and, 68; faith and, 12, 112; *homoousios* and, 25; infallibility and, 144; magisterium and, 106; in Nicene Creed, 34–35; in Paul VI,

167; as Pneuma, 13; revelation and, 42; Tradition and, 13, 103; Word and, 111, 160
Homogeneous Evolution of Catholic Dogma, The (Marín-Sola), 120
homoousios, 24–26, 38, 138
Humani generis (Pius XII), 166, 168
human rights, 152–53
Hume, David, 165
Husserl, Edmund, 99

idealism, 73, 80, 104, 142, 158n50, 165
Idea of a University, The (Newman), 33, 110
identity, 32–33, 73, 75–76, 83–84, 106, 109, 125, 159, 161, 172
Ignatius of Antioch, 135
Immaculate Conception, 52, 127–29, 128n69, 131
Immortale Dei (Leo XIII), 151–52
Incarnation, 53, 146, 160–61; in Arius, 21; assertion of, 129; Daughter Zion and, 137; in Günther, 144; in John of the Cross, 53; language and, 7; in Paul VI, 167; rationalism and, 142–43; revelation and, 92, 162n56, 170; Son and, 28; as speaking, 43; time and, 145; truth of, as self-evident, 158
indifferentism, 150–52
infallibility, 64, 105, 130, 135–36, 139, 144, 146–47, 153
Innocent I, 52
intellect, 2–3, 57n34, 74, 76–78, 81, 93–94, 94n57, 106, 115, 144, 158n50, 163–65
intelligibility, 81–82, 143, 171
Irenaeus of Lyons, 16, 135
Isaac, 44, 133
Isaiah, Book of, 6, 31, 124

James, Book of, 31
Joachim of Fiore, 53n19
Joel, Book of, 31
John, 103
John, Gospel of, 7, 18–19, 21, 23, 28–30, 49–50, 53, 68, 72, 75, 111, 123–25, 129, 137, 176
John of St. Thomas, 80n23
John of the Cross, 53
John Paul II, 135–36, 168
Joshua, 44
Journet, Charles, 153
Jude, Book of, 176
Justin Martyr, 16

INDEX 189

Kant, Immanuel, 71, 73, 91, 100n76, 165
Kasper, Walter, 171, 171n80, 172, 176
Kelly, J.N.D., 21, 24n31
Kings, Book of, 56n26
knowledge, 2; analogical, 72; attention and, 79; connatural, 111–14, 117; God and, 85–86; identity and, 73, 75–76, 83–84; instrument of, 78; language and, 79–80, 82–83, 85, 87; meta-empirical, 72–73; perception and, 79; presence and, 81; realism and, 75; representation and, 88; revelation and, 82, 85; sense, 77

language, 7; God and, 93, 95–96; knowledge and, 79–80, 82–83, 85, 87; magisterium on dogmatic, 162–69; revelation and, 85
Lateran Synod of 649, 126
law, 45, 61, 66–67, 121, 149–52, 155–56
Leibniz, Gottfried Wilhelm, 164
Leontius of Byzantium, 11
Leo the Great, 173
Leo XIII, 150–52
Le Roy, Édouard, 162–63
Locke, John, 80
logic, 2; of antecedent and converging probabilities, 126–37; in De Lubac, 116n30; God and, 75; identity and, 161; inevitable, 110–19; in Newman, 110, 123; Scripture and, 109
logical justification, forms of, 119–26
Logos, 19–20, 75, 138, 159. *See also* Word
Loisy, Alfred, 113–14
Lonergan, Bernard, 4, 16, 25, 73, 88–90, 124
Luke, Gospel of, 18–19, 53, 62, 127–29, 132, 135
Lumen gentium (Second Vatican Council), 148
Lysis (Plato), 38

Maccabees, Second, 29
magisterium, 15, 61–64, 70, 103, 106, 153–54, 162–69
Marcion of Sinope, 16
Marín-Sola, Francisco, 3, 112, 120–23, 120n43, 120n45, 125, 126n63, 127–29, 136
Maritain, Jacques, 74, 74n7, 78n19
Mark, Gospel of, 47, 137
Mary, 57, 127–29, 131–34, 136, 159, 161
Mass, 49, 58, 162

materialism, 21, 23–24, 38, 76, 91, 139, 142, 147
Matthew, Gospel of, 7, 19, 21, 30–31, 34, 48, 51, 53, 61, 65, 69, 90, 123, 125, 148, 173
Maximus Confessor, 11
Metaphysics (Aristotle), 38, 164–65
Milestones (Bonaventure), 54–55
Minerd, Matthew, 121n49
Mirari vos (Gregory XVI), 150–51
Modernists, 47, 49, 53, 71–72, 99, 162
Montanists, 53n19
Moses, 28, 30, 44–45, 51–52, 56n26
Murphy, Francesca Aran, 92n50
Mysterium fidei (Paul VI), 167

narrative, of revelation, 6–7
neo-Platonism, 20, 38, 174
Nestorianism, 159
Nestorius, 35
Newman, John Henry, 4, 7–9, 11–12, 33, 42, 57n34, 63–65, 87, 103, 106–7, 109, 109n7, 110, 123, 130, 134–35, 145, 172–75
Nicene Creed, 10, 34, 89
Nichols, Aidan, 1–2
Noah, 45
Nutt, Roger, 153

Ordinario sacerdotalis (John Paul II), 135–36
Origen, 20, 38
Osborne, Thomas, 80n23
ousia, 24–26

Page, Carl, 102
pantheism, 139, 147
Papias of Hierapolis, 99
Parmenides (Plato), 38
Paul, 7, 36, 43–44, 47–48, 51–52, 56, 61, 66, 69, 103, 146
Paul VI, 167
penance, 155–56
Peter, 44, 51, 120
Peter, First, 32, 60
Peter, Second, 32, 56, 90n44
Philippians, Epistle to, 20–21, 28, 51
Pius IX, 52, 127, 147, 150–52
Pius V, 15
Pius XII, 166, 168
Plato, 38, 75n10
Platonism, 20, 101
pluralism, 2, 104, 151

positivism, 2–3, 76, 91, 113, 165
pragmatism, 168
Prestige, G. L., 24
probabilities, antecedent and converging, 126–37
Protestants, 56, 63, 71, 147, 173, 175
Psalms, Book of, 29

Quanta cura (Pius IX), 150–51

Rahner, Karl, 4, 119, 156–59, 158n51, 159
Ratzinger, Joseph, 4, 52n16, 54, 60
realism, 73–75, 88–92, 122, 165
Reformers, 71
Reid, Thomas, 164–65
representation, 88
resurrection, 6, 21, 42, 96, 100, 132, 162
Resurrection, 133, 176
revelation, 3, 42–55; accessibility of, 103; Church and, 148; as "closed," 3–4, 169; as cognitive, 3; cognitive character of, 84–85; as communal, 51–52, 61; dogma and, 139, 141; as experimental, 71; faith and, 45, 74, 87–88, 118–19; freedom and, 150; God and, 3, 49, 133; historical facts and, 70; historicity of, 96–104; Incarnation and, 92, 162n56, 170; knowledge and, 82, 85; language and, 85; as narrative, 6–7; in Newman, 7; as propositional, 3; realism and, 75; as realist, 3; recipient of, 12–13; Tradition and, 53, 105–6
Revelation, Book of, 16
Romans, Epistle to, 7, 21, 36, 43, 47–49, 74
Rousselot, Pierre, 4, 117
Rule of Athanasius, 25, 89
rule-theory of meaning, 80

Sabatier, Auguste, 71
salvation, 44, 46–47, 51, 53, 73, 85, 96, 104, 128, 147, 159
Samson, 44
Samuel, 51
Samuel, Book of, 56n26
Saul, 44, 51
Schillebeeckx, Edward, 4, 118–19
Schleiermacher, Friedrich, 54n21, 71
Schultes, Reginald, 121n49
scientism, 168
Scripture, 65–69, 90–91, 104, 113–14, 119;

in First Vatican Council, 140; logic and, 109; Tradition and, 55–60
Second Council of Constantinople, 126
Second Council of Nicaea, 126
Second Council of Orange, 15, 127
Second Vatican Council, 44, 46, 49, 147–54, 169
Seewald, Michael, 1, 1n4, 172, 175–76
Sens commun, Le: La philosophie de l'être et les formules dogmatiques (Garrigou-Lagrange), 162
sexuality, 136–37
Sokolowski, Robert, 3
Son: in Arius, 17, 19, 26; baptism and, 21; in Council of Nicaea, 22–24, 27–28, 30, 138; Father and, 31–32, 123–24; God and, 125; *homoousios* and, 25–27; in John, 30; revelation and, 42; Rule of Athanasius and, 89
soul, 20, 71–72, 94, 120, 165n66, 175
state, Church and, 151–52
Statesman (Plato), 38
Steiner, George, 75, 75n10, 78, 158, 158n50
Suarez, Francisco, 120n45
substance, 10, 17, 22–27, 123–24, 160n54
Summa contra gentiles (Aquinas), 164–65
Synod of Carthage, 127
Synods of Toledo, 126–27

theological parameters, 2–3
Thessalonians, First, 62
Third Council of Constantinople, 125–26
Tilley, Terrence, 91, 91n46
Timothy, 52, 66
Timothy, First, 7, 56, 66, 69, 90n44
Timothy, Second, 7, 56, 67, 69, 90n44
Titus, 52
Topics (Aristotle), 121, 128
Tractatus de divina traditione et scriptura (Franzelin), 143–46
Tradition, 141; in Blondel, 114, 114n23; faith and, 12; in Franzelin, 143–44; fundamental theology and, 42; Holy Spirit and, 13, 103; as pneumatological, 4; revelation and, 53, 105–6, 113, 171; Scripture and, 55–60, 119; women and, 136
transubstantiation, 155, 162
Trinity, 146, 155; in Arius, 26; *Catechism of the Catholic Church* and, 8; faith and, 49; in Paul VI, 167; reason and, 142–43;

Trinity (*cont.*)
    revelation and, 142, 170; Scripture and, 91; Son and, 28
Tübingen school, 1
Tyrrell, George, 53, 72

Unfolding Revelation (Walgrave), 1

Veatch, Henry Babcock, 3, 78n17, 81n25, 84n33, 88
Vedantic Hinduism, 174
Vincent of Lérins, 69, 109, 109n7, 141, 148n31, 154

voluntarism, 156
von Harnack, Adolf, 175

Walgrave, Jan, 1, 115n26
Whole of Dogma, 116–17
women, 136
Word, 3, 12–13, 47, 50, 72, 111, 129, 139, 144, 159–61, 168. *See also* Logos
wordless experience, 7, 7n1

ALSO IN THE SACRA DOCTRINA SERIES

Bread from Heaven
An Introduction to the Theology of the Eucharist
Bernhard Blankenhorn

Ecclesiology
Guy Mansini, OSB

An Introduction to Vatican II as an Ongoing Theological Event
Matthew Levering

Fundamental Theology
Guy Mansini, OSB

John Henry Newman on Truth and Its Counterfeits
A Guide for Our Times
Reinhard Hütter

The Godly Image
Christian Satisfaction in Aquinas
Romanus Cessario, OP

The One Creator God in Thomas Aquinas and Contemporary Theology
Michael J. Dodds, OP